Leibniz's Final System

Gottfried Wilhelm Leibniz was one of the central figures of seventeenth-century philosophy, and a huge intellectual figure in his age. This book from Glenn A. Hartz (editor of the influential *Leibniz Review*) is an advanced study of Leibniz's metaphysics.

Leibniz's Final System explores a complicated topic, widely discussed in contemporary commentaries on Leibniz, namely the question of whether Leibniz was a metaphysical Idealist, Realist, or whether he tried to reconcile both trends in his mature philosophy. In recent years, the debate has centered on whether it is possible to maintain compatibility between the two.

Taking his cue from Leibniz's claim that "sectarianism" is a mistake, Hartz portrays Leibniz as a "theory-pluralist" for whom philosophical accounts are theories rather than absolute truths. While inconsistency between truths is problematic, inconsistency between theories is not. Hartz is thus free to examine separately and in great detail both the familiar monads-only Idealist theory and the largely unexplored Realist theory of matter and animals. He shows that Idealist and Realist passages are about equal in number and are typically found in the same texts throughout the mature period.

As the first major work on Realism in Leibniz's metaphysics, this key text will interest international Leibniz scholars, as well as students at the graduate level.

Glenn A. Hartz is Professor of Philosophy at Ohio State University and is editor of the *Leibniz Review*.

Routledge Studies in Seventeenth-Century Philosophy

Leibniz's Final System

Monads, Matter and Animals

Glenn A. Hartz

 Routledge
Taylor & Francis Group

LONDON AND NEW YORK

First published 2007
by Routledge
2 Park Square, Milton Park, Abingdon, Oxon OX14 4RN

Simultaneously published in the USA and Canada
by Routledge
270 Madison Ave, New York, NY 10016

Routledge is an imprint of the Taylor & Francis Group, an informa business

© 2007 Glenn A. Hartz

Typeset in Garamond by
Taylor & Francis Books
Printed and bound in Great Britain by
Antony Rowe Ltd, Chippenham, Wiltshire

British Library Cataloguing in Publication Data
A catalogue record for this book is available from the British Library

Library of Congress Cataloging in Publication Data
A catalog record for this book has been requested

ISBN10: 0-415-76993-0 ISBN13: 9-780-415-76993-8 (hbk)
ISBN10: 0-203-96796-8 ISBN13: 9-780-203-96796-6 (ebk)

For Pamela

Contents

List of Figures

Preface

This book began in earnest when I read an undergraduate paper by Hillary Rosenberg at the University of Michigan in 2000. In the midst of expounding passages in the Arnauld Correspondence (LA 74–8; 90–102), she wrote:

> At first Leibniz maintains that only things with a soul are real beings. In some parts of the text, Leibniz claims that the body itself, separated from the soul, cannot be considered a real substance because, just like a machine or a pile of rocks, it is a being of aggregation, not a unity, and so can be divided and destroyed. ... However, Leibniz hedges on the definition of real objects, and he opens the door for the existence of other real beings besides animated objects. He now claims that aggregates can be real since they are composed of simple units and "there is no plurality without true unities." Here Leibniz allows more objects into reality. Instead of only animate objects being real, his reality test incorporates ... pluralities (inanimate objects) because they are *composed* of true unities. If they were not composed of beings with true unity, then these pluralities would be deprived of all reality and thus imaginary. Leibniz wants us to be wary of considering pluralities as real because he doesn't want extension to contribute to realness. [W]hen we use reason to get to the heart of the aggregate and perceive that it is composed of true unities, we can realize that pluralities are in fact real.

That is a stunning exposition of Leibniz's argument. The ebb and flow an interpreter feels as she confronts his work is captured perfectly here. Leibniz "at first" is an Idealist (as I will say). However, he "hedges" on that and "opens the door" to Realism – where even beings by aggregation, because they are composed of true unities, are real. Those unities at the "heart of the aggregate" account for the fact it is not merely "imaginary" and that its reality is owed to something other than extension.

Now it struck me as odd that this paper, which so genuinely represents the mind of Leibniz, would receive a lackluster response in many graduate schools. Why? Because it is not properly Idealist. She had not – poor undergraduate! – yet learned the fine art of filtering out the Realist "hedgings" and "howevers" that keep getting in the way of a pure Idealism. Should she choose to pursue a career in Leibniz studies, she'd have to be "told," I thought.

Indeed, these Realist themes had always seemed important to me, and appear in my earlier work (Hartz 1992) as providing the key to uniting much of the metaphysics of monads with Leibniz's theory of bodies and animals. It occurred to me that I might check to see how many times Realist themes like these appear in the mature corpus – roughly 1686–1716.

The result was – and still is – astonishing. An intensive examination of some main parts of the mature corpus turned up over two hundred endorsements of Realism – almost exactly the same number as Idealism receives therein. The Realist passages offer a paradigm that contrasts starkly with the familiar Idealist one, but which has been largely unexplored. Complicating the task of exploring it was the fact that this paradigm was nearly always found in the same works – sometimes the same paragraph, sometimes the same sentence – as contained the Idealist one. One could not simply say that Leibniz at some point changed his mind or that his thought evolved, say, from Realism to Idealism.

Indeed, it was impossible to say at the outset whether Realism would prove a viable metaphysical scheme. Among other questions, I asked: "Do Realist themes together form a coherent pattern or a systematic theory?" and "Is there a viable concept of rationality that allows adherence to two incompatible theories in the same body of work?"

In this book I argue that these questions can be answered positively.

The results are important not just for Leibniz scholarship, but for philosophy in general. For it turns out that the long-neglected Realist theory is *intrinsically* interesting – philosophically exciting. The familiar Idealist picture is also interesting in its own way – though it leads in a very different direction. Both are explored in detail here so the systems can be compared and fruitfully assessed in light of each other.

At the end of the day, my apology for writing this book is this: for too long those who would understand Leibniz's philosophy have been treated to a one-sided, partial view of it. Both sides must be presented and fairly described. If, after that is done, an interpreter is drawn to one of the sides more than to the other then that is fine and may even be quite plausible. But only "after that is done."

On then, to an examination of both sides.

Acknowledgements

My interest in Leibniz goes back to graduate school, when José Benardete gave me the topic for my dissertation. This was the issue of the "filler" for matter – i.e., "What fills matter up with being, distinguishing it from empty space?" Indeed, looking back now, that could receive Leibniz's answer only by being entertained from a Realist rather than an Idealist perspective. For, as I found in my research into his dynamics, Leibniz's answer is given in terms of the forces of mind-independent substances or "true unities." Had he been a Berkelesque Idealist, his answer would have appealed to some sort of "noetic stuffing" that fills in sense-data or phenomena.

Along the way, many people have been of assistance. I hope I don't forget anyone, but if I do they must realize their reward, like all of ours, is in heaven – Plato's if not God's. Somewhere out there is an invisible "Realm of Excellence in Philosophical Thought," and thanks are due to all who contribute to it.

The help of philosopher Rick Groshong has been the most crucial factor in the writing of this book. He read several earlier drafts and his comments have been of enormous benefit. Massimo Mugnai and Philip Beeley have also offered detailed comments that improved the text dramatically. Conversations with Patrick Lewtas have been invaluable. Students with whom I've worked also have helped, directly or indirectly, with the final product – Hillary Rosenberg, Seth Yalcin, Ryan Nichols, Roy Cook, Andrew Arlig, Cristina Moisa, and James Harrell.

My teachers have had a profound influence on my style and approach – among them, Donald Yehling, José Benardete, Jonathan Bennett, C. L. Hardin, and William P. Alston. Philosophers Robert M. Adams, Richard Arthur, Martha Bolton, J. A. Cover, Daniel Garber, Mark Kulstad, Sukjae Lee, Samuel Levey, Paul Lodge, Ralph Hunt, Peter Ross, Donald Rutherford, Heinrich Schepers, R.C. Sleigh, Jr, Eric Sotnak, Marshall Swain, James van Cleve, Catherine Wilson, R. S. Woolhouse, and anonymous referees have helped shape the final draft.

To The Ohio State University I am most indebted for several quarters free of teaching duties, and principally for a year's sabbatical in 2000–2001. Generous support from my Dean, John Riedl, has enabled this project to take shape over many years. Philosophy Department chairs Marshall Swain, Daniel Farrell, and George Pappas have also been supportive.

Terry Clague, commissioning editor at Routledge, has given the project strong backing, as has assistant editor, Katherine Carpenter. H. T. Mason and Paul Lodge have helped by granting me permission to make use of their translations – respectively, of the Arnauld and the De Volder correspondences. Selections from *G. W. Leibniz: Philosophical Essays*, edited and translated by Roger Ariew and Daniel Garber, 1989, reprinted by permission of Hackett Publishing Company, Inc.; all rights reserved. Excerpts from *Leibniz: Determinist, Theist, Idealist*, by Robert Merrihew Adams, © 1994 by Robert Merrihew Adams, are used by permission of Oxford University Press, Inc. Excerpts from *Gottfried Wilhelm Leibniz: Philosophical Papers and Letters*, edited by Leroy E. Loemker, 1969, are reprinted with kind permission of Springer Science and Business Media. Passages from *Leibniz's 'New System' and Associated Contemporary Texts*, translated and edited by R. S. Woolhouse and Richard Francks are quoted by permission of Oxford University Press. Reproduced with permission are extracts from *Leibniz: New Essays on Human Understanding*, edited by Peter Remnant and Jonathan Bennett, 2nd Edition, 1996, © Cambridge University Press and from *Leibniz and the Rational Order of Nature*, by Donald Rutherford, 1995, © Cambridge University Press. Permission to quote from Bertrand Russell's *The Philosophy of Leibniz* is granted by Routledge and the Bertrand Russell Peace Foundation.

Of course the person who stands, invisible, behind the writing of every word is my wife, Pamela, without whose constant support this project could have never have been seen through to completion. Words cannot convey my gratitude to her.

List of Abbreviations

A	*G. W. Leibniz: Sämtliche Schriften und Briefe*, Darmstadt and Berlin: Berlin Academy, 1923.
Ad	R. M. Adams, *Leibniz: Determinist, Theist, Idealist*, New York: Oxford University Press, 1994.
AG	*G. W. Leibniz: Philosophical Essays*, R. Ariew and D. Garber (ed. and trans.), Indianapolis: Hackett, 1989 (printed with revisions in 1999).
C	*Opuscules et fragments inédits de Leibniz*, L. Couturat (ed.), Paris: Alcan, 1903; repr. Hildesheim: Georg Olms, 1961.
Clarke	*The Leibniz-Clarke Correspondence*, H. G. Alexander (ed.), Manchester: Manchester University Press, 1956. Cited by the number of Leibniz's letter and section: e.g., '5.47'.
DM	G. W. Leibniz, *Discourse on Metaphysics*, cited by section number.
G	*Die philosophischen Schriften von Gottfried Wilhelm Leibniz*, C. I. Gerhardt (ed.) 7 vols, Berlin: Weidmannsche Buchhandlung, 1875–90; repr. Hildesheim: Georg Olms, 1978.
GM	*G. W. Leibniz: Mathematische Schriften*, C. I. Gerhardt (ed.) 7 vols, Berlin: A. Asher; Halle: H. W. Schmidt, 1849–63; repr. Hildesheim: Georg Olms, 1971.
L	*Gottfried Wilhelm Leibniz: Philosophical Papers and Letters*, L. E. Loemker (trans. and ed.), 2nd edn, Dordrecht: Reidel, 1969.
LA	*The Leibniz-Arnauld Correspondence*, H. T. Mason (ed. and trans.), Manchester: Manchester University Press, 1967; repr. New York: Garland, 1985. (Pagination cited is margin pagination, which follows G volume 2).
Mon	G. W. Leibniz, *Monadology*, cited by section number.
NE	*G. W. Leibniz: New Essays on Human Understanding*, P. Remnant and J. Bennett (trans. and eds), Cambridge: Cambridge University Press, 1981; 2nd edn, 1996. (When the pagination differs, first edition is given first, second edition second).

NS	G. W. Leibniz, *A New System of the Nature and Communication of Substances, and of the Union of the Soul and Body*, cited by paragraph number.
PNG	G. W. Leibniz, *Principles of Nature and Grace, Based on Reason*, cited by section number.
PW	*Leibniz Philosophical Writings*, G. H. R. Parkinson (ed.), M. Morris and G. H. R. Parkinson (trans.), London: Dent, 1973.
R	B. Russell, *A Critical Exposition of the Philosophy of Leibniz*, 2nd edn, London: George Allen & Unwin, 1937; repr. London: Routledge, 1992.
Rd	D. Rutherford, *Leibniz and the Rational Order of Nature*, Cambridge: Cambridge University Press, 1995.
T	G. W. Leibniz, *Theodicy: Essays on the Goodness of God the Freedom of Man, and the Origin of Evil*, E. M. Huggard (trans.), A. Farrer (ed.), La Salle: Open Court, 1985.
WF	*Leibniz's 'New System' and Associated Contemporary Texts*, R. S. Woolhouse and R. Franck (trans. and eds), Oxford: Oxford University Press, 1997.

1 Introduction

I felt – as many others have felt – that the *Monadology* was a kind of fantastic fairy tale. At this point I read the *Discours de Métaphysique* and the letters to Arnauld. Suddenly a flood of light was thrown on all the inmost recesses of Leibniz's philosophical edifice. I saw how its foundations were laid, and how its superstructure rose out of them.

Bertrand Russell (R xiii-xiv; 1992 xvii-xviii)

In these pages I develop an understanding of the mature philosophical system proposed by G. W. Leibniz (1646–1716). The "mature" system is usually dated to 1686 and thereafter. The *Monadology*, written in 1714, is the most familiar work that sets forth the main doctrines.

I aim to discover what Russell here calls the "superstructure of Leibniz's philosophical edifice." Sudden flashes of insight are supplemented by a sustained effort to understand the precise details of the various metaphysical accounts and to push for maximum coherence among them. The analyses, which are based on a thorough study of the relevant texts, build upon one another – culminating in a complex series of definitions that capture all of Leibniz's constraints on a given type of object.

The end result is this. While not all themes from the mature philosophy can be made to cohere with one another, two very important features do fit together on the analysis offered here. Those two features are monads – Leibniz's famous purely spiritual substances which perceive and strive – and animals. Typically these two elements are seen as exclusive alternatives, so that taking one means leaving the other behind. Here they live in harmony. The task of saying exactly how they can coexist peacefully is a long and difficult one. But it is well worth doing, since it unifies Leibniz's mature vision of the universe in a way hitherto unimagined.

In a word, I offer the reader *freedom*. Freedom from the expectations of tradition and time-honored readings of Leibniz that have managed to gain ascendancy. Freedom from preconceived notions about what Leibniz's system should look like. Freedom from the narrowness and bias found in some mainstream commentaries – a bias which is as noxious to Leibniz studies as it is to historical studies generally. The "readings" I'm talking about find, in certain select claims, Leibniz's deepest, most important philosophy and then discount or explain away or render metaphorical those that won't go along. One of several Leibnizian paradigms becomes the lens through which to view all the texts.

My paradigms flow out of the texts. If they don't align logically I nevertheless derive them in all their pluralistic splendor. They are viewed as theories of Reality, not absolute pronouncements about Reality. So concern over consistency across these models can be set aside, granting the texts freedom to lead us to the theories they portend.

"Portend" indeed. The theories are seldom there waiting to be expounded. They are often inchoate suggestions that need the aid of various techniques to bring out their full complexity, interconnectedness, and promise. Leibniz often did not stay on one philosophical topic for long. Like the proverbial fox who "knows many things," he jumps about from topic to topic. This discourages systematic theoretical development, of course. And this book is meant to remedy that a bit.

I consider use of theory-building techniques an important part of charitable philosophical commentary. The division of labor in Leibniz interpretation calls for both close textual studies that examine the nuances of the historical context and more free-ranging interpretive inquiries that seek to discover the contours of the theories and arguments those texts need to be rendered fully intelligible. I believe there is no competition between these camps. Each has its legitimate sphere. Neither can be done properly without the other.

While this study falls clearly into the "interpretive inquiry" category, it incorporates some textual research of its own and is built on rafts of earlier historical studies. Without people bringing texts up from the "mines," and armies of others refining the raw ore into properly transcribed and edited editions, the interpreter would have no hope of turning out the pure metal of intelligible commentary. It is my hope that this book will help justify existing historical studies – and inspire new ones – because it will grant them a legitimacy they did not have before. For example, under the influence of "Idealism," there has been a tendency to view discussions of such "Realist" themes as the doctrine of animals and Leibniz's claim that bodies are collections of substances as concerned with some of the shallower areas of his thought. Those studies will now have a claim to full legitimacy as inquiries into Leibniz's deepest thought.

Ideally, interpretive and historical inquiries might be carried out by the same person in the same work. I have gone some distance towards making a textual case for the theories I attribute to Leibniz but in a work of this size there is a sharp limit on the textual detail one can consider. Leibniz's mature thought is daunting in its complexity, even when one limits oneself to a given time period. There is no way a single work devoted to the mature philosophy could present an adequately nuanced textual study *and* a detailed look at the theories the texts convey. I'm afraid the reader will often have to settle for a mere glimpse of the full textual picture. But I mean to get things off on the right foot by featuring, when possible, passages from the major mature works among the passages that launch the theories.

In addition, little in the way of biographical facts about Leibniz and his contemporaries will enter into what follows. Fortunately, these facts are readily available in other studies, and I have no doubt that such facts often bear interestingly on the theories presented here.

1.1 Overview of this Book

Here is a somewhat simplified *précis* of the mature metaphysics. In the world outside us there are *monads* (which are also called "simple substances"). Monads are soul-like or mind-like individuals; they are indivisible, simple, real, and perfectly one. Created by God at the dawn of time, they are the "building blocks" for everything else. Often Leibniz indicates that collections of monads – "aggregates" as he calls them – retain some reality they borrow from their constituent monads. This gives them a degree of derivative reality. Aggregates comprise rocks, corporations, and corpses. Leibniz also allows *animals* (sometimes called "composite" or "corporeal" substances) to be the constituents of aggregates. They play exactly the same role in aggregates as do monads. So it is often simply said that "substances" compose aggregates, where that term covers both monads and animals.

When the substances in an aggregate achieve something analogous to machine-like order and arrangement, they are said to compose a "primitive machine." Primitive machines combine to form "natural machines" – that is, complex machines composed of lower-order machines, composed of other lower-order machines, to infinity. Leibniz often refers to a natural machine as an "organic body." An organic body is fit to perform the role of providing a temporary body for an animal when God assigns it to a "dominant monad." The dominant monad is designed to have a specific sequence of bodies; at any given moment it combines with one to compose an animal. An animal persists forever – its dominant monad shedding its current organic body and taking on a new one – unless annihilation was in its plan or "complete concept."

In Figure 1.1, the structure of these various elements is portrayed. Here S = a substance (that is, a monad or an animal), m = a primitive machine, n = a natural machine (that is, an organic body), D = a dominant monad, and A = an animal. An interesting feature of the diagram is that it builds upon itself an infinite hierarchy of animals – something Leibniz explicitly held to characterize all of nature. Thus when the Ss are monads, what one might call a "basic animal" is formed; when the Ss are basic animals, "higher-order animals" are formed, with yet higher order animals formed of them – and so on to infinity.

The book is structured in such a way as to achieve a clear understanding of every major doctrine. The rest of Chapter 1 is devoted to principles of

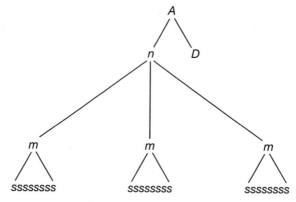

Figure 1.1. Diagram of the Mature Metaphysics

interpretation that play a role in the entire work. Chapter 2 seeks to clarify Leibniz's motivations for starting with substances. Chapter 3 examines Leibniz's complex rules about combining them so as to get aggregates, or composite objects like crystals and planets. That same chapter includes a brief explanation of Leibniz's views of the continuum, space, and time. Chapter 4 is an overview of his doctrine of aggregates, with Chapter 5 devoted to an exclusive look at the Idealist analyses of aggregates, and Chapter 6 the Realist accounts. Chapter 7 is an intensive look at the question of whether Realism and Idealism are compatible. In Chapter 8, some of the material from the Idealist and Realist analyses of aggregates is used to explain Leibniz's doctrine of animals. Finally, Chapter 9 is a look back at the mature system.

On texts: often they will be quoted, though sometimes groups of texts are handled as collections. For a few main mature works, a comprehensive representation of endorsements of some key doctrines is provided in the "Doctrine Tables" in the Appendix. These Tables are used throughout the book to help establish the relative weight accorded to various beliefs. Dates (when available) and references to transcriptions and English translations are provided to help those interested in locating a claim chronologically or doing further research. When a passage is quoted, any translation cited, though generally reliable, is not always followed exactly. Some unremarked changes are made along the way in the interest of accuracy and consistency of translations within this book.

The novice reader of Leibniz must realize that the mature corpus is gigantic, scattered, unwieldy, only partially edited, and even more partially translated reliably into English. (All the main works are in French or Latin.) To help combat the problem this creates for a book in English devoted to his mature thought, I highlight the main mature works and correspondences. These works are reliable sources of his mature thought because there is general scholarly consensus (with some exceptions, of course) that they are the places where Leibniz most tellingly put down his philosophical ideas. As a result, these works have attracted the most intensive scholarly attention, and generally reliable transcriptions and translations exist.

The issue of the corpus is relevant to this study in the following way. The interpretation offered here does not depend on new manuscripts found in Leibniz's archives or on esoteric, difficult-to-find texts. It can make its case completely given what is already known about his thought. In fact, the arguments could be advanced using only five mainstream mature works – the *Discourse on Metaphysics* (1686), the correspondence with Antoine Arnauld (1612–94) which was conducted between 1687 and 1690, the *New System* (1695), the correspondence with Burcher De Volder (1643–1706) during the years 1699–1706, and the *Monadology* (1714). Reliable editions and translations of these works are generally available. I will cite three of them by abbreviation and section number – e.g., DM 1, NS 3, Mon 61.[1] The page number in the Arnauld exchange (i.e., G 2) will follow 'LA,' and I will refer to the De Volder correspondence by the page number in G 2 (accompanied by a translation page, if available).

Now even though these works will be in the spotlight, and appear in the Doctrine Tables thoroughly analyzed, the doctrines advanced in them are sometimes better and more fully expressed in his occasional writings and his correspondence with people other than Arnauld and De Volder. So sometimes these other passages are cited or quoted. The goal throughout is to make the book self-contained and at the same time to provide sufficient scholarly apparatus to enable readers to pursue the issues in more detail, should they so wish. Detailed notes on the historical context cannot be made here, but I have always tried to represent in my interpretation of the passages any crucial contextual factors that are needed to understand it aright.

While there is a sustained attempt to make the material accessible, it sometimes becomes complicated. At such times, diagrams and concrete examples are used to illustrate the analyses.

1.2 Idealism v. Realism

Now as this distinction represents the book's main "fulcrum," it is important to be clear at the outset about the sense I'm placing on those terms.

"Idealism" and "Realism" are rough terms, admitting of varying interpretations. I ask the reader to leave aside the many connotations these titles have accrued over the years as philosophical systems have come and gone. There is no attempt to represent these as titles Leibniz himself would have used, though I think Leibniz would have agreed that the relevant themes extracted from his philosophy belong in these categories.

A very clear picture of what I mean by the terms will emerge presently as Leibniz's claims are examined in detail. But for now, the following general characterization will give the reader an initial bearing.

Idealism   In the universe there are only minds and mind-dependent objects.

Realism   In the universe there is at least one object that is neither a mind nor mind-dependent.

"The universe" is taken here as equivalent to what is sometimes called "reality" – the whole vast configuration of things. I aim to build upon these sparse characterizations, step by step, a more full-blooded, distinctively Leibnizian conception of them. Thus Leibnizian Idealism will include specific claims about minds and their objects, and Realism claims about mind-independent objects.

Now one can very nearly tell the entire history of philosophy by reference to the two major world systems that fit beneath these general titles. To name but a few: Plato, Berkeley, a prevalent interpretation of Kant, and twentieth-century phenomenalisms of various sorts cluster around the Idealist theme. And Democritus, Aristotle, Locke, and recent "scientific realist" positions uphold the Realist strand. Unremarkably, they are seen as alternatives: a theorist must be on one side or the other.

Leibniz is commonly regarded as an Idealist. Indeed, his thought leans towards Idealism in many ways, and there can be no question that he has an Idealist theory on offer. But what is astonishing is that he also presents a Realist theory, right alongside the Idealist one. Realism has been largely neglected in favor of Idealism for many reasons. Prime among them is the fact that Kant's work was influential on later thinkers, who have exalted the Idealist elements to the exclusion of Realist ones.

In this work I am not much concerned with the historical reasons for the ascendancy of Idealism. But it must be said that the majority of scholars view this interpretation as the right way of looking at his philosophy.

I will be going against the grain by presenting arguments to the effect that Leibniz was as much a Realist as he was an Idealist. Instead of getting the "best of both worlds," he *gets both worlds*. The "Summary of Doctrine Tables" in the Appendix shows why I say that. For Idealism is endorsed 245 times, and Realism 251 times in the five main works. That's almost an exact division of his commitments between the two theories. (A preliminary look at the larger mature corpus has revealed the same approximately even bifurcation.) And, as the Summary and individual Doctrine Tables illustrate, there is no sense in which he began as a Realist and ended up a pure Idealist or vice versa, so that one theory predominates in a particular time period or set of texts and the other in another. If his thought had this "Darwinian" feature, evolving over time, the task of explaining its inconsistencies would be easy. But it's far otherwise, I'm afraid. The *Monadology*, written very late in his life and supposedly backing pure Idealism, provides an arresting case. Though Idealism predominates (with 47 endorsements), Realism retains a significant foothold (with 32).

When commentators confront these divergent themes living side by side in the same works, something must be done to dispel the sense of incoherence. The Idealist strain typically rises to the top, and Realist elements are either ignored, distorted, or made metaphorical so that they appear innocuous. As long as there is no real conflict with Idealism, Leibniz's rationality, it is thought, is preserved.

But that is short-sighted – on two fronts. First, all of us who would understand Leibniz miss out on the richness of his system. Realism never gets explored. In this study Leibnizian Realism is explored with as much passion and imagination as Leibnizian Idealism. Second, as Rick Groshong has noted, it is philosophically bankrupting. On my interpretation, Leibniz is an Idealist facing Realist worries, and a Realist facing Idealist misgivings. A consistent Realist like Reid mocks Idealism and hopes the reader stays with "common sense"; a consistent Idealist like Berkeley makes similar maneuvers with respect to Realism and hopes the reader hangs on to phenomenalism. Leibniz is different from these "consistent" theorists in that he adopts Realism yet tries to address Idealist concerns, and also adopts Idealism while yet confronting the full fury of Realist concerns. I don't want to miss out on what can be learned from his failures and successes in this rare endeavor.

1.3 Genius

Because of the depth and originality of his contributions to a wide range of disciplines and his mastery of nearly everything known at the time, Leibniz is clearly to be reckoned among the world's geniuses. A recent book on creativity puts down, as two marks of genius, constructing "novel combinations" and "connecting the unconnected."[2] Call these *synthesis* and *reconciliation*. Both are exhibited throughout Leibniz's philosophy, as they were in his political career and mathematical and theological writings.

He often made daring attempts to forge alliances between political factions that were quite set against one another. In theology he aspired to reconcile Protestant and Catholic differences. He also tried to remove the tension between East and West, going so far as to seek a Christian interpretation of all Chinese religions. His founding of learned academies where scholars of all sorts would interact further testifies to his synthetic and reconciliatory efforts.[3]

This, then, is the man whose thought I aspire to understand. It is unremarkable that in his metaphysics Leibniz is also inclined to push for novel connections and to reconcile such apparently contradictory systems as Realism and Idealism. On the whole, commentators have dismissed rather than welcomed the reconciliations, claiming that Leibniz can't have all the different claims on pain of contradiction. They want to save Leibniz from himself by discounting select themes and passages. The search is on for the "esoteric" Leibniz who kept himself well hidden in the popular, "exoteric" works.[4] One distills out a purified liquid from the vast vat of text, making sure nothing embarrassingly inconsistent-looking remains.

Such commentators should remember that they are studying someone who thought a person on the other side of the world who takes herself to be merging with the universe is actually, unwittingly, worshipping the Christian God. He denigrates atomism as "imperfect" because it is tied to "the crude concept of a corporeal substance which depends only on sensory imagery," and yet goes on to say that this "corpuscular philosophy" is "excellent and most true in itself."[5] In his hands, Plato's thought (Idealism) merges with Aristotle's (Realism) (DM 27). His *Theodicy* received the complaint (as paraphrased by Catherine Wilson) that "Leibniz wanted to reconcile everybody, the Socinians with the Lutherans, the Lutherans with the Calvinists, the Calvinists with the Catholics, the Molinists with the Predeterminists, the Predeterminists with the Jansenists" (Wilson 1989, 270). He persists in trying to reconcile free will and determinism when the prospects seem utterly hopeless (see Riley 1999).

In fact, Leibniz seldom saw a dilemma he didn't want to *engulf*. He assimilates the claims and suggests ways to minimize cognitive dissonance. Or he just lives with the dissonance.[6] There is much more tolerance for inconsistency and ambiguity than is typically allowable. In this, Leibniz is very much a child of his times – when "there was no such thing as a specialist" (Reston 1995, 25). A hundred years after Galileo made his mark at the Academy of Florence by calculating the size of Dante's *Inferno* using St. Peter's cone as a guide to the length of Lucifer's arm, Leibniz was at work on his mature philosophy.[7] In it, mathematical, metaphysical, theological, logical, and scientific themes would be welded together into a daring, imaginative synthesis fully characteristic of the Renaissance ideal of universality and eclectic comprehensiveness.

Twentieth-century English-language commentary has largely lost sight of that Renaissance spirit. Beginning with Russell, the "inconsistency" charges have mounted. Charitable interpretation has given way to logic-chopping, with interpreters forcing Leibniz's thought into a preconceived mold rather than allowing it to remain fluid. But no matter how much the contemporary mind rebels against it, the desire to meld the unmeldable and bridge the unbridgeable is indomitable. It triumphs over the commentators because the nice, neat, tidy logical structure they manage to dream up is a hopeless fabrication destined to be smashed to bits on the stones of the corpus. Again and again these idealized "interpretations" fall to the ambiguities and subtleties apparent throughout the full range of Leibniz's writings.

Explanatory richness, depth, and range were, in the end, more important to him than surface consistency. In that glorious age, it was more important to have explanations (often made possible by fertile analogies) than it was to come up with strictly consistent systems of thought. The analytic mind of today does Leibniz a disservice if it underestimates the degree to which the ambiguities were *meant* – were deliberate attempts to coalesce different ideas even in the absence of a fully detailed explanation of the reconciliation.

He had a vision of how the parts fit into the whole, but not all the detailed questions were answered – or even answerable. The consummate rationalist, Leibniz saw most explanatory gaps as mere limitations on knowledge. An infinite intelligence could explain how the puzzle goes together – to the last piece, to the last detail.[8]

1.4 Four Levels of Ontic Involvement: Solipsism, Substance, Animal, and Aggregate

Leibniz's overall system, though it presents a detailed account of the outer realm, is designed to collapse back into solipsism when under pressure from skepticism, rather as a turtle under threat withdraws into its shell. Thus the texts operate – often simultaneously – on different levels.

At the deepest *Solipsist Level*, or "solipsism," there is I (and God).[9] God is included because otherwise I would have no sufficient reason.[10]

In a few passages, Leibniz seems comfortable with solipsism. For instance, in an early piece dating to the late 1670s, he writes:

> And if some Platonist were to say that the whole of his present life is a well-cohering dream, and that his soul will awaken at death; perhaps he could not be refuted *a priori* without knowing the reason for a universe which underwent no interlude of this sort. ... And the same would apply to someone who denied that any bodies or any other substances exist apart from the person that thinks.
> ("Metaphysical Definitions and Reflections" A VI 4 B, 1396 (N. 267)/
> Leibniz 2001, 241)

But the comfort often doesn't last. As he says immediately after this, while solipsism "would in itself be possible," it is "not consistent with the primary reasons of things." In particular, there is no reason why there should be "one of you in the universe, when there could be so many other thinking substances more perfect than you. ... " (ibid.). That is, God would have no sufficient reason for making you and no other being. (This argument survives into the mature period as a theological argument for an infinity of monads – see Chapter 5.)

In addition, in this text he says the "causes of phenomena" must lie outside you. He lists two possible "first principles of sensation":

i) I, who perceive, exist.
ii) The things I perceive are various.

Leibniz continues,

There are some who inculcate only the first of these, which they express as *cogito ergo sum*. But they leave out the second, which is much more fruitful. For two things above all occur to someone experiencing, that the perceptions are various, and that it is one and the same person who is perceiving. From this it is not only inferred that there is a percipient, but also that the reason that perceptions are so various must be outside the percipient; and therefore that there are other things besides me. From the first I arrive at a knowledge of myself, from the second at a knowledge of the world.

(A VI 4 B, 1395[N.267]/Leibniz 2001, 239)

So while Solipsism remains a possibility in itself, it has little chance of being the way things actually are.

Instead, one must indulge a more generous ontology at the *Substance Level*. "Substance," as it will sometimes be known, comprises everything in Solipsism plus other purely spiritual simple substances or "monads" – like human minds and souls of donkeys.

In a very interesting mature passage, Leibniz comments on the viability of Solipsism and Substance:

For it would not be impossible for a creature to have long and orderly dreams resembling our *life*, such that everything it believed it perceived by the senses was nothing but mere *appearances*. ... [T]he existence of intelligible things, and particularly of this I who thinks and is called mind or soul, is incomparably more certain than the existence of sensible things, and thus, ... it would not be impossible, speaking with metaphysical rigor, that, at bottom, there should only be these intelligible substances, and that sensible things should only be appearances.

(1702, Letter to Queen Sophie Charlotte, G 6, 502–3/AG 188–9)

First, he recognizes Solipsism as minimally adequate: I might be having a "long and orderly dream" where all my perceived objects are "mere appearances." Second, he recognizes Substance as equally legitimate, since within it there are "intelligible substances" in addition to "this I who thinks," and all perceived things are still only appearances. The connection between Solipsism and Substance on the one hand, and "phenomenalism" – roughly the view that bodies are mere appearances – is clearly made here. And two years later he endorses Substance again:

And if anyone concedes to me that there is an infinity of percipients, in each of whom there is a fixed law of the progression of phenomena, that the phenomena of these different percipients correspond with each other, and that there is a common reason for both their existence and their correspondence in the thing which we call

God, this is all that I claim in the matter, and all that I think can be claimed.

(21 January 1704, to De Volder, G 2, 264/L 535)

Still, it might turn out that there are some things in the universe that are neither thinking substances nor mere appearances. If so, one ushers in the quite different *Animal Level*. Here doubts concerning the mind-independent reality of animals are held in check.[11] "Animal" includes everything in Substance, and, in addition, human beings, donkeys, and palm trees.[12]

Finally, holding in abeyance yet further doubts about the extra-mental unity and reality of heaps opens up the most inclusive ontology of all, the *Aggregate Level*. This adds to the contents of Animal diamond rings, rainbows, herds of sheep, and brass balls in the physicist's lab.

So there are these levels:

Solipsism	God and I
Substance	God and all simple substances
Animal	God and all simple and corporeal substances
Aggregate	God, all simple and corporeal substances, and all aggregates.

That appears rather austere. But actually each level houses much more than is mentioned. For instance, space, time, and numbers are present at every level. Every level contains God, and these three items ultimately have their being in God. As for extension, it can be viewed as a quality of mind-independent bodies (in Aggregate) or of sense-data (appearances or "phenomena") entertained by simple substances at all levels. Even if (as in Solipsism) I were the only finite perceiver, extension could be instantiated in the representational content of my mental states. So derivative or secondary ontologies are nested within some items in this primary ontology.

Notice that the Idealist/Realist split is readily apparent here. Solipsism and Substance fall under Idealism, since there only minds and their ideas or appearances exist. But Animal and Aggregate are Realist theories, where mind-independent objects gain being. The fact that all four exist in Leibniz's mature philosophy explains why there is so much "redundancy" in it – with bodies, for example, being explained as appearances in my mind (Solipsism) *or* all minds (Substance) *or* the corporeal component of animals *or* aggregates of substances.

The four ontic levels are also going to create quite a strain within his metaphysics. Leibniz often doesn't help alleviate the tension because, rather than staying at one level, he routinely switches back and forth between them. Sometimes there is what appears to be a categorical denial of explanatory commerce between the levels – as in the famous mill example at Mon 17, where it is said that motions of pulleys and levers (Aggregate) can never explain perception (Solipsism/Substance). Such passages lead many to declare a complete separation between them and to downplay texts that seem recklessly to disregard those more sober pronouncements.

But the overarching scheme needs the interlevel moves. Otherwise the accounts become "balkanized" and don't fit into a unified pattern.

Some theorists note the "inconsistency" of holding simultaneously to the "monadology" (Substance) and to claims that, astonishingly, grant matter mind-independent existence (Aggregate).[13] In response, some have removed the inconsistencies by construing the doctrines as if they all intended to tell the same story at the same level. But such well-intentioned efforts have the same cheapening effect on Leibniz's system that a well-meaning restorer's brush has on a masterpiece. This artificial "consistency" quickly brings the larger scheme to ruin. Why? Because the system is deliberately designed to explain properties of objects on a certain level of analysis by means of properties and concepts from a foreign, quite different level. Properties of objects at the alien level help explain what otherwise would remain unaccountable.

For instance, the "original limitation of creatures" (Solipsism, Substance, Animal) finds a "perfect image" in Kepler's "natural inertia of bodies" (Aggregate).[14] Mechanism (Aggregate) is said to be disillusioning if one tries to find reasons for it within mechanism: the ultimate foundations must be found in Substance (G 3, 607/L 655). Animals roam freely through the *Monadology*.[15] A body's exertion of force (Aggregate) is said to be somewhat similar to one's first-person sense of striving (Solipsism, Substance) (G 2, 270/L 537). Teleology (Substance, Animal) and mechanism (Aggregate) are wedded in a general harmony (Mon 79) and in an explanation of Snell's Law (DM 22). All of a mass's states (Aggregate) can be read in the soul or "entelechy" (Substance) – even its trajectory around a curve.[16] Thus mechanical causes are "concentrated in souls" (G 4, 562/WF 116), and "whatever happens in the mass or aggregate of substances according to mechanical laws, the same thing is expressed in the soul or the entelechy ... by its own laws."[17]

Animals and monads (Substance) are often said to be in masses or bodies (Aggregate) – furnishing those bodies with reality, activity, force, and heterogeneity. An entelechy (Substance) provides the primitive force whose modification appears in a body (Aggregate) as derivative force.[18] And the fact that bodies (Aggregate) move is evidence that monads (Substance) must differ qualitatively (Mon 8). World-apart themes (Solipsism) are followed immediately by endorsements of mind-body (Substance-Aggregate) parallelism and the *per se* unity of corporeal substances (Animal) (DM 32–4).

It is more than an accident that the same "interlevel" technique shows up so often. It seems to define one main sort of Leibnizian explanation. In it, one explores imaginatively and creatively the possibility of liaisons between objects and processes that are usually deemed completely disparate. So there is no way to pull the levels apart without pulling the mature metaphysics apart.

1.5 Interpretive Options

I have tried to determine the main interpretive alternatives available to someone addressing the issue of inconsistency in Leibniz's thought. The ones that have a significant following can be divided into two broad types: Incompatibilism (with several varieties falling under it) and Compatibilism.

(A) *Incompatibilism*: Leibniz's two main systems of Idealism and Realism are, in Russell's words, "hopelessly inconsistent" (R 117).

1 *Mystery*. Proponents of Mystery leave the inconsistencies unresolved and unexplained – "shrouded in mystery" (van Biéma 1908, 164).
2 *Indifferentism*. Indifferentists claim that Leibniz did not defend one system over the other (Garber 2004, 2005).
3 *Exclusive Idealism*. In order to avoid attributing inconsistencies to Leibniz, only the Idealist part of the mature system is endorsed on his behalf. Selection of the favored part is based on philosophical (Furth 1976) or historical (R 1–2) criteria.
4 *Exclusive Realism*. Every apparently Idealist-leaning text is construed as consistent with an animals-only ontology, so that all monads are actually animals or "corporeal substances." This interpretation is found in Fischer (1902), Martin (1964), and most recently Phemister (2005).
5 *Contextualism*. The inconsistencies are explained principally in terms of historical and philosophical influences and tensions Leibniz inherited and did not successfully resolve. Thus Catherine Wilson writes that combining his main metaphysical schemes "ruins the attempt at coherence" and that those schemes represent "Leibniz's never-to-be overcome indecision about perception" (Wilson 1989, 81). But reasons for the incoherence can be found in the context: "we can identify precisely the nexus of conditions which drove Leibniz" to adopt the claims which he "could not reconcile" (1989, 193). And more recently she says these claims "do not form a system." It is an "object-based failure" or "basic mistake" to suppose, with Leibniz, that they do (1999, 373, 384).

(B) *Idealist Compatibilism (often simply "Compatibilism" herein):* Compatibilists wrestle with the supposedly inconsistent themes and arrive at a philosophical reconciliation – a new synthesis in which all logical tensions are resolved and a final consistent mature system, compatible with nearly all the texts, emerges (Ad, Rd). (As far as I know, there are no "Realist Compatibilists," so I devote this category wholly to the Idealist sort.)

Note how theorists in these camps approach Leibniz's rationality and corpus.

On *rationality*, arguably all of them fail to sustain respect for it. Mystery theorists and Indifferentists give up the quest for understanding and on their watch the system – and along with it Leibniz's rationality – disintegrates.

Exclusivist Idealists believe that the Realist parts were put there mistakenly or through ambivalence or forgetfulness – which impugns Leibniz's rationality.

Exclusive Realists, on the other hand, believe the Idealist parts were put there mistakenly — perhaps as concessions to historical influences. Thus Pauline Phemister claims Leibniz's Idealist elements "can be explained by his desire to be accepted into the Cartesian debates on the relation of the soul to the body" and that "Created monads, as complete corporeal substances, are the true substances" (Phemister 2005, 3, 76). She claims remarks to Bernoulli are "more accurate" than *Monadology* §1, since the *Monadology* was guided by "pragmatic considerations" (ibid., 74). Undercutting select Idealist works and passages in order to bolster others that tell a different story undercuts the rationality of the one who penned all of them.

Contextualists usually leave one perplexed as to the philosophical reasons for the inconsistencies. In their view Leibniz is a victim of historical forces beyond his control that led him into contradictions, and his rationality is left undefended. Finally, Compatibilists, despite their admirable goal of defending Leibniz's rationality, arguably fail to do so. For, as will be argued at length in Chapter 7, they reconcile the inconsistencies by modifying Leibniz's doctrines or by constructing systems which themselves harbor inconsistencies. Either way, Leibniz's rationality is not secure.

On the *corpus*. While theorists espousing Mystery and Indifferentism embrace the entire set of writings, they can't provide an interpretive context for the incompatible theories found therein. Exclusive Idealists treat seriously those passages advancing only one of the two theories, chopping the corpus to pieces in an effort to save its author's reputation. Going the other way, Exclusive Realists treat seriously only passages favoring animals, using them to filter out Idealist elements. Contextualists, by contrast with the Exclusivisms, are textually inclusive — and thus in much better shape. Also, unlike Mystery and Indifferentists, Contextualists sometimes discover historical and philosophical factors that "explain" — in the sense of giving historical and philosophical reasons for — the logical inconsistencies. Finally, Compatibilists also are textually inclusive. But their requirement that Idealism and Realism be consistent across-the-board often makes it difficult for them to understand those texts because when considering one theory, incompatible elements from the other one keep getting in the way.

If I had to choose one of these, Contextualism would get my vote. It is textually inclusive and sometimes finds reasons for the inconsistencies, tracing them illuminatingly to historical and philosophical sources. It seems better than the Compatibilist extreme of denying there are inconsistencies, and the Mystery-Indifferentist extreme of giving up the quest for understanding why they're there.

1.6 Theory-Pluralism

> Our biggest fault has been sectarianism, limiting ourselves by the rejection of others.
>
> Leibniz (G 4, 524/WF 85)

[My] system appears to unite Plato with Democritus, Aristotle with Descartes, the Scholastics with the moderns, theology and morality with reason. Apparently it takes the best from all systems and then advances further than anyone has done yet.

Leibniz (NE 71)

It is not to be wondered that historians do not agree about "the real Leibniz." Leibniz, more than any other philosopher, was all things to all men.

Lewis White Beck (1969, 202)

The interpretation I recommend is *Theory-Pluralism*. In terms of the categories laid out in the last section, this is similar to the Incompatibilist position, as it holds that Realism and Idealism are inconsistent. However, unlike any of those interpretations, this one takes Realism and Idealism to be *theories of Reality* rather than descriptions of It. That is, all of the other theorists treated Realism and Idealism as "Truths" about the way the world is. Theory-Pluralism does not account them Truths, but only theories. The 'Theory' in "Theory-Pluralism" is meant to mark this difference in the way Realism and Idealism are regarded. Indeed, in my view, Idealism would often better be called "the Idealist theory" and Realism "the Realist theory" – though in what follows I will not always uses these longer titles in the interest of economy.

There is nothing unusual about such a supposition: typically philosophical claims are regarded as theories about what's True rather than as Truths. Theories are sets of Truth-*claims* designed to explain the things we know – our "evidence base." The commentator thus is not "forced to choose" which one to "purchase," as I had written before (Hartz 1992, 511). The theories are, for the Leibniz I'm defending, just tantalizing possibilities in this life of "window-shopping." How better to avoid what Leibniz calls in the epigraph "sectarianism" and the limitations involved in "rejecting others?"

The familiar case of scientific theories provides a nice analogy for philosophical theories. As Carl Hempel writes, scientific theories seek to explain "a system of uniformities" and "to afford a deeper and more accurate understanding of the phenomena in question" by construing them as "manifestations of entities and processes that lie behind or beneath them, as it were" (Hempel 1966, 70). Analogously, metaphysical theories aspire to explain the uniformities in its wide-ranging evidence base, attributing them to entities and processes behind or beneath them. Thus one of Leibniz's theories sees in the law-like behavior of moving bodies, evidence of the forces of substances in them. And, like scientific theories, metaphysical ones like Realism and Idealism will not be provably True or False (Hempel 1966, 80–1). They will have to be assessed on other, more indirect criteria such as explanatory power, how well they fit with the evidence, and simplicity.

This maneuver resolves in a single stroke the logical problems that drive all the other interpretations. For instance, the inconsistencies are baffling to all Incompatibilists because, they rightly believe, Idealism and Realism can't both be Right. And to protect Leibniz from incoherence, Compatibilists battle long and hard to resolve the many contradictions between them.

But when Realism and Idealism are regarded as theories designed to explain Reality, inconsistency between them is no more a problem than that between the Ptolemaic and Copernican theories of astronomy – where two incompatible theories attempt to explain the "Way the Universe Is." Similarly for Realism and Idealism: there is but one Way Things Are, and two incompatible theories seek to explain It. This sort of Pluralism frees one up to examine Realism and Idealism separately and without sinking into puzzlement or feeling pressured to choose only one or forcing them to fit.

Leibniz himself addressed the Ptolemaic/Copernican issue, and what he says shows him leaning in this direction. In a work of 1689 he offers some advice to Catholic authorities as they try to deal with this theologically charged controversy. In it he advises tolerance of both sides, saying "the Copernican account is the truest theory, that is, the most intelligible theory and the only one capable of an explanation sufficient for a person of sound reason" while "the Ptolemaic account is the truest one in spherical astronomy" (C 591–2/AG 92). "For," he adds, "the nature of the matter is that the two claims are identical; nor should one look for a greater or a different truth here."

The two theories are "identical" in that they explain a single thing – Truth. They differ in their explanations and so are "true" relative to their respective purposes – to explain the Truth according to the principles either of spherical or elliptical astronomy. Looking for Truth *in the theories* is a mistake: "the truth of an hypothesis," he writes, can only consist in its "greater intelligibility" (C 592/AG 92). Each theory gains *prima facie* assent even though sometimes one may seem more "intelligible" because, in Leibniz's words, the "other hypotheses" confront "innumerable perplexities." With this perspective, "philosophical freedom" can be restored to all parties (C 592/AG 93). As he writes more than a decade later, the Catholic Church must recognize that the Ptolemaic theory is not "more than an hypothesis" (NE 515) and that suppression of the Copernican doctrine is unreasonable.

Freedom indeed lies on the path marked out by Theory-Pluralism. Avoiding passionate commitment to one theory as "the Truth" means having the luxury of standing back, taking a deep breath, and letting the theories fight it out among themselves without feeling that one's favorite must "win" and all the others must "lose." One sits in the "stands" far from the blood and sweat of conflict on the field of combat, observing the action and assessing the opponents' strengths and weaknesses.

This phenomenon is quite common in science, with different theories thriving simultaneously within separate "conceptual schemes" and it is assumed access to a "godlike, omniscient point of view" (which could tell us which theory is True) is denied (Freudenthal 1996, 152). One seems well advised to avoid what Gideon Freudenthal calls "dogmatism," where:

> Statements of the relevant conceptual scheme are claimed not only to be valid within it and according to its standards but also to adjudicate the truth-claims of this very theory and those of competing theories. Being at the same time both party and judge, it is no wonder that one's own party wins – not because of a psychological inclination of the judge but because logical standards of judgment belong to this very theory or conceptual scheme.
>
> Freudenthal (1996, 153)

Following this method, one ends up "excluding all but one view." And:

> If the cognitive realm is conceived from the point of view of one conceptual scheme, then different views appear as mistakes. And mistakes should be eliminated. Hence, if we wish to avoid oppressing all but one conceptual scheme as if they were mistakes, we have to use different criteria both within conceptual schemes and outside of them: within the system we enforce consistency; among the systems we allow the plurality of incompatibles.
>
> Freudenthal (1996, 153)

The "plurality of incompatibles" is what Theory-Pluralism is keen to emphasize. The assertions of a scientist – or a philosopher – within a given scheme "have truth value," but such a theorist must recognize that those working within other schemes "are entitled to exactly the same kind of truth-claims, however incompatible with his own" (Freudenthal 1996, 152).

Hence there are quite "different criteria" within a scheme and outside it. Within a scheme consistency is enforced among its truth-claims. But *not* consistency of truth-claims *across* schemes. If that were enforced, the legitimate variety of approaches appears a "mistake" – the very word some commentators use to characterize Leibniz's mixture of Idealism and Realism. It has been said that Realism indicates Leibniz's "ambivalence," his "indecision," his tendency to seek popularity and the favor of princes – a puzzling, paradoxical, wayward set of doctrines. And the "oppression" of alternative doctrines Freudenthal mentions is all too familiar in Leibniz studies. A proponent of a particular viewpoint – which is both "party and judge" – typically takes on the task of refuting alternative interpretations rather than allowing them to coexist with her own. The resulting view becomes, as Leibniz predicted, sectarian and limiting.

Nevertheless, a completely non-sectarian approach seems as aimless as a sectarian one is limiting. Neither extreme is fruitful. One can imagine watching several viable opponents competing on the field of battle; but if there were hundreds, the "competition" would be a free-for-all "state of nature," with thousands of contestants, each out for themselves.

Science's openness to other theories has its limits because of its demand that a viable theory with its own "truth-claims" fits the evidence in a fairly strict sense. Indeed, I think a fairly restricted Theory-Pluralism is more plausible than Leibniz's own. From my perspective, a "viable" theory is not just any assemblage of words that is consistent with the evidence. Sometimes, as in the case of the Ptolemaic theory, there are just too many (as Leibniz says) "perplexities" to allow it even to remain a theory for a person of "sound reason." Somewhere in the course of making all its *ad hoc*, theory-saving adjustments, it passes into the realm of the non-viable – the safely ignored. It has now passed from viable to idle because its fit with the evidence is effected only by a most questionable array of special assumptions and adjustments.

And the Ptolemaic theory isn't even the most extreme example of a theory being maintained despite a lack of fit. At one point Leibniz lists among "philosophical sects" in which resides "more good sense than we had realized" the "vitalistic philosophy" of the Cabbalists and Hermetics (G 4, 523–4/WF 85). While he restricts this to a certain favorite part of those theories, the "philosophy" he mentions can only be properly understood within the larger systems – in which astrology and religious magic are countenanced.

Fortunately, for our purposes we need not follow Leibniz down this path to ultra-openmindedness. We can stop well short of "ultra," taking it that, at a minimum, Idealism and Realism (and the many views that fall under these rough categories) remain viable theories – that neither can claim a clear victory on the criterion of fitting the evidence. I shall be restricting 'Theory-Pluralism' hereafter to this more minimalist form of the doctrine unless otherwise noted.

1.6.1 Theory-Pluralism v. Truth-Pluralism

Theory-Pluralism must be sharply distinguished from "Truth-Pluralism," according to which Idealism and Realism are *both* True. Given that they are incompatible, that claim is incoherent. And Theory-Pluralism does not affirm it. Instead, it says that Idealism and Realism are possibly true accounts of Reality: only *one* can be True.

Now Theory-Pluralism has a particularly important impact on traditional arguments for Exclusive Idealism. The case for this interpretation is usually made by appealing to the fearful logical results of letting Realism "in." Thus Bertrand Russell claims early in his book that "philosophic error chiefly appears in the shape of inconsistency" (R 3), and he builds his main case for ignoring Realism (in his terms, doctrines clustering around "Perception yields knowledge of an external world" and true unity for animals – R 4, 149–50) on the belief that it is "hopelessly inconsistent" (R 117) with

Idealism (which he derives from "Every proposition has a subject and a predicate" – R 4). But inconsistency between *theories* is not an "error" at all, and the inconsistencies Russell finds in Leibniz's philosophy do not – if construed as claims belonging to separate theories – compel one to take on Exclusive Idealism.

It is hard to overestimate the importance of this point. Exclusive Idealism has been sustained largely by the need to avoid the dreaded contradictions that await one in holding Idealism and Realism to be True. So, it is thought, a clean break must be made right from the start: simply ignore the Realism and circle the wagons round the familiar Idealist passages. Otherwise. . . .

That rationale is now resolved into smoke. The proponent of an Idealist *theory* has nothing to fear from a Realist *theory*. Holding them simultaneously is perfectly rational.

Still, a look at the texts shows that a few of them could be seen as leaning in the "hegelian" direction of Truth-Pluralism – one recently championed by Graham Priest (1987).[19] For instance, in one place he says there is a "common center of perspective" within which Pythagoreans, Skeptics, Aristotle, Plato, Parmenides, Democritus, Plotinus, Cabbalists, and Hermetics are all "reunited" (July 1698, G 4, 523–4/WF 85; cf. G 4, 305). Leibniz seems to have in mind here the limited claim that these disparate systems contain points of commonality with his own. But if one emphasized the bit about "reuniting," it might seem as if he is claiming that somehow Reality might be made up wholly of numbers *and* of atoms; might have bodies in it *and* have no bodies in it. Those claims, which fall in with Truth-Pluralism, are incoherent. And there's no reason to push the passage in that direction.

Indeed, elsewhere in Leibniz's thought he upholds the ultimacy of logic. Against Descartes, it is something that God must abide by and is not determined by the divine will. (Similarly on the "Euthyphro" question: right and wrong are already established independently of God's commands – Riley 1999.) He does sometimes toy with the possibility of alternative logics, but defends pretty staunchly the principle of non-contradiction and bivalence (NE 362; see Levey 2002). In the end, if God affirmed contradictions he wouldn't be rational, while the whole of Leibniz's system is based on the assumption that he is. And he writes that while much having to do with the external senses may be doubted and remains at best highly probable, the two "mathematical sciences" of "arithmetic and geometry" are not merely probable. They are "exempt" from doubt – so much so that even if I were dreaming in a solipsist world, I could rely on my mathematical discoveries as certain (see the 1702 Letter to Queen Sophie Charlotte, G 6, 499–508/AG 186–92).

Consider a court case. The date is inflexible: it must be held today. Yet on this day the defense attorney has been taken deathly ill and no one in his office knows anything about the case. The prosecuting attorney is ready to proceed. The judge tells her that, as she knows the case better than anyone else available that day, she must present the defense as well! Her job is to argue as vehemently as possible against the accused, then as forcefully as possible defend that same person before the jury. This is a tall order. But, summoning up as much objectivity as she can, she sets to work. She aims her best arguments at the accused, then meticulously picks apart those arguments, searching for their subtle weaknesses. That evening the newspapers quote arguments from the prosecution and defense, attributing them (of course) to the same person. The jury never returns a verdict.

Leibniz puts himself in a similar situation. (Indeed, the allegory is strengthened by the fact that he took his degree in law, writing a dissertation on juristic antinomies, where valid grounds exist for both of the opposing sides.) He offers a vicious attack on Idealism and a triumphant defense of Realism. The same man, in the same works, launches a jarring assault against Realism and a smashing defense of Idealism. Since they come from the same pen, they look like contradictory claims because they are. The "jury never returns" in Leibniz's case means this: we metaphysicians remain in a "veil of tears" pending (in Leibniz's mind) our time of enlightenment in heaven. The two theories must remain, for us, deadlocked because there are valid grounds for both opposing sides. God some day will divulge which one is True.

The allegory is of course imperfect. One main difference is that the prosecution-persona is taken on for a while and "then" the defense-persona emerges to rebut the prosecution's arguments. If Leibniz's writings were to follow this exactly, we could expect them to have stretches of pure Idealism before or after stretches of pure Realism. And there would be a fairly clear dividing-line between the two "voices." But I'm afraid that's not what's there. Instead, there is a blending of the two voices – sometimes juxtaposed in the same letter, the same paragraph, even the same sentence.

For a theorist of this sort, Theory-Pluralism seems made to order. For it then doesn't matter that there is frequent "switching" back and forth. He is just running with two theories simultaneously, and saying contradictory things is predictable when one does that.

It is quite natural that Leibniz should be found on both sides of an issue if, as Beck says in the epigraph, he is all things to all people. In the realm of politics, if there is a party which aspires to be all things to all people, it will often be committed to inconsistent goals since some of its constituents will want A to happen, and others of its constituents will want A not to happen. The party has trouble knowing where to stand with respect to A.

Similarly, Leibniz wants to give realists Realism and idealists Idealism. And, amazingly, he does. But just as astonishing is his apparent blindness to the lack of fit between them at crucial junctures – that is, in terms of the analogy, when Realism says A and Idealism says not-A. To maintain his position as go-between, he must say – and does say – A and not-A. Indeed, something has to give if, in line with Leibniz's claim in the epigraph, one aspires to "unite Plato with Democritus" – that is, *unite Idealism with Real-*

ism! Plato, like Berkeley, dismisses bodies as appearances; Democritus, like Locke, offers a theory of composition for real bodies: A and not-A. Leibniz's claiming to "unite" them leads one to believe that he will wrap up all their doctrines up in a single consistent theoretical package. Leibniz probably wanted people to believe he could do that. He may even have believed, at the height of a metaphysical reverie, that he had done it. But he did not, I think. What he ended up with was a sophisticated, rhetorically nuanced blending of elements of both.

He would make my task of defending Theory-Pluralism a lot easier if he had qualified his endorsements, saying each looks consistent with what else we know, but that its status as Truth is somewhat in doubt since we remain ignorant of so many things. Occasionally he writes in this tentative vein. He writes in 1702 that Solipsism is "not impossible" – where everything is a "dream" and every object an "appearance" (G 6, 502–3/AG 188–9). Two years later he says that if the reader "concedes" to him an infinity of percipients with all their phenomena corresponding to each other given that God is their common cause, then "this is all that I claim in the matter, and all that I think can be claimed" (G 2, 264/L 535). And eight years later he writes that it is a mere "hypothesis" that the perceptions of the soul correspond to something "outside" (G 2, 451/L 605). I take it these positions are at best possible because, while they accord sufficiently with the evidence base, that same base can also be explained by other theories.

But more often there are bold, brash claims, with all "ifs" left out. Thus the *New System* declares the pre-established harmony between soul and body "something more than a hypothesis" (NS 17), and the *Monadology* makes the bold claim, "the monads have no windows" (Mon 4). These passages are written in the language of Truth, not theory. A is, he seems to be saying, the Way Things Are. And this is what sets the reader up for disillusionment when, a few lines or paragraphs before or after, he is just as triumphantly declaring for not-A and producing all manner of arguments concluding that *not-A* is the Way Things Are.

The fact that Leibniz often presents himself as a purveyor of Truth makes the Theory-Pluralism here envisaged difficult to attribute uniformly to Leibniz-the-historical-figure. In order to justify this departure from the sense of the texts, a strong rationale must be provided, according to the rules of acceptable interpretation. So here is my strong rationale: if I don't make that move, Leibniz's rationality is annihilated, and along with it the rationality of any commentary upon it. Often justifications for going against the sense of a text read something like this: "without this move, his thought is less coherent because it then would not jibe with other things he says." My justification for this departure is: *without this move, Leibniz has no thought.* That is the strongest rationale imaginable.

Now even before I had adopted this sort of Pluralism as a way of resolving inconsistencies, I had become so used to finding them in Leibniz's thought that they no longer seemed particularly unusual or problematic.

The tendency to be on both sides – there are usually just two – of an argument is fully characteristic of his thought.

For instance, in Michael Murray's review of a book by "strong essentialists" J. A. Cover and J. O'Leary-Hawthorne, there is this:

> Does God choose to create Adam, all other facts about Adam thus following necessarily? Leibniz says no. The superessentialist and strong essentialist try to maintain consistency here by holding that Leibniz really means "yes" but that he can fly under the radar as long as he avails himself of counterparts. The problem here is that the appeal to counterparts to ground contingency at this point precludes us from taking Leibniz at his word. The counterpart theorist contends that individuals have all properties ... necessarily, but that we can ground claims about contingency in the existence of counterparts. This is surely trying to have it both ways.
>
> Murray (2000, 79)

The details of contingency and counterparts do not concern me here. I'm interested only in Murray's assumption that Leibniz has a single, monolithic view – so one can take him "at his word" and not try to "have it both ways."

Indeed, the authors' reply appeals to places where Leibniz does not to take *himself* at his word:

> Well, we intended to ... address what has seemed to many scholars as a persistent sense that *Leibniz himself* is trying to have it both ways, and by considering general strategies for understanding *his own efforts* at flying under the radar.
>
> Cover and Hawthorne (2000, 95–6)

Like Murray, I instinctively want to put the question, "Wasn't Adam's fall from grace determined to happen and hence not free?" When Leibniz faces it he says Yes and No. It was determined but was also free so long as 'free' is defined – I would add, *as possibly true theories would* – in terms of counterparts or "inclining without necessitating" or "infinite analysis" or "hypothetical necessity." Even with all the pressures in his system leading him to say Yes and leave it at that, he goes on to give multiple detailed accounts that allow him also to say No. And while this position might be construed as "Yes and No," I view it as "*Some theories say Yes, some No.*"

I think that Idealism has captured so many minds and hearts because of Leibniz's power of persuasion as he speaks the language of Truth. As one reads along, one almost can't help saying, "He must believe this is True!" But equally powerful Realist presentations cut short any Idealist exuberance. Those passages seem betrayals of all that has gone before – evidence of a sudden inexplicable reluctance to run the final victory lap for Idealism. He flies beneath his own radar, doesn't take himself at his word, and has it both ways.

Indeed, when he sees Berkeley "running the victory lap" in his *Principles* of 1710, Leibniz writes that there is "much here that is correct" and "agrees with my views." However, immediately he hedges: "But . . . we have no need to say matter is nothing. . . . " Instead, matter is a "result of substances" and the author should have gone on to "infinite monads, constituting all things."[20]

This brief passage is more powerful than any other in the corpus in showing Leibniz's attitude towards Exclusive Idealism. Having been presented with an excruciatingly pure, "consistent," and all-encompassing statement of it, he spends most of his time objecting to it. All his reasons accord perfectly with Theory-Pluralism. He is not content to let the monads merely perceive and bodies be "nothing." Monads not only perceive, they *constitute*. And there's a thought which is only intelligible in Realism, for in Idealism minds can't constitute anything – and least of all bodies.

1.6.2 Restrictions on Theory-Pluralism

Returning now to Pluralism generally: Leibniz places at least four restrictions on its scope as applied to metaphysical theories.

1 Pluralism will not apply to such "factual" matters as the shape of the earth or the location of Egypt: it is False that the earth is flat and that Egypt is in North America. It will apply only to such metaphysical claims as "material atoms are the basic building-blocks of the world," or "there is nothing in reality except minds and their ideas."
2 Metaphysical schemes that are theologically unacceptable can be left out: his main critique of Newton commences with the claim that "natural religion" is in "decay" in England (Clarke, 1.1). (Nevertheless, parts of Cabbalism are retained despite its allegiance to pantheism.)
3 Theories which are inconsistent with something in the evidence-base are also proscribed. For instance, Descartes's claim that bodies are mere extension can be ignored since it is inconsistent with the fact that bodies move and act. But as I've said, for Leibniz this restriction doesn't rule out nearly as much as it does for scientists and many philosophers.
4 Usually theories that represent bad philosophy are eliminated. Spinoza's idea that objects are modes of God can be safely eliminated because it's such a bad idea to confuse the finite with the infinite. I say "usually," for again things are not always so clear. He finds formidable philosophical objections to atomism yet remains open to it. Recall, he wrote that this doctrine is tied to "the crude concept of a corporeal substance which depends only on sensory imagery," yet the "corpuscular philosophy" is "excellent and most true in itself" (GM 6, 236/L 436). So while *some* philosophies are just too far afield even to qualify for Theory-Pluralism's indulgence, others are not. And I have been able to discover neither what determines whether some set of ideas is "too far afield" nor what makes inconsistencies with the evidence too egregious.

As I am interested only in a minimal Theory-Pluralism, I needn't determine a precise boundary around viable philosophical theories – though that remains a worthy historical inquiry. I am making the more limited claim that within the boundary are Idealism and Realism. Neither of these is (1) factual, (2) theologically unacceptable, (3) inconsistent with the evidence, or (4) an example of doing philosophy poorly.

1.6.3 Why Leibniz Presents Himself as a "Purveyor of Truths"

Even with these qualifications in place, the issue of truth might seem to present a lingering problem for Pluralism. In response to my "court case" scenario (where a single lawyer presents the prosecution and the defense) presented earlier, lawyer and philosopher Patrick Lewtas writes (in private correspondence):

> The prosecutor works within an institutional system where the roles of the players are well-defined. Prosecutor and defense must present the best cases they can. Neither searches for truth. In fact, truth isn't even a goal of the system as a whole. The metaphysician, on the other hand, wants truth. If his method can't uncover it, then he fails utterly. Worse, if he can build two equally good cases for two inconsistent positions, then I think he should feel pushed towards a wide-ranging and deep skepticism. He should question whether his methods are any good at all. If our clearest thinking leads to incoherence, then what confidence can we have in any thinking?

In part, the reply to this challenge is now apparent: Leibniz the (minimal) Pluralist does not pursue "truth" in this sense. What Lewtas calls a "failure to uncover truth" would, in my terms, be a failure to uncover *Truth*. And a failure to uncover *that* is not a failure at all if the metaphysician's goal is to uncover theories. That metaphysician has given up the quest for Truth, and will settle for the humbler goal of finding the best theories – approximating Truth as best they can with positions that are theologically viable and immune to philosophical refutation.

But that is only partially satisfying, I think. The last bit in Lewtas's challenge remains hauntingly unanswered: "If our clearest thinking leads to incoherence, what confidence can we have in any thinking?" That is, if our best philosophy leads to A and not-A, why do philosophy at all?

Indeed, this points to what is perhaps the deepest purely philosophical explanation for Leibniz's tendency to uphold the appearance of "purveyor of Truth" rather than "suggester of theories that aim at Truth." If he came off as a mere "suggester," it would undercut the immense confidence he places in "Reason." Reason is supposed to lead us through the gloom of Falsehood into the brilliant light of Truth. If the best it can do is to eliminate obvious losers and present us with "possibly right" options, it's a very lame enterprise. Freedom is a great thing, but Reason isn't supposed to leave things *that* open-ended.

Also the difference in background beliefs between contemporary scientists and Leibniz is crucial in this regard. For while they believe that a "godlike, omniscient point of view" is completely inaccessible, Leibniz didn't. He assumed not only that there was one, but that we ourselves could get close to accessing it if we worked hard enough. (Someone once quipped that Leibniz thought there were a *few* things God knows that he hadn't yet discovered.) So there were theological beliefs leading him to adopt an insanely optimistic view of Reason's capacities.

In addition to all these factors, there is a natural and predictable tendency for advocates of a theory to make assertions that are unabashedly truth-claims and not hedged round by qualifications. Thus someone stating Boyle's law doesn't bother to say, "assuming the kinetic theory of gases is correct." They just state the law. I think it is the same with philosophical theories: once one is "in" a given viewpoint, one just *says it* – even though, as in Leibniz's case, it is acknowledged that one's claims are theory-laden "truths" rather than Truths.

My principal claim here is that Theory-Pluralism is the most fruitful way to *interpret* his writings. When Leibniz says, confidently, "in the end, there are simple substances alone," I say to myself, "All right. But what else might be True?" and note – without being fazed by it – that just before he had written "a substance is either simple ... or it is composite" (C 13–14/ PW 175). How could he, or anyone, declare – as if they were *describing* the Way Things Are – that substances are simple only, or also composite, or that monads have no windows, or that mind-body parallelism is more than a theory?

When the other interpretations take Leibniz's claims as Truths rather than theories of Truth, any sign of pluralism will be seen as portending "Truth-Pluralism," and thus as a dire threat to his rationality. For me, this point has thrown a new light on the plight of typical commentators. With a specter like Truth-Pluralism leering at you across the table, you're likely to pull out all the stops to end its encroachment on Leibniz's thought.

1.6.4 Theory-Pluralism's Explanatory Power

I can summarize the discussion of Theory-Pluralism by indicating its explanatory power.

First consider the difference between it and the "Contextualism" examined earlier. Contextualism took it that there was no philosophical resolution to the inconsistencies – that they had to remain logical mistakes. But Theory-Pluralism *has* a philosophical resolution: the inconsistencies belong to different theories that need not square with one another. Holding multiple, redundant theories (all except one "in reserve" on any given occasion) gives Leibniz a potent arsenal of techniques and doctrines with which to construct a theory or confront an objector. That is an eminently reasonable philosophical strategy.

The power of "reserves" is evident in the *New Essays*. There he confronts Locke's claim that souls are "indifferent to any parcel of matter" (*Essay* II, 27, 14). It would seem this is an accurate criticism. And it is – against a pure Idealist for whom there are no mind-independent "parcels of matter." But Leibniz does not concede the point because he has Realism in reserve: "On my hypotheses," he says, souls are "united in an orderly way" with certain portions of matter which make up their "bodies" (NE 240). (Here he says explicitly that he holds "hypotheses.")

If I'm right, what the Contextualist finds as the philosophical and historical influences – Wilson's "nexus of conditions" – that lie behind the inconsistencies are not regrettable. They are not carrying him along, against his will, towards contradiction. Instead, they simply help him fill in the "logical space" of possible theories about the world – all of which can be entertained, simultaneously, as possibly true. Influences like *that* are welcomed rather than feared.

The "welcoming" opens up myriad possibilities for me that are not present in other interpretations. The typical commentator tries to say which view was "the one" he "really" held. I have no need of doing that. If there are inconsistent views afoot, I feel no pressure to suppress all but one. There is no need to fix a precise time for a "revolution" from one scheme to another. There always are many theories in the air. Some go in and out of vogue in Leibniz's writings. Some have already been fairly well described in his works. Some have been discovered by others. Some are revealed here for the first time. Some will come along later. What a wonderful research program opens before us!

And even if the reader is convinced, on balance, that one of the other strategies is better, they can still enjoy the benefits of the analyses offered in this study. Adopting Theory-Pluralism is not a precondition to reading this book with profit.

A final payoff for Theory-Pluralism is that it explains an oft-noticed feature of Leibniz's system: its "doctrinal conservativeness." That is, Leibniz almost never, within the mature period, turns his back on former beliefs. Instead others are *added* and the whole lot goes forward as the new synthesis. For example, he begins with animals as his model substances, and later adds spiritual monads without taking the animals away. Often this is seen as a peculiar trait. Is he unwilling to walk away from doctrines he committed himself to in published writings – even when they sort ill with the new ones he wants to add?

On Theory-Pluralism, the puzzle disappears. For within it, a theory is a theory, and can be continued in that status even when other theories – delicious alternatives never before contemplated – come along. Doctrinal conservativeness is a natural upshot of Theory-Pluralism's freedom, where doctrines are held loosely enough to allow their fellows a chance.

Again this has a dramatic effect on traditional arguments for Exclusive Idealism. For it is often assumed that anyone who wants to put spiritual monads in the "substance slot" must first clear animals out of that category. Hence the familiar story is told, according to which Leibniz arrived at his final system of pure Idealism. But: *he never gets there because he doesn't have to.* On other interpretations he seems to be courting an inexplicable madness in taking on so many incompatible elements and appearing hardly to notice the jarring inconsistencies. On Theory-Pluralism, he's doing about what one could expect him to do: welcoming in discordant elements because the claims he makes are relativized to the theory in which they have their home. "In the end, there are simple substances alone" is true according to the Idealist theory, but there are simple and composite substances in the Realist one. He can say both, without embarrassment, in the same paragraph because, while stated in the "language of Truth," they are actually truth-claims at home in separate theories which need not, for us in our current condition of ignorance, compete for exclusive allegiance.

1.7 Idealism's "Canonical Metaphysics"

As Idealism (in this section taken to be, not a theory, but a set of Truths) largely holds the field in Leibniz interpretation, it is important to understand something about it at the outset.

As I said earlier, Idealists tend to identify with Leibniz's logical concerns and hold that the universe houses only minds and mind-dependent objects. Leibniz's distinctive form of Idealism is revealed when one examines several specific doctrines associated with it. These are presented below as a list of beliefs that will be called, jointly, the "Canonical Metaphysics" – so named because they are often taken to be his definitive positions.

Here 'Canonical' conveys nothing honorific. It simply designates the "received view" of Leibniz's philosophy. The main reason for choosing just these doctrines is that they are consistent and together form a coherent set. They also present a fantastic, alluring, fascinatingly simple and elegant picture of the universe.

A short list of Canonical tenets is as follows. These all seem to emanate from Leibniz's famous "complete concept theory of substance" (Mercer 2001, 474), according to which, in Leibniz's words, "the nature of an individual substance or complete being is to have a concept so complete that it is sufficient to make us understand and deduce from it all the predicates of the subject to which the concept is attributed" (DM 8: A VI 4 B, 1540 (N. 306); see also LA 43, 46; C 520/AG 32). Each substance has complete independence (except not from God) and is immune to changes going on outside it – including, as in "Solipsism," the annihilation of everything outside it.

Idealists are content to settle on "Substance" rather than advocating the extreme of Solipsism, and that is why their position looks like this:

The Canonical Metaphysics

1 The only substances are monads (Mates 1986, 49).
2 Relations are either purely ideal or reducible to intrinsic states of the relata.[21]
3 The "predicate in subject" doctrine holds universally. In particular, when the predicate is "perceives a body," the body thus perceived is wholly in the subject doing the perceiving (R 117).
4 Bodies – and all their primary qualities, including extension – are eliminatively reduced to phenomena in the representational content of monads' perceptual states (Furth 1976).
5 Universal harmony and mirroring holds between all the perceptual states of all the monads (G 2 450–51/L 604–5), but not between the perceptual states of monads and a mind-independent universe (since there isn't one) (Furth 1976, 116–23).
6 "Parallelism" as a view of mind and body is denied because there is no mind-independent body to be in states that parallel mental states (Furth 1976, 120; Mates 1986, 206–8).
7 The "aggregate thesis" – roughly the claim that a body contains or is constituted by monads – is denied in light of 4's eliminative reduction. (Furth 1976, 121; Mates 1986, 204[22]).
8 Animals are not true unities, but mere aggregates of monads – "substances by courtesy" (Latta 1898, 110; Sleigh 1990, 100; Rescher 1991, 46, 221).

These eight are considered, together, the Canonical Metaphysics. 4 is singled out for special treatment in the Doctrine Tables, because I thought it important to count the explicit endorsements of "Phenomenalism" separately. The Doctrine Tables show where these claims are found in the five major works, and the Summary reveals that they contain 190 Canonical claims and 55 Phenomenalist endorsements.

1–8 present an austere and quite coherent metaphysic of the world, remembering now that this "world" is not a physical universe. It is a community of minds, all in their private states, often enjoying harmonized perceptions of animals and bodies.

I bring forward Idealism and its Canonical doctrines at this early stage because it is an essential backdrop for understanding Leibniz's philosophy. The debate between Pluralism and Idealism will become acute when the Realist elements are discussed – principally in Chapters 6 and 8. But at a larger, programmatic level, the first stone has already been cast: I argued for Theory-Pluralism (in which Realism and Idealism coexist) over Exclusivism (used to sustain Idealism).

In what follows there will be no attempt gratuitously to intensify the conflict between my interpretation and Idealism. For instance, the critique of extension will be preserved to the end. That critique in large measure defines Leibniz's mature philosophy, and there can be no question of editing it out. But given the requirements inherent in Leibniz's own thought, many of these Canonical doctrines must be accorded a restricted range of application, making room for Realist themes that are also found in the texts.

1.8 Realism's "Aggregate Thesis"

It is important as a backdrop for this study also to characterize Realism as it is understood here. The "aggregate thesis" is the label typically affixed to a group of claims that seem to require bodies to be mind-independent. It conveys the idea that bodies must in some sense be composed of or constituted by substances.

The Aggregate Thesis

Composition	Every body is composed of substances.
Containment	Every body contains substances.
Divided	Every body is actually divided into substances.
Force	Every body has derivative active force that supervenes on the primitive active force of the substances it contains.
Mass	Every body is a "mass" or aggregate of substances.
Plurality	Every body is a plurality.
Presupposition	Every plurality presupposes genuine unities.
Reality	Every body has some residual derivative reality because of the presence in it of primitively real substances.
The Ss	Every body *is* substances.
Supervenience	Every derivative quality of a body must arise from the primitive qualities of the things it contains.

In the Doctrine Tables, these are tracked individually as they are less familiar than Idealism's Canonical doctrines. The Summary shows that there are 150 endorsements in the five major works. Added to these in the category of Realism are 101 references to animals for, as I argue in Chapter 8, animals can't be properly understood by any Idealist analysis – Exclusivist or Compatibilist. And even if the reader is unsure that animals belong in Realism, the 150 Aggregate Thesis endorsements are a significant body of work that needs to be explained, and they alone will suffice, until Chapter 8, to provide the textual basis for Realism.

1.9 Supervenience

Supervenience – one of the aggregate thesis doctrines above – will play a crucial role in my discussions. So a word about it is in order now.

   If supervenience is viewed, as it typically is, as a relation between families of properties, then it is quite a separate matter from mereology, or the study of parts and wholes. Still, the topics are related. Jaegwon Kim calls a key principle closely allied to supervenience "mereological determinism": " … the Democritean credo that wholes are completely determined, causally and ontologically, by their parts, that if you make a replica of an object by putting it together atom by atom, particle by particle, you get the 'same' object."[23] Thus a lake is reducible to the collection of its constituent water molecules.

Supervenience, by contrast, is often viewed as a non-reductive relation, and need not involve mereology at all.[24] With respect to mereology, one can claim that moral goodness supervenes on – is determined by – purely descriptive features without presupposing a particular answer to the question, "Is the object reducible to parts which have purely descriptive properties?" Moreover, mereology may actually be sundered from supervenience in some cases. For example, the properties of magnetic fields supervene on – are determined by – those of moving electric fields. But it is unclear how one might construe the electric field as part of the magnetic field. Perhaps this is sheer property-to-property supervenience, with no "mereological determinism" story tied to it.

However that may be, Leibniz takes the usual tack and presents mereological and property supervenience in tandem. Within Realism's "aggregate thesis" mereological supervenience is represented in "Composition," where bodies are composed of substances. Property supervenience is represented in "Supervenience," according to which bodies derive their main qualities from the qualities of their component substances.

So define supervenience as follows:

Supervenience   Property B *supervenes on* property A iff[25] for any object x
composed of ys and any world wi, if the ys have A in wi, then
x has B in wi.[26]

Fragility (in the definition, "Property B") supervenes on chemical bonds (A) just in case a body (x) composed of appropriately bonded molecules (ys) in some world (wi) must be fragile. The mental supervenes on the physical just in case an object composed of purely physical material in some world must be mental. Derivative force, as Leibniz will say, supervenes on primitive force just in case a body composed of primitive-force-bearing substances in some world must have derivative force.

It is important to note that the "subvenient property" (Property A) that characterizes the ys will typically be a relational property that they jointly instantiate. It will not be a monadic quality that each possesses in isolation: it is chemical relations (often ionic bonds) between molecules that ground fragility, and relations between large numbers of neurons that ground mental states.

When one moves to Leibnizian substances as the constituents, the need for relational properties presents a problem – at least for the Idealist's

Canonical program. Within that program relations are under severe pressure to yield to eliminative reductions of one sort or another – reductions that transform every relation into intrinsic features of the items purportedly related to each other. And so it will be difficult, in the broadly Idealist theory, to give any details about how a body's properties – say, its forces and extension – are grounded in properties of its constituent substances.

At the moment, I must leave the matter at that fairly abstract level. Along the way I will add details as I develop a specifically Leibnizian concept of supervenience.

2   Substance

Leibniz is intent on starting at absolute rock-bottom. There can be no hint of convention or arbitrariness at this stage. Everything here must be completely determinate. The items he arrives at in this quest for a foundation are called "substances." They are self-sufficient and independent of everything else – except God. Thus they are mind-independent objects *par excellence*, and the building blocks for all else that exists.

A proper understanding of substances is crucial for any interpretation of Leibniz. In this chapter I offer some of Leibniz's reasons for starting with substances and some of his arguments for the nature of substances. This will launch the larger project designed to come to terms with the mature metaphysics – which by all accounts shines the spotlight on these premium individuals and seeks to explain everything through them.

It is helpful to think of substances as functioning in the way "theoretical entities" function in scientific theories. Such entities as germs and elastic, moving atoms are postulated by the theory as a way of explaining a set of regularities in the world. The existence of such things can't be directly confirmed, but they are used to rationalize and make more intelligible what is observable. Similarly, substances (except in the case of the one which is oneself) can't be directly observed but can be used to explain what is known, or what is in the "evidence base."

2.1 *I*

Begin with *I*. The most basic metaphysical datum is that I am an active, real unity that perceives and strives.[1] I am in categorical, wholly inner states picked out by monadic predicates. "I act," "I am real," "I am one," "I perceive," "I strive" – these can be true even if I am the only finite object in the universe. *I* has primacy not merely in epistemology and the ontology of mind; it pervades one's account of both worlds – the inner and the outer.

The curse of modern philosophy is that it leaves one with explanations that are hopelessly bifurcated. (And: the curse is with us still: as Peter Unger writes, "At least since Galileo," there has been in force a "restriction of qualities to minds," so that only spatiotemporal properties and propensities characterize what's physical. This leads straight to "a *deeply segregated* worldview," while its denial would help lead to a *"deeply integrated"* one (Unger 1999, 94, 82).) There is the province of bodily mechanism – extension, mass, gravitation, laws of motion. And then in another explanatorily airtight compartment over *here* are mental states and their associated paraphernalia – desires, beliefs, willings, feelings, flashes, bangs. Concepts of mechanism never really tie in with those of mind. Explanations are either mechanical or mental, but never, illuminatingly, partly both. Explanatory unity is occluded.

But at all costs such unity must be preserved – yes, even across a divide as seemingly unspannable as mental and physical. Finally even these two meet up in *I*. In his Realist theory, Leibniz will try to restore empirical relevance to the free-floating Cartesian soul by making it the form of a living body – rather as Aristotle dragged the Forms out of Plato's Heaven and back into the world of plants and animals. He will even try to restore a measure of reality to sticks and stones by putting souls or animals in them.

The "deeply segregated worldview" is a Cartesian legacy. For Descartes is quite clear that mind and body are completely different, and that while the mind grasps the concept of body, nothing can be learned about the nature of body by studying the mind, and vice versa. In his Idealist theory Leibniz is in much the same predicament: body is a phenomenon in a mind and minds can't help us figure out the nature of bodies, nor bodies that of minds. The passage that comes to mind is at Mon 17, where it is said that motions of pulleys and levers can never explain perception.

But Leibniz is not always such a dutiful dualist, hanging on tightly to the bifurcation. He also has the Realist theory, where he overcomes it. The details of how this is done must wait until Chapter 6, but in general it is accomplished by declaring, in line with the "Aggregate Thesis" (1.8), that bodies are *constituted by minds*. Here segregation disappears, for the key to understanding the nature of bodies lies precisely in understanding the nature of minds. Again, just to anticipate a bit, one can see here another reason to give the Realist theory a closer look: it offers hope that fruitful explanatory analogies can be found between mental and physical – that after all we might be rescued from Descartes's explanatory impasse.

At the most general level, one's metaphysic is either "inside out" or "outside in."[2] That is, one begins either with knowledge and ideas and works one's way out, explanatorily, to external reality, or with external reality and works back into the mind and its contents. It seems the outside-inners won't be able to use their outside tools inside – to explain the datum that stares back at us every waking moment. No amount of nuancing or spin can transform a piece of vacuous, infinitely divisible extension into a true unity of the sort I find myself to be. Nothing in the stock of outside concepts can explain how a pile of inert atoms could be a creature capable of activity. No assembly of levers and pulleys can explain a perception. *Start outside and you'll never get in.*

But then isn't it also true that: *Start inside and you'll never get out?* That all depends on how much one can grab on the way out. Some empiricists are inside-outers who try to get along with mere sense-seemings – try to construct from sheer seemings an account of the outer. With such pathetically impoverished and subjective data, it is no wonder they never make it out. Thus as Locke stretches forth his hands and touches the "foot-ball", he has no chance of becoming acquainted with external solidity (*Essay* II iv 6). What he has found is a feeling – mere internal solidity. Of course sense-seemings get selected because epistemic concerns drive the empiricist program: knowledge and certainty are paramount.

Not so Leibniz. Empiricists demand knowledge; Leibniz settles for *explanation*. While Leibniz, like them, is an inside-outer, he does not make indubitability a main concern. So he can accept much more than seemings from the inner. There is also reason, which is considered a trustworthy source of concepts, principles, and analogies that help one construct a world – to derive a story about the external realm. One engages in what Unger calls "extrapolative analogical thinking" that helps connect familiar properties with ones that are necessarily hidden from us (Unger 1999, 80). I indicated (in 1.4) how such thinking is involved in Leibniz's "interlevel explanations."

I will examine several considerations that favor the prominence of *I* in metaphysics. These are not intended to be knock-down arguments; they are offered as powerful reasons to take a close look at metaphysics done inside-out.

(1) Intelligibility

Occult concepts doom the prospects for clear explanations from the outset. One's root notions need to be intelligible and clear – which is why *I* is the anchor. No concept is more opaque than one that makes no connection with the inner. When De Volder complains that the "modes of action in the mind are too obscure," Leibniz responds, "I thought they were most clear; indeed, that they alone are clear and distinct" (G 2, 261, 265/L 535). On the nature of force, he declares "there is nothing in nature more intelligible than force" (Bossuet 1909, 6:529/WF 34), and that this "principle of action is most intelligible, because there is something in it analogous to what is in us, namely, perception and appetite" (G 2, 270/L 537). With feet firmly planted on the inner, I can reach forth to the outer – to other minds, the external world, and God.

(2) Priority of Quality Over Quantity

The reductive ideal of modern mechanism was embodied most palpably in Descartes's attempt to reduce all qualities of bodies to mere extension. Quality would be reduced, without remainder, to Quantity. Nature's thoroughgoing mathematization would at last be realized.

Leibniz regards this as quite implausible. How could Quantity – extended-ness, spread-out-ness, sheer amount – be the ultimate reality from which the world of appearance springs? That would require radical emergence – the kind that precludes even an "in principle" intelligible explanation. The world of appearance is chock-full of qualities. And qualities must arise from qualities. A bankrupt "hollow" shell can never bring forth an array of objects complete with qualities.

So while the reduction to Quantity may seem appealing because of its elegance and relative simplicity, it cannot be reckoned a philosophical account of the world. As with so many reductions, too much is lost along the way.

(3) Privileged Access Enriched by Reason

For all I know, I live in a solipsist world – the demon scenario makes that clear enough. Something in our privileged-access, first-person experience must provide at least an analogy or hint as to what (if anything) is outside us. Reason comes to the aid of *I* in this regard, furnishing it with analogies, parallels, concepts, and metaphysical principles – all of which help connect inner and outer. Some examples:

1 Reflection on what it's like to be a conscious being provides a basis for our knowledge of other minds and God.
2 The representative content of our perceptions furnishes a hint about the nature of objects in the external world.
3 Awareness of striving and exerting effort gives us analogous knowledge of what it's like for external objects to exert forces.
4 Being an active, real, unified substance in categorical states gives us a feel for what it's like for external objects to have some measure of categori-city, activity, reality, and unity.
5 Awareness of what it's like to be a composite unity is a guide to what it is to be a non-human composite unity – say, a donkey.
6 Knowledge of what it's like to be a goal-oriented being gives us insight into the nature of other teleologically-driven objects – like Winston Churchill, angels, and God.[3]
7 Direct acquaintance with solidity, impenetrability, and inertial resistance helps us understand what these qualities come to in external objects.[4]

In connection with this last case involving solidity, Locke was looking for solidity on the *wrong side of the foot-ball*. Grasping the ball's solidity was never on. But having a sense of what it's like to be solid – from the inside – was. All one needs to ease the transition from inside to out is what Leibniz has – a generous theory of analogy that postulates a rough resemblance based, not on knowledge, but on a plausible hunch. On the Realist picture, the ultimate origin of the activity, motion, and force in the hand is a mental substance with its own native versions of those qualities. On that picture, the same sort of story is told about the foot-ball. The ball's solidity is taken to be a visible effect of the forces in its constituent mental substances. By comparison, Locke has no such "analogy-bridge" across which to convey explanations from felt solidity to external solidity. The felt foot-ball is a mind-dependent "idea," while the external one is not and is not constituted by anything remotely similar to what's mental. So Locke is stuck with as "deeply segregated" a worldview as Descartes.

It's entirely unremarkable that Locke never had a chance at external solidity. Solidity of that sort is caught up in the scientific story about the world – which tells us how hard, cold, and impersonal "objective reality" is.[5] It asserts that there are only primary qualities "out there." So necessarily "viewpoints" and subjectivity are left behind. Which means that Locke's feeling can't convey any information about outer matter.

(4) Categoricity

There is a fascinating argument to the effect that, necessarily, our concepts of all the properties of outer objects are dispositional. By "dispositional" properties I mean ones that attribute to an object potentialities to act in a certain way given the actions of other things.[6] Typical examples include impenetrability and resistance, which are powers to act that await the presence of other objects before they are manifest. By contrast, "categorical" properties are occurrent states – fully manifest in the object and not at all dependent on other things.

When one looks at the list of "primary qualities," it seems they all vanish into dispositions despite their seeming categoricity. Thus solidity – Locke's main hope for a categorical primary quality – is a disposition of physical things to act on perceivers or each other. Mass similarly crumbles into dispositions to interact with other massive objects.[7]

Some recent discussions have concentrated on the relationality of motion, impenetrability, and mass. So long as mass, say, is defined scientifically as a disposition to react lawfully with other massive objects, one is left without an account of categorical mass.[8]

Another version concentrates on the human epistemic condition. Since one has to examine physical things through the five senses, one can only learn what the object will do to one in these sense modalities. "[W]hat [man] knows is not a sun and an earth, but only an eye that sees a sun, a hand that feels an earth."[9] (What man knows is not a foot-ball, but only a hand that feels a foot-ball.) The ball feels heavy and looks roundish. But these qualities are all the results of the ball's exercising its dispositions on human senses. They are none of them categorical qualities of the ball: what form, if any, size, shape, motion, solidity, and mass take in the object is beyond knowing.

A more intractable, broadly Kantian version is due to Simon Blackburn, who writes,

I believe that science never gives us genuinely categorical properties at all ... [T]he empirical relation between surface reflectance properties, and the disposition to appear red is the relation between one kind of disposition and another ... [N]othing in our understanding and nothing in science give us any conception of what a categorical property can be, nor how it could ground a disposition. Categorical grounds remain entirely noumenal, and talk of them is, as near as makes no difference, meaningless.

Blackburn (1997, 3)

This argument is perhaps the most powerful because it claims that our best science will never discover a single categorical physical quality. There are only sheer powers, dangling completely free of what *is*. The best science can do is to connect the powers in something like an infinite connect-the-dots game, where each dot is itself composed of dots that need connecting with other dots, and so on. So one is left with an intolerable conception of the natural world as "simply made up of dispositions" (Blackburn 1997, 5). Put bluntly by Bertrand Russell: "We know nothing of the intrinsic quality of the physical world ... We know the laws of the physical world, in so far as these are mathematical, pretty well, but we know nothing else about it" (1927, 264).

In this predicament Blackburn looks to Hume for some consolation, saying that one may have to settle for categoricity only in subjective experience – in the manifest image, with its healthy viewpoint, rather than the viewpointless scientific one. A string quartet playing softly, a pungent perfume, the report of a shotgun – these are all categorical "as they present themselves to us" (Blackburn 1997, 15). Yet they are, as Blackburn owns, hopeless as the categorical grounds of the dispositions and powers of physics.

Extending Blackburn's argument: in order for experiences to ground physical dispositions, they would have to be such that just the physical categoricity could be refined out of them, leaving the subjective categoricity behind as noetic dross. Thus Locke might reach forth and ask, "Just the solidity this time please; none of the feeling." But to no avail: categoricity is as inseparable from subjectivity as the primaries are from the secondaries. Berkeley's familiar argument thus can be extended: since categoricity is incarnate only in secondary qualities, it is unknown – indeed, unknowable – in the primaries.

Now it is all but explicitly acknowledged in Leibniz's texts that physical-quality-categoricity is unknowable.[10] Nevertheless, says Leibniz, there must be a base, an inherent nature, a "filler" for matter.

A revisionary turn must be taken. Enter panpsychism – cum supervenience. "Cum supervenience" because Leibniz does not use "protomental" properties to ground full-blown mental properties, as some panpsychisms do. In those panpsychisms, upper-level mental properties (say, "is a mind") are derived from primitive mental properties ("is a rudimentary faint sensation"), and there is no need for supervenience of one kind of property on another.

In Leibniz's Realist theory, an "enriched panpsychism" holds that the physical supervenes on what's mental in such a way that the mentality of the subvenient states gets thoroughly "washed out" long before the physical emerges from it. This gives us what appears to be a freestanding physical realm – one that seems physical all the way down.[11] Indeed, one that can be studied profitably, as it is in the "mechanical philosophy," as if it were physical all the way down. Leibniz at one time took it to be freestanding and purely physical, but was pulled up by some questions that seemed unanswerable if that is the way things are.

One such question is: how is categoricity to be accounted for? The physical can't answer that, and so physicality must not really be fundamental.

Leibniz's enriched panpsychism avoids Blackburn's charge of "noumenalism" because the categoricity envisaged here is not instantiated in a physical property – "I know not what" – that somehow grounds the dispositions of physical objects. Rather, it is a categoricity of perfectly knowable mental properties.

To sum up the considerations for the primacy of *I*: Something in the natural world must explain the instantiation of categoricity, activity, reality, and unity in us. Nothing in the outer realm can do that. In fact, the explanatory direction seems just the opposite. The "blooming, buzzing confusion" out there seems to presuppose categorical sources of unity, activity, and reality. The dispositions of material things cry out for categorical bases;[12] their plurality, things that are one; their motion, an already-existing source of activity; their measure of reality, a hidden, deeper, reality beneath. Unless there are some items that are, to begin with, categorical, active, real, and one, it is impossible – without taking on radical emergence and the explanatory infelicities it entails – to derive collectivities that have powers and are, in a derivative sense, active, real, and unified.

2.2 Gunk and Simples

Every non-nihilist mereology must postulate, at the limit of its wholes' decomposition, either *Gunk* (parts that contain parts that contain parts, to infinity) or *Simples* (partless parts). In this section I will examine the positive and negative consequences of siding with Gunk or Simples.

Under each of these are two varieties, depending on whether the parts are "homogeneous" with (of the same kind as) the whole, or "heterogeneous" (different).

First consider the two varieties of Gunk:

a) Homogeneous Gunk: each of its infinity of parts is of the same general kind (e.g., material, extended) as the whole.

b) Heterogeneous Gunk: at least one of its infinity of parts is of a general kind different from that of the whole.

Since Heterogeneous Gunk metaphysics are virtually non-existent, set b) aside.

Among Homogeneous Gunk metaphysics, a notable case is Descartes's view of matter as an undifferentiated "substance" – Extension. Leibniz also, though he firmly rejects Descartes's offering, recognizes two different construals of matter on which it turns out to be Homogeneous Gunk. These construals will be explained in detail in Chapter 3, but they are mentioned here briefly to illustrate Gunk metaphysics. When Leibniz considers matter as extended mass – infinitely divisible into bits that are also extended mass – it is Homogeneous Gunk. And there is another, quite distinct, sense of "matter" on which it is Homogeneous Gunk. This is the construal of matter as a phenomenon. Matter as a phenomenal appearance is Homogeneous Gunk because the appearances are said to be infinitely divisible into sub-appearances: "Phenomena can therefore always be divided into lesser phenomena which could be observed by other, more subtle, animals and we can never arrive at smallest phenomena" (G 2, 268/L 536).

Now Leibniz *also* offers a Simples construal of matter, according to which it is composed of monads or (more generally) substances. He gives reasons for supposing that this last construal is more metaphysically accurate than the other two. I will examine them presently.

But at the moment note that science will be of little help in coming to terms with Gunk v. Simples. For any simples – like quarks – that science discovers, there is always the possibility that they are underlain, not by smaller simples, but by gunk. So: when one reaches the ground floor analysis of composition, metaphysics is pretty much on its own. The choice must be based on something like a firm conceptual hunch.

Again: a revisionary plunge must be taken. By atomists Democritus, Epicurus, Boyle, Gassendi, Newton, and Locke no less than by Leibniz. Why? Because atoms have not yet been discovered and are so small as to be unlikely to be found any time soon. Yet the atomist forges ahead, postulating them as "indivisible, unalterable, permanent, completely solid, corporeal existences" (Epicurus, in Oates 1940, 4) or "solid, massy, hard, impenetrable, movable" (Newton 1952, 400) simples at the bottom. Leibniz, for his part, postulates mental simples – the monads. Both moves involve stipulation and going beyond the data of sense.

Of course one might not want to choose between a conservative program and revision. I can imagine an agnostic saying:

> Gunk? Simples? Who knows? It's all right with me either way. If we get our medium-sized dry goods it doesn't much bother me what the ground floor looks like. Philosophers are always asking questions that can't be answered anyway ...

This pragmatic approach is more popular today than in the past, when no doubt it would have been scorned as metaphysics beneath contempt. How can a philosopher reach a crux like the ground floor and simply demur?

The revisionist forges ahead, aware that risks are being taken. However, they would rather take the risks than lose out on the explanatory power emanating from a determinate ground floor. With this foundation laid, one can get on with the task of providing an explanation of the qualities of composites, and one can explain the composite's scientifically important additive properties – e.g., how an extended object of mass 12 can arise from 12 extended bits of mass 1, and each of the bits of mass 1 can arise from myriad atoms each with a non-zero but very small mass.

Gassendi once remarked on the advantages of atomism – and even noted its contrast with gunk-metaphysics:

> [I]t does not do a bad job of explaining how composition and resolution into the primary elemental particles is accomplished, and for what reason a thing is solid, or corporeal, how it becomes large or small, rarefied or dense, soft or hard, sharp or blunt, and so forth. For indeed these questions and others like them are not so clearly resolved in other theories where matter is considered as . . . infinitely divisible.
> . . . it accounts for the innermost source and root, as it were, from which all movement and all activity arises.
>
> Gassendi (1972, 399–400)

As I've said, Leibniz is very much interested in "the innermost source" of motion and activity.[13] He finds the "root" in genuine individuals – simples but not atoms. With atoms one sinks in a quagmire of gunk.

This argument reappears in Kant. As James Van Cleve argues in his exposition of Kant's "Amphiboly," (what I've been calling) 'gunk' would have to be "constituted entirely by relations" – which in Bradley's phrase means it would share with space the apparently impossible feature of being "essentially a relation of what vanishes into relations, which seek in vain for their terms" (Van Cleve 1988, 233–6).

The fact that Leibniz rejects atoms as the "basis" should not blind us to the fact that atomism and Leibniz are in firm agreement about one thing: any adequate metaphysic must be a Simples metaphysic. "Theories of masses," as they are sometimes called today, need to discuss gunk because they are concerned with the agglomeration of parts in such things as bath water and succotash (Zimmerman 1995). The question of the unity of such masses is never raised seriously, nor is there concern with individuation conditions that go beyond mereological essentialism.[14] Of course one could stipulate that a "spoonful of cornmeal" – even infinitely-finely-ground cornmeal – is "one thing." But because this is a mere convention, there could be no pretense that such "things" have any sort of unity or integrity. Its being held together by a physical boundary of some sort would hardly make it an individual.

By contrast, simples have a chance at more than arbitrary, "merely boun-ded," conventional unity and wholeness. Simples just might be individ-uated.

Because he rejects Gunk metaphysics, Leibniz tosses aside the Cartesian concept of body as space: that makes it gunk endlessly "searching in vain for its terms." Ironically, atoms, though supposedly simples, fare no better on the issue of individuation. Though the parts are never so inextricably bound to one another, they are nevertheless there (geometrically) to infinity. And that ruins any individuality they might possess. As Leibniz says, "Whatever is divisible has parts, which can be distinguished even before their separa-tion" (G 7, 552/R 248). Atoms are gunk parading about in sheep's clothing, as if they were simples.

Now the dialectic of our project requires that I keep atomism alive at the moment. I will not take Leibniz to have eliminated atomism with his "gunk in sheep's clothing" argument above. Instead, atomism will be given the benefit of the doubt so one can see how it fares on other grounds.

Returning now to the original classification of theories, there are two kinds of Simples metaphysics:

a) Homogeneous Simples, where there are partless parts of the same general kind as the whole; and
b) Heterogeneous Simples, where there are partless parts of a different general kind from that of the whole.

Atoms, considered merely as material bits and not as specifically, say, hydrogen atoms, are the most familiar Homogeneous Simples. They, like the wholes they compose, are material. Thus Newtonian atoms are material and the bodies "compounded of them" (Newton 1952, 400) are also mate-rial. A traditional atomist's composite bodies are material all the way down to the simples. Supervenience wouldn't be needed here except to provide a "glue" between the atoms so that composites can be formed. The glue unites K atoms to constitute a K composite.

Supervenience of a richer sort than mere adhesion is needed to account for composites which seem radically different from the constituent simples. Thus some scientific realists represent "Heterogeneous Simples" – say, ones who believe everything material can be reduced to a set of fundamental particles and their associated forces. It is heterogeneous because such things as quarks are of a kind dramatically different from that of the wholes they compose. Leibniz himself holds a Heterogeneous Simples metaphysic for matter construed as "secondary matter" or a congeries of substances. For material bodies that are "aggregates of substances" are not homogeneous with the substances that constitute them.

Every Heterogeneous Simples mereology will need a rich and active rela-tion of supervenience. Some regular determinative relation (possibly passed along through intervening steps) will have to hold between K*-simples and the supervening K object. Indeed, there is, predictably, a systematic connection between mereology and supervenience in metaphysics of this sort. The simples that make up the composite must also furnish the ultimate "subvenient" properties for the composite's properties.

Leibniz calls his simples "substantial realities" (G 4, 491/AG 146) or "true atoms of nature" (Mon 3). Unlike physical atoms, these are metaphysical as science will be not be discovering them anytime soon. Whereas atomism awaits the day when science discovers its simples, Leibniz deliberately forgoes any such hope. These simples will be visible only to the intellect. And they will not be what one would expect matter to be composed of – unless one is thinking rather than sensing or imagining. Again the revisionary turn is upon us.

Perhaps all the "revisions" are already too much of a strain. The reader might well think: "First he turns our metaphysic inside out; now he writes off the material world as a delusive appearance arising from a spiritual substrate. Is a materialist account of the material world too much to ask?"

Yes, it is. Try it. Leibniz did. He considered materialism, but was not satisfied on some weighty issues. The challenges he posed are as relevant today as they were in his day. The size and nature of physics's simples has changed, but the conceptual issues remain largely the same.

2.3 Simples

In all systems simples are functionally defined:

> *Simple*: x is a simple = $_{df}$ x is a partless part of some whole.

In this section there is no attempt to make 'part' and 'whole' obey Leibniz's strictures – to be examined in the next chapter – on these terms. For example, there is no requirement that x be a proper part: x might *be* the whole of which it is the partless part. Also the "wholes" here intended are not guaranteed to have true unity or even loose spatiotemporal integrity.

Simples need not be small. They may have no size whatever – like the purely spiritual monads. Or they could be huge: on an "objectivist" interpretation of Spinoza's attributes, Extension – though infinitely large – is a heterogeneous simple that helps (with Thought) to compose Substance. But the simples I am concerned with will be either unextended or extended and small.

Typical material simples are "simples" only relative to the kind of whole they are taken to compose. Material atoms might compose some molecules, which in turn together compose a pane of glass. The molecules could be taken as simples with respect to the glass, but their simples – the atoms – are closer to the ultimate simples of this reduction of the glass to its parts. The atoms are also wholes relative to their parts – protons and neutrons – which are wholes relative to their parts – quarks and gluons. (The absolutely ultimate simples – if indeed there are simples "down there" – would be some items probably not yet discovered.)

It might seem that *all* simples – not just material ones – are relative in this way. Indeed, Leibniz has been charged with being "quite arbitrary" in insisting on "theoretically indivisible" bits rather than merely something simple "in contrast to the complex" (Nason 1945, 478, 464). This "insistence" is anything but arbitrary. As will become clear, the absolute, unqualified simplicity of his simples is demanded by his argument against merely relative, qualified simples. That argument is designed to show that supposing simples are relative and qualified is literally incoherent. At this point I must leave the matter there, with the promise that it will be expanded upon later as Leibniz's arguments are examined in detail.

As I said in the last section, in a Heterogeneous Simples Metaphysic there is a systematic connection between mereology and supervenience. A typical composite has properties that supervene on its constituents' subvenient properties. Thus glass's fragility supervenes on the subvening properties of the molecules – say, their various chemical bonds. And perhaps goodness supervenes ultimately on physical properties had by a person's cells. A composite's ultimate constituents are simples, and the simples' proprietary properties must provide the deepest subvenient base for the composite object's supervening properties. Thus simples will often be treated as both the building blocks of wholes and the possessors of properties on which the whole's properties supervene.

That Leibniz was thinking of these two concepts in tandem is evident from the following passages. "What is in a composite can come only from its simple ingredients" (Mon 8). "There must be force and perception in these unities themselves, for otherwise there would be no force or perception in all that is formed of them" (G 7, 552/R 248). "Where there is no true unity, there is no true multiplicity. And where there is no reality not borrowed, there will never be any reality, since this must in the end belong to some subject" (G 2, 267/R 242). If the composite is real, reality must be bubbling up from the simples. If the composite is plural or many, then genuine "ones" must compose it. If the composite is active, the simples must be active.

Summarizing these thoughts, the following rule inflicts two "burdens" on simples:

Simples Rule: Every Simples Metaphysic that individuates its composites must meet the following conditions:

i) the simples themselves must be individuated (the "individuation burden"); and
ii) all the composites' qualities must supervene intelligibly on the simples' properties (the "supervenience burden").

Composite-individuation depends on simples-individuation. And a composite's qualities must be explained ultimately by appeal to its simples' qualities. Variegated composites can't arise out of blank, homogeneous, qualitatively bankrupt simples.

Is the Simples Rule warranted, or just rationalist overkill? A skeptic might say,

> There are clear cases where variety at one level of analysis arises from what is homogeneous at a deeper level. Countless snowflakes, each with a unique shape, are composed of chemically identical H_2O molecules. Why should it be any different in metaphysics?

While there is no time to settle the matter here, I note that this Rule is a deep assumption Leibniz brings to the table – an assumption without which his approach to explanation is unmotivated.

The individuation burden predominates in the corpus: again and again he says genuine unities must be found at the bottom. The supervenience burden appears less frequently, but is a persistent theme tied to rationalist strictures on explanation. Roughly, these entail that if a composite has a certain quality, one should not reach a "gap" in the explanation of this quality as one proceeds from simples to composite. That would violate "continuity" constraints on explanation. In a fascinating text, the rules governing continuity and intelligibility are laid out in some detail:

> I would not like to be compelled to resort to miracles in the ordinary course of nature, or to admit absolutely inexplicable powers and operations. For, with the aid of 'what God can do', we may give too much leeway to bad philosophy by admitting these 'centripetal powers' and 'immediate attractions' at a distance, without being able to make them intelligible; I do not see what is to prevent our Scholastics from saying that everything simply comes about through 'faculties', and from promoting their 'intentional species' which travel from objects to us and find their way into our souls. If that is acceptable, 'Everything will now happen whose possibility I used to deny' [Ovid].
>
> Whenever we find some quality in a subject, we ought to believe that if we understood the nature of both the subject and the quality we would conceive how the quality could arise from it. So within the order of nature (miracles apart) it is not at God's arbitrary discretion to attach this or that quality haphazardly to substances. He will never give them any which are not natural to them, that is, which cannot arise from their nature as explicable modifications. So we may take it that matter will not naturally possess the attractive power referred to above, and that it will not of itself move in a curved path, because it is impossible to conceive how this could happen – that is, to explain

it mechanically – whereas what is natural must be such as could become distinctly conceivable by anyone admitted into the secrets of things. This distinction between what is natural and explicable and what is miraculous and inexplicable removes all the difficulties. To reject it would be to uphold something worse than occult qualities, and thereby to renounce philosophy and reason, giving refuge to ignorance and laziness by means of an irrational system which maintains not only that there are qualities which we do not understand ... but further that there are some which could not be comprehended by the greatest intellect if God gave it every possible opportunity, i.e. [qualities] which are either miraculous or without rhyme or reason.

(NE, Preface, 61, 66)

Thus, an ideal observer introduced to the secret natures of things should be able to tell how the qualities of a composite arise from, or supervene on, the qualities of the simples.

Now arguably atomisms can shoulder up neither burden.

(1) Atomism on the individuation burden

Atomists recognize the vast variety in composites and yet are content to stop their quest for explanation of that variety when they arrive at material atoms. Since atoms have no inner, qualitative marks of distinction, such atoms are individuated only spatiotemporally. They have mere "positional individuation."

Of course, in a Newtonian world, with Space and Time anchoring all objects in their eternally frozen reference frame, such an otherwise "thin" account of individuation seems in order. It is because of their association with this metaphysical Gibraltar that atoms are securely distinguished one from another. And then of course their positions can account, by straightforward agglomeration, for the spatiotemporal position of the composite.

But Leibniz rejects any such account of Space and Time. Spatiotemporal identity for simples like atoms is completely inadequate even to get them on the ontological map.

(2) Atomism on the supervenience burden

Set aside individuation worries for the moment and simply put atoms on the map. They then face the supervenience burden. How well will atoms do? The historical test case is found in Locke, who puts down the sweet scent and blue color of a violet to the "texture" and "different motions and figures, bulk, and number of such particles" (*Essay* II viii 13–14).

Set aside the vacuous spatial properties "bulk" and "figure" and the explanatorily otiose "number." Locke's subvenient base for blue and sweetness consists of texture and motion. To the extent that "texture" depends on spatial position at a time, it is vacuous and can't distinguish atoms from regions of space of the same size. Insofar as texture involves change, it reduces to motion. So the entire subvenient base is motion of solid atoms. But the explanatory gap that opens up between moving solid atoms on the one hand, and blue and sweet on the other, is a yawning chasm. It seems as though there is, at best, brute association between them.

Of course, even if suitable ways were found to shoulder up the individuation and supervenience burdens, atomism still faces Leibniz's "gunk in sheep's clothing" argument. According to this argument, atom-simples are really complex – are merely for practical purposes waved on as "one." But metaphysicians aren't moved by practical purposes. Simples by convention won't do. Their individuality would be completely arbitrary and unprincipled. Writes Leibniz: "What reason can anyone assign for confining nature in the progression of subdivision?" (Clarke, 4.PS). And,

> shall one say ... that the substance of the composite of these things [chain links joined in such a way that they cannot be separated] is as it were in suspense and depends on the future skill of the man who will wish to separate them? (LA 102). "Superficial philosophy, such as is that of the atomists and vacuists, forges things which superior reasons do not permit. (Clarke, 5.26)

In the end, the Simples Rule requires that simples be individuated qualitatively. Purely quantitative, spatiotemporal individuation fails, and even if it didn't, the bloodless simples it furnishes can provide no basis for a composite's supervening qualities.

There is not time here to inquire into the possibilities of non-atomist materialisms with simples. But it is clear that all the viable ones will have simples that are extended – and that is of course enough to rule them out as genuine simples. Whether one is talking about mass-bits or perhaps pieces of Cartesian Extension – such as Spinoza's "simplest bodies" – they all are susceptible to the "gunk in sheep's clothing" argument.[15]

2.4 Monads

The simples of Leibniz's late-mature system are substances. Sometimes these are said to be "simple substances," or the famous monads.[16] Other times, "composite substances" – also called "corporeal substances" or animals – are equally considered as falling into the category of substance. Since what unifies animals and ultimately gives them the status of simples is a dominant monad (which inherited that job from "substantial forms" in the early mature period), I shall confine my remarks to what is true of monads. This involves a simplification, but not a distortion, of the mature system.

Monads bear the individuation and supervenience burdens in this system. They are the "metaphysical points" found at the end of every whole's decomposition, and their properties provide the ultimate subvenient base for the properties of wholes in this Heterogeneous Simples metaphysic.

Leibniz says monads are mind-like and have the ability to perceive and strive. Selections from the *Monadology* present the orthodox picture:

> The *monad*, of which we shall speak here, is nothing but a simple substance, which enters into composites – *simple*, that is, without parts.
>
> Now where there are no parts, there can be neither extension, nor shape, nor divisibility. These monads are the true atoms of nature and, in a word, the elements of things.
>
> The passing state, which involves and represents a multiplicity in the unity or in the simple substance is nothing but what is called *perception*. . . .
>
> The action of the internal principle which produces change or passage from one perception to another may be called *appetition*. . . .
>
> If we wish to give the name of 'soul' to everything which has *perceptions* and *appetites* in the general sense I have just explained, then all simple substances or created monads can be called souls. . . .
>
> (Mon 1, 3, 14, 15, 19)

It should be said at the outset that there is nothing mysterious about monads. If there are any such things, each of us is one. I know exactly what monads are like because I live the "monadic life" all the time. I perceive a welter of things in a single unified state. I strive for various things, am aware of an inward force, am active and real. I find myself in categorical states. All these things could be true even if there were no other object around.[17]

Also, Leibniz did not know more about monads than anyone else can know. He got his information from (1) inner experience and (2) arguments about what the world must be like if it is to be explained adequately. On (1) Leibniz had no advantage over us, and his arguments (2) will be examined shortly. Their premises are accessible to evaluation by anyone.

What is distinctive and somewhat surprising about Leibniz's monads is that they come in an infinite variety of grades. From humans they proceed through angels and on to God, the highest monad. And among finite things they grade off into a very low level of mentality – the so-called "naked monads" (Mon 24).

Most of us would be hard-pressed to accord a mental life to hermit crabs, though I think it begins somewhere around that level of complexity. Leibniz, however, boldly projects an analogy between us and the constituents of a rock. Those constituents – low-level monads – are similar to us in that they have mental states. That's how all of nature is seen to supervene on a single kind of substrate – the mental.

Monads are partless. But unlike atoms or quarks, their simplicity has nothing to do with size or the relative difficulty of separating them.[18] They are partless because they are, in the broadly dualist tradition, mental, or *non*-spatial. The concept of spatial partitioning or physical division does not apply to them in the least. They have a logical guarantee of partlessness – making their status as simples, in a way, unarguable. Whereas every material simple, because it is extended, has only a fake, conventional simplicity, the monads have genuine simplicity. They *couldn't* have parts. That's the kind of reason a rationalist loves to give. As to their origin: since only God is beginningless, monads must be created *ex nihilo* (Mon 6).

Of course there had better be more to say than just that they are mental. Otherwise this position would involve postulating mere "spiritual some-things-or-other" – which would be quite as unintelligible as unknowable material "substrata" that are supposed to underlie and provide a home for physical properties.

The need to color monads with quality is explicitly acknowledged in the texts: "[M]onads must have some qualities, otherwise they would not even be beings" (Mon 8). *No ontology without quality*, Leibniz seems to be saying. If simples had no qualities, they would collapse under (i) the "supervenience burden," and (ii) the "individuation burden." I have marked these in brackets in the continuation of Mon 8:

> And if simple substances did not differ in quality, there would be no way of perceiving any change in things, since [(i)] what is in a com-posite can come only from its simple ingredients; and [(ii)] if the monads had no qualities, they would be indistinguishable from one another, since they also do not differ in quantity. Consequently, assuming a plenum, in motion, each place would always receive only the equivalent of what it already had, and no one state of things would be discernible from another.
>
> (Mon 8)

Recall from Chapter 1 the importance of interlevel explanations. Note the interlevel play here – to be defended in detail later on when we look at the various analyses of aggregates. Monads (from Substance) are used unabash-edly to explain such features of the "evidence base" as the knowledge that bodies (Aggregate) exhibit variety and motion.

Note again how important it is that monads bear the supervenience burden. If a composite were to have genuinely emergent qualities – qualities whose roots can't in principle be traced by an ideal knower to the simples' subvening qualities – the continuity and unity of explanation will have been broken. In particular, if the composite can derive its qualities from the mind thinking of them (as in phenomenalism), there is no need to include the monads' qualities in one's explanations. And then, after all the work to get simples up and running, they would turn out to be explanatorily otiose in the larger scheme.

On this striking Realist theory of the world, Substance reaches forth and touches Aggregate, imparting reality to it – rather as Michaelangelo's divine being leans over and offers the touch of life to a languid Adam. As will become apparent in the next section, all of Leibniz's non-theological arguments for monads rest foursquare on that theory.

2.5 Arguments for Substances

[T]he real world that lies behind what appears to sensory perception, is composed of (of all things!) *minds*; it is chock-full of minds. How does Leibniz know that? Not by looking around, not by deriving testable consequences from the hypothesis. He knows the existence of his own mind by introspection; as for the others, he concludes their existence from the goodness of God, which requires the existence of everything that is compossible with what exists. Nothing that can be observed would ever be accepted by Leibniz as casting the slightest doubt on this ontology.

Mates (1986, 242)

How does Leibniz argue for substances? 'Substances' for my purposes will refer indifferently to monads ("simple substances") and to the animals ("corporeal substances") that predominated in the early-mature period and survived into the latest years. All substances have in common indivisibility and true unity (GM 3, 542/AG 168).

One can divide the arguments into non-theological and theological.[19] Of course, as the extract reveals, it is often said that there aren't any non-theological arguments. Leibniz, it is said, never "looked around," never used "observation" to establish his ontology. That is misleading because there are non-theological arguments whose first premise is: (look around!) "there are bodies."

I will not here dwell on the theological arguments, as they require one to establish claims about the existence and nature of God. My quarry remains Leibniz's theory of the natural world, and the arguments that were advanced without special theological assumptions.[20]

There are four main non-theological arguments, with a fifth less fundamental one added at the end of this section. They are given in abstract form without a detailed textual defense. More complete textual elaboration for most of these will appear in later chapters.

Four Non-theological Arguments for Substances

Some crucial claims that play a role in these arguments are as follows:

Presupposition   Every plurality presupposes genuine unities that are contained in it.

Containment   Every body contains substances.
Supervenience   A supervening quality of a body arises from the primitive
                qualities of the things it contains.
Intelligibility   Supervening qualities must arise intelligibly from primitive
                qualities.

(1) Divisibility Argument

1 There are extended bodies. (Premise)
2 Every extended body is a plurality that is divisible into smaller extended bodies, each of which is itself a plurality divisible into smaller extended bodies, to infinity. (Premise)
3 There are pluralities that are divisible into extended bodies. (from 1 and 2)
4 Every plurality presupposes genuine unities that are contained in it. (Presupposition)
5 If the division of extended bodies into smaller extended bodies is endless, then there are no extended genuine unities contained in extended bodies. (Premise)
6 The division of extended bodies into smaller extended bodies is endless. (2)
7 There are no extended genuine unities contained in extended bodies. (5 and 6)
8 There are non-extended genuine unities contained in extended bodies. (3, 4, and 7)
9 Only substances are non-extended genuine unities. (Premise)
10 There are substances that are contained in extended bodies. (8 and 9)

(2) Reality Argument

1 There are derivatively real extended bodies. (Premise)
2 Every object's derivative qualities must arise (naturally) from the primitive qualities of what is contained in it. (Containment, Supervenience)
3 Derivative qualities must be "explicable modifications." (Intelligibility)
4 Derivative reality is an explicable modification only of primitive reality. (Premise)
5 If 1, 2, 3, and 4, then there are primitively real things. (Premise)
6 There are primitively real things. (1–5)
7 Only substances are primitively real. (Premise)
8 There are substances. (6 and 7)

(3) Activity and Force Argument

1 There are extended bodies that possess derivative activity and force. (Premise)
2 Every object's derivative qualities must arise (naturally) from the primitive qualities of what is contained in it. (Containment, Supervenience)

3 Derivative qualities must be "explicable modifications." (Intelligibility)
4 Derivative activity and force are explicable modifications only of primitive activity and force. (Premise)
5 If 1, 2, 3, and 4, then there are things that possess primitive activity and
force. (Premise)
6 There are things that possess primitive activity and force. (1–5)
7 Only substances possess primitive activity and force. (Premise)
8 There are substances.

Finally, the "Aggregate Argument" is a most abstract argument for substances, based on Mon 1, 2, and 8 (here quoted in part):

§1 The *monad* ... is nothing but a simple substance which enters into
composites – *simple*, that is, without parts.

§2 And there must be simple substances, since there are composites; for a
composite is nothing but a collection, or *aggregate*, of simples.

§8 And if simple substances did not differ in quality, there would be no
way of perceiving any change in things, since what is in a composite can
come only from its simple ingredients.

And the argument based on this passage is:

(4) Aggregate Argument

1 There are aggregates that have a variety of qualities. (§2, 8, Premise)
2 Every aggregate is "nothing but" a collection of "simple substances" that
"enter into" it, and the qualities of every aggregate "come from" the qualities of its "simple ingredients." (§1, 2, 8: Containment, Supervenience)
3 There are simple substances that have qualities. (1 and 2)

Evaluation of the Arguments

It is noteworthy that the first premises of all the arguments claim that there
are bodies. This is unmistakably robust Realism, claiming there is something
material outside the mind. The bodies are said to presuppose substances, or
draw their reality, activity, and force from them.

The bodies that launch these arguments can't be in the mind of a perceiver, as Idealism requires. For if they were, it would be impossible for
mind-independent substances to bolster them with their reality, activity,
and force. Indeed, in largely expository passages, Russell writes that though
Leibniz "invented what may be called a spiritualistic or idealistic theory of
matter,"

what his theory started with was still matter. Accordingly, the problem with which he began was not: Does matter exist? But, what is
the nature of matter? ... The question, Does matter exist? is thus one
which Leibniz never thoroughly faced.

[H]e believed himself, on a purely dynamical basis, to have shown matter to be the appearance of something substantial. For force, which he regarded as equivalent to activity, is required by the laws of motion, and is required in each piece of matter. That there must be entelechies dispersed everywhere throughout matter, follows from the fact that principles of motion are thus dispersed (G 7, 330).

(R 70, 107)

Now in light of this one can see with piercing clarity the source of Leibniz's problems with consistency: arguably for all four arguments, if the conclusion is true, the first premise must be false. They begin with Realism and end with Idealism. The existence of mind-independent matter is the fundamental first premise, but the substances he establishes with those very arguments threaten to eliminate it in favor of phenomena or appearances in minds. As Russell says, in Leibniz's ontology matter seems to be "gradually transform[ed] into psychology" (R 70). When Leibniz seeks refuge from extension in indivisible substances, everything else in some sense gets reduced to the substances. Mind-independent bodies disappear.

That is what De Volder learned late in his correspondence with Leibniz – that really, beneath all the talk of extended bodies and masses was an Idealist reduction waiting to liquidate all those things in favor of spiritual monads. De Volder writes,

I had asked where the forces in corporeal substances flow from, but indeed you seem to eliminate bodies completely and place them in appearances, and to substitute for things only forces, not even corporeal forces, but perception and appetite.

(G 2, 275/AG 181)

Leibniz replies:

I don't really eliminate body, but reduce it to what it is. For I show that corporeal mass, which is thought to have something over and above simple substances, is not a substance, but a phenomenon resulting from simple substances, which alone have unity and absolute reality. I relegate derivative forces to the phenomena, but I think that it is obvious that primitive forces can be nothing but the internal strivings of simple substances, strivings by means of which they pass from perception to perception in accordance with a certain law of their nature, and at the same time harmonize with one another, representing the same phenomena of the universe in different ways.

(G 2, 275/AG 181)

On realizing this reduction threatened to undermine any serious regard for the physical world, De Volder rebelled. And so do I.

Leibniz knows he's in peril of losing the coherence of his view. As I would say, the two theories he's trying simultaneously to maintain are tearing away in different directions. He feels constrained to try to relate the monads to extension in some interesting way – all without violating his own rules about their being indivisible and spiritual. De Volder had already read what was perhaps his best attempt:

> for all changes, of both spiritual and material things, there is a place, so to speak, in the order of succession, that is, in time, and for all changes, of both spiritual and material things, there is a place in the order of coexistents, that is, in space. For even if they are not extended, monads have a certain kind of situation in extension, that is, they have a certain ordered relation of coexistence to other things, namely, through the machine in which they are present. I think that no finite substances exist separated from every body, and to that extent they do not lack situation or order with respect to other coexisting things in the universe. Extended things contain many things endowed with situation. But things that are simple ought to be situated in extension, even if they don't have extension, though it may be impossible to designate it exactly, as, for example, we can do in incomplete phenomena.
>
> (G 2, 253/AG 178/L 531)

Notice what is at stake here. Leibniz is trying desperately to sustain Realism – in essence, to preserve the truth of the first premise in the arguments for substances. Without "extended things" and "machines," there would be no bodies for the substances to be in, no bodies needing to borrow their reality, activity, and force from substances. So he keeps extended things around, assigning monads "a certain kind of situation in extension" – which is vague and non-committal enough to appear (he hopes) to remain consonant with his Idealist theory – where the monads are completely untainted by extension.

This notion that after all monads have a stake in extension – though extended things are not real – understandably caused confusion. When he writes such things to Lady Masham (1658–1708), she lets him have it:

> 'Force', I presume, cannot be the essence of any substance, but is the attribute of what you call a 'form', 'soul', or 'atome de substance', of the essence whereof I find no positive idea, and your negation of their having any dimensions makes their existence, I confess, inconceivable to me, as not being able to conceive an existence of that which is nowhere. If the locality of these substances were accounted for by their being, as you [say] they are, always in organized bodies, then they are somewhere: but if these 'atomes de substance' are somewhere, then they must have some extension, which you deny of them.
>
> (G 3, 350/WF 209–10)

The weakness of Leibniz's reply shows the depth of the hole he has dug for himself:

> The question whether it is *somewhere or nowhere* is purely verbal; for its nature does not consist in extension, though it agrees with extension which it represents. So one should place the soul in the body in which is located the point of view according to which it represents the present state of the universe. To want anything more, and to tie the soul down to dimensions, is to try to think of souls as being like bodies.
>
> (G 3, 357/WF 215)

I am often in the same position as those original correspondents. I cannot see how to make the two ends meet. Indeed, to this day people call Leibniz everything but a bald-faced liar for representing himself as committed to an outside world and at the same time nurturing with such complete abandon claims that would prove its undoing.

Of course, if Theory-Pluralism is right, the two ends need not meet at all. We can, looking on as interpreters, get Leibniz out of this jam pretty quickly by simply saying that while substance is interestingly related to extended things in the Realist theory, it is not in the Idealist one. Supposing the two claims must somehow be blended without diminishing either one is probably rationalist overkill and it certainly can't be done – even by a genius.

Elimination Argument

Before leaving the arguments, however, I include another one that also requires the Realist theory. Here I simply quote selectively from a version offered to Arnauld.

> If there are aggregates of substances, there must also be genuine substances from which all the aggregates result. One must therefore necessarily arrive:
>
> 1 either at mathematical points [Points] or
> 2 at atoms [Atomism] or else
> 3 one must acknowledge that no reality can be found in bodies [Phenomenalism], or finally
> 4 one must recognize certain substances in them that possess a true unity. [Realism] (LA 96)

The Elimination Argument works only if 1–3 are eliminated. Points and Atomism are easily dismissed. But Idealism's "Phenomenalism" (3) must also be rejected. Only if it is can Leibniz infer (4) – which invokes the Realist picture of substances in mind-independent bodies.

3 Mereology

I must pause, before plunging into the details of Leibniz's views of aggregates and animals, to examine the complex set of rules laid out for the use of "part," "whole," and related mereological terms. The reason this must be done first is that he aspires to use substances as the "building blocks" for all else. Before one can in any intelligible sense build something derivative out of fundamental, primitive substances, one needs to know the "rules for building." His mature mereology provides those rules.

Now on typical materialist schemes – Newtonian atomism provides a nice example – the relevant rules are largely spatiotemporal. Newton has Space and Time, with its regions fixed eternally and granted absolute uniqueness, as a backdrop against which to individuate extended atoms and their composites. Thus, suppose Atom A snugly fits Region One, Now. If at the same time another atom, B, snugly fits an adjoining Region, they can together compose a larger object, AB, just in virtue of holding these positions.

Immediately one can see that way of agglomeration won't work for Leibniz. First, he does not begin with extended atoms, but with non-extended substances – the sorts of things that remain altogether untouched by these relations. Second, as I will explain presently, he does not believe there are any absolute beings, Space and Time. He remained skeptical of these and offered an alternative (broadly "relational") conception of them – one that does not offer "spatiotemporal individuation" for any objects.[1]

One might well wonder: What is left, if one puts spatiotemporal relations aside, to do the aggregating? That is a good question, and one that will occupy me throughout the book. For now, it is important to look at Leibniz's mature doctrine of space, time, extension, divisibility, and dividedness.

Exactly why are those five topics the main players in coming to terms with Leibniz's mereology? Because they all emanate from his thoughts on the problem of the continuum. I will not attempt a comprehensive treatment of the gigantic topic of Leibniz on the continuum. Recent work has helpfully examined Leibniz's early thought on this topic and some of its historical precedents (see Beeley 1996, Levey 1998, Leibniz 2001, and Mercer 2001), in many cases drawing interesting connections between it and his mature positions. Other studies have featured the mature thought (e.g., Mugnai 1992, Levey 1999, and Crockett 1999), but in any case the matter is too complex to be given full consideration here.

My goal is more modest. I will explain those texts and doctrines which, it turns out, play a pivotal role in his mature theory of aggregates and animals.

3.1 Some Historical Roots of the Divisibility Argument

In 2.5 I examined Leibniz's "Divisibility Argument." It has some interesting historical precedents. No claim is made for comprehensiveness, but here are a few of the connections that are particularly important for understanding the impact of continuum issues on Leibniz's doctrine of matter.

Aristotle once examined some arguments used by atomists to show that one must reach bodies as "indivisible magnitudes" at the bottom of matter's decomposition. It is this general line of argument that is eventually taken over by Leibniz to show the need, not for material atoms, but for indivisible substances.

316a 15–35: For to suppose that a body (i.e. a magnitude) is divisible through and through, and that this division is possible, involves a difficulty. What will there be in the body which escapes the division?

If it is divisible through and through, and if this division is possible, then it might *be*, at one and the same moment, *divided* through and through, even though the dividings had not been effected simultaneously; and the actual occurrence of this result would involve no impossibility. Hence whenever a body is by nature divisible through and through, whether by bisection, or generally by any method whatever, nothing impossible will have resulted if it has actually been divided – for if it has been divided into innumerable parts, themselves divided innumerable times, nothing impossible will have resulted, though perhaps nobody in fact could so divide it.

Since, therefore, the body is divisible through and through, let it have been divided. What, then, will remain? A magnitude? No: that is impossible, since then there will be something not divided, whereas *ex hypothesi* the body was divisible *through and through*. But if it be admitted that neither a body nor a magnitude will remain, and yet division is to take place, the body will *either* consist of points (and its constituents will be without magnitude) *or* it will be absolutely nothing. If the latter, then it might both come-to-be out of nothing and exist as a composite of nothing; and thus presumably the whole body will be nothing but an appearance. But if it consists of points, it will not possess any magnitude. For when the points were in contact and coincided to form a single magnitude, they did not make the whole any bigger ...; hence, even if all the points be put together, they will not make any magnitude.[2]

It is a beautiful argument against (in my terms) gunk, saying that when one takes matter to be gunk it ends up having no constituents at all and is reduced to "nothing." With "nothing" as its constituents, a body will be "nothing but an appearance" – in Leibniz's terms bodies will be mere phenomena! Indeed, in the LA 96 version of the "Elimination Argument" expounded in 2.5, the atomist's three alternatives for body's ultimate decomposition are mentioned explicitly by Leibniz: (i) mathematical points (the atomist's "points without magnitude") (ii) atoms ("points with magnitude") and (iii) (as Leibniz says) "no reality can be found in bodies" (the atomist: composed of "absolutely nothing," the whole body is "nothing but an appearance").

Incorporating some of the material from this passage, a version of the Divisibility Argument can be put as follows:

1 Matter ultimately decomposes into divisible objects or into indivisible objects. (Premise)
2 Suppose matter ultimately decomposes into divisible objects. (Assumption for reduction)
3 Then the divisible objects are not the objects left at the end of matter's *ultimate* decomposition (since those objects can be further decomposed).
4 But, by 2, the divisible objects are the objects left at the end of matter's ultimate decomposition.
5 Matter does not ultimately decompose into divisible objects. (2–4, indirect proof)
6 Matter ultimately decomposes into indivisible objects. (1 and 5)

Atomists, with their severe restriction of the real to body and void,[3] proceed as follows:

7 All objects are material. (Premise)
8 Matter ultimately decomposes into indivisible material objects. (6 and 7)

Leibniz accepts (1)–(6) but rejects (7), replacing it with the assumption that "a body is divisible through and through." Thus he affirms:

7′ Every material object is divisible. (Premise)

And then, unwilling to accept that matter is "nothing but an appearance," he takes the revisionary plunge. As Leibniz looks through the universe, he finds something that, while not material, is indivisible – the soul. Atomists like Lucretius are wrong about the soul: it is not particulate, not composed of fine material atoms. And so:

8′ Matter ultimately decomposes into indivisible non-material objects. (6 and 7′)

One arrives at the somewhat surprising conclusion that when one plumbs the depths of matter there are, hiding in it, non-material soul-like substances.

Again, to recap the argument: if things with magnitude have infinitely divisible parts, their very claim to reality is in jeopardy: they end up frittered away to nothing. So if things with magnitude are to have a share of reality – as they surely seem to have – there must be indivisibles at their foundation. These foundations cannot themselves have magnitude or be divisible, else they'd fall to the same argument. The foundations must be simple and yet related, in some metaphysically robust way, to what has magnitude.

It is probably the Divisibility Argument that more than any other accounts for Leibniz's ferocious attack on Cartesian natural philosophy. When Descartes said that matter's essence is extension, he *wandered out into point-blank range of the Divisibility Argument*. If matter is extension, it is continuous. If continuous, its reality is lost in endless division. As only unities ("indivisibles") are real, placing real unities in bodies is the only viable way to account for matter's reality.

Again the argument appears in Epicurus' "Letter to Herodotus," which shows clearly how atomists compressed together the issues of divisibility and reality:

> Therefore we must not only do away with division into smaller and smaller parts to infinity, so that we may not make everything weak and in our conceptions of the totals be compelled to grind away things that exist and let them go to waste into the non-existent, but also we must not suppose that in finite bodies you continue to infinity in passing on from one part to another, even if the parts get smaller and smaller. For when someone once says that there are infinite parts in something, however small they may be, it is impossible to see how this can still be finite in size; for obviously the infinite parts must be of *some* size, and whatever size they may happen to be, the size [of the total] would be infinite.
>
> Furley (1967, 13–14)

Infinite division will render things "weak," will "grind away things that exist and let them go to waste into the non-existent." In Leibniz's terms, "[W]hatever can be divided into parts has no reality unless there are in it things which cannot be divided into parts" (G 2, 261).

As David Furley notes, this argument seeks to establish finite decomposition on conceptual grounds. Paraphrasing the argument, Furley writes:

> We must reject infinite divisibility, he says, for otherwise we should make everything weak – that is to say, when we tried to get a firm mental grasp (περίληψισ) on the atoms, we should find them crumbling away into nothingness. Every time we thought we had arrived at the irreducible minima, we should have to admit that even these

minima are divisible. And so our search for the reality of the atoms would be endlessly frustrated.

Furley (1967, 13)

It's not just that physical atoms will "crumble away" if subjected to an infinite number of decomposings. The point of the passage is that, within the confines of a thought experiment, such decomposings would make the body one is imagining vanish (Furley 1967, 14). This is what makes the argument so Leibnizian in spirit. It cites conceptual constraints as the reason there must be simples. One finds here none of the modern appeal to the invincible hardness of atoms.[4] As is now apparent, Leibniz parts company with atomists only on ultimate metaphysical commitments. The two parties agree that simples are inevitable, but disagree about what the simples are.

The passage from Epicurus also shows why the atomist must steer a delicate course between finite and infinite. She commences the decomposition of finite things but must pull up before it proceeds to infinity. If she doesn't, she forfeits her account of (i) decomposition and (ii) composition. (i) Composites disappear into nonbeing if they can be broken down into ever-smaller bits to infinity. And (ii) sizeless atoms, even if infinite in number, will not add up to finite extended composites. If, on the other hand, atoms have size but are infinite in number, every composite will be infinite in size – which is disconfirmed every waking moment.

3.2 Space and Time

[T]he notions of space and time, with motion conceived as a mathematical function of these, form a conceptual grid that the mind imposes upon phenomenal change.

McGuire (1976, 308)

The doctrine of part and whole that Leibniz applies to body is developed in large measure by working out these relations for ideal mathematical entities like space, time, points, and lines. "Ideal" here is a term of art.[5] It indicates roughly that the items have their being only in the mind and not in the world. The "mind" envisioned here is not a particular individual mind; it is more like "the reasoning intellect." God as well as finite minds are intended.

Leibniz uses 'ideal' to designate items that are abstract and continuous or of use in analyzing continuous quantities. They are among the principal conceptual tools of mathematicians and geometers, comprising, in addition to space and time: "mathematical motion," "mathematical bodies" (like straight lines, points, and perfect circles), relations, infinite quantities, and infinitesimals. All of these are helpful aids in various sorts of explanations, but they can't "stand up to the finest analysis" (LA 119) and hence do not exist in their own right. Humans are acquainted with them because they are built into reason itself – rather as Kant's noumena are. Any rational mind, including God, has access to "the ideal." But, as in the case of Kant, it is maintained that what is found wholly within should stay there: space, time, and infinitesimals do not exist in nature. On the other hand, natural objects seem to be spatiotemporal because, as McGuire says above, this abstract conceptual grid is laid over perceived objects – rather as a scrim is superimposed on a stage scene.

Focusing specifically now on space and time: they represent a nice mathematical fiction, enabling one to keep track of the motions of bodies. In a fertile mature passage representative of this body of thought, Leibniz writes,

> Matter is not continuous but discrete, and actually infinitely divided, though no assignable part of space is without matter. But space, like time, is something not substantial, but ideal, and consists in possibilities, or in an order of coexistents that is in some way possible. And thus there are no divisions in it but such as are made by the mind, and the part is posterior to the whole. In real things, on the contrary, units are prior to the multitude, and multitudes exist only through units. (The same holds of changes, which are not really continuous.)
> (11 October 1705, to De Volder, G 2, 278–9/R 245)

There are plenty of points there, and many deserve more detailed analysis than they can receive here. I will settle for the modest goal of explaining this one passage, acknowledging that there are many similar passages (see, e.g., Hartz and Cover 1988) which help illuminate it.

The principal point in this text is that space and time are ideal, while bodies are real. Space and time are "prior" to their parts. This means space and time themselves are given conceptually, *en bloc*, with no prior concrete parts or bits provided. No actual parts are required since space and time are mere conceptual grids marking out possible parts. Regions of space or moments of time are taken arbitrarily, and can be any size one likes. One can assign a metric – any metric at all – to the manifold since it is simply an ordering or mapping of possibilities. All that flexibility is convenient for mathematical purposes. But the fact that it can be carved up any way one likes and its parts assigned arbitrarily raises suspicion about its ontological integrity. How could such a thing be determinate or unified? There are no fixed unities with which to build a spatiotemporal manifold; there are no qualities on which it might supervene. So in Leibniz's mind it cannot be metaphysically basic.

By contrast, in this passage bodies are said to be posterior to or dependent on logically prior substantial discrete "parts." Bodies are "multitudes" that exist only through "units." Note that this claim can't be understood except in the context of Realism. If bodies were, as in Idealism, mere appearances in minds, they couldn't be posterior to or dependent on mind-independent substantial units. The main contrast between "ideal" and "real" assumes that the "discrete" bodies fall on the real side of things – i.e., are mind-independent collections of mind-independent units rather than continuous mind-dependent phenomena that can exist without mind-independent units.

In general this passage illustrates why Idealists have traditionally had such trouble with the mature continuum doctrine. It says things that must be false in Idealism – most glaringly that bodies are real because they contain discrete substances. Since their phenomenal bodies can't contain anything like that, Idealists are forced to look for some other way of understanding such claims. These "other ways of understanding" the claims will, of course, be examined in due course.

For now, I note that on this topic the most dramatic difference between Leibniz and many of his (and our) contemporaries is that space and time are not accorded a fundamental ontic status from the outset. Where are the metaphysical credentials of space and time? Before giving them the job of holding the world of objects and events in their lap, one must ask: How could something like a spatiotemporal manifold exist in its own right? Because Leibniz knew that mathematical devices are typically abstract idealizations used for convenience, he refused to take these postulated mathematical constructions at face value. Instead, he relegated them to the scrap heap. Outside the divine intellect,[6] they are eliminatively reduced to mere conceptual structures in rational minds.[7]

Consider another argument due to Leibniz. Those who make space and time basic face a "conflict of fundamentals" problem: to wit, too many "big things" in one's ontology. With God already at the ground floor, Space and Time get in his way. "Space and God's immensity are not the same thing," Leibniz reminds Clarke (Clarke, 5.36). If they were, the infinity of Space would compete with the deity's infinite immensity, and the eternity of Time with his eternity (Clarke, 5.44). In addition, space's divisibility would contaminate the deity with divisibility (Clarke, 5.51). If one refuses to debunk spatiotemporal relations, about all that's left is to merge God with Space and Time, as Henry More (Grant 1981, 223–8) and Newton did – with predictably disastrous results.

In Leibniz's system, space and time are safely tucked away in reason. To say space is infinite and time is eternal is simply to say that there is no end to the number of Rs that can hold between possible simultaneous objects or successive events. God then remains the only concrete, actual being laying claim to eternity and infinity (Carlin 1997, 9–10). Mathematics still has its useful tools – and those tools have been explained – but they are not an ontological extravagance cluttering up one's metaphysic.

It has been said that Leibniz was one of the first to suggest sundering space from God, thus freeing up discussions of space from the theological issues in which they had for so long been entangled (Grant 1981, 261–4). But really Descartes owns that legacy. Not that he advocated discussing Extension without mentioning the deity in the same general vicinity. But he first irrevocably broke the tie between spirit and extension. His dualist bifurcation cut so deeply that space became, for the world of spirit, a metaphysical excrescence – something that spirits can do without and to which they need not bear any relationship whatever. This was quite foreign even to his contemporaries – who felt constrained to say that space is somehow a property of God, or is God, or is related to God's nature in some important way. For Descartes, God is a spiritual being and *ipso facto* not related to space (except as its creator) in any meaningful way. His creating a physical world involves God's creating space (indeed, for Descartes, just space) because it is not already there – a container coeternal with God, as it were – waiting to have matter dumped into it.

Descartes also owns another radical truncation: a material world freed up from all traces of mind. Before, under the thraldom of Aristotelian metaphysics, the extension of physical objects came from their being associated with a somewhat mentalistic feature – a form. Now suddenly, in his hands, bodies had become self-contained units, standing on their own as bleeding chunks of sheer virgin extension.

These two moves left space and its contents a self-contained system. Descartes thought space deserved the honored title of 'substance,' and accordingly called it 'Extended Substance.' What justified this title was its independence from all other things and its comprehensiveness, its indefinite extent – its all-encompassingness within the kind, *extension*, as it were.

For Leibniz, by contrast, extension and mind would, in many texts (this qualification, though strictly speaking needed, will often be dropped in the interest of economy of expression), remain closely connected. First, every finite spirit is tied to some parcel of matter or other for the duration of its existence – even in the afterlife. There is no absolute separation of matter and mind except in God.[8] Second, Leibniz's reversion to the Aristotelian form/matter model for animals guaranteed a close connection between the physical and what is broadly mental. Finally, extension is booted out of the category of substance. It has none of the marks distinctive of substances – it has no active force or causal powers. It is only an empty shell with no qualities that could give it reality.[9] Reality will come to extended things only by placing substances in them – which requires a very close association between what is broadly mental and the extended.

It is important to see how perfectly the Cartesian legacy prepared the philosophical world for Leibniz's assault. An influential figure had promoted extension from the status of a tag-along accident of stuffs and animals all the way to the principal feature – even the principal Substance – of the physical world. It had drowned all qualitative variety in the vast ocean of its utter emptiness. Overnight the world went from a place probably over-full of qualities to one that had none. The qualitative bankruptcy imputed to the physical world ensured that the Cartesians who followed couldn't leave his view unaltered. The "altering" they proposed was perhaps the only one he left open: divine tinkering (occasionalism).[10] The "only one": because matter's causal powers had been stripped away and were replaceable only by supernatural powers *ex machina*.

3.3 Extension

> [E]xtended phenomena are in reality only the simultaneous action of a plurality of actual and coexisting substances.
>
> McGuire (1976, 308)

In Leibniz's system, "extension" is used in two different ways, depending on the context. (1) "Extension" is sometimes used in rather a Cartesian sense to pick out what one would typically call "space" (e.g., G 4, 568/L 583/WF 122). (2) More typically, "extension" is predicated of bodies. As (1) has just been addressed, I move directly to (2).

Here extension is a feature or accident that belongs to a physical thing. In this case "being extended" is a property of the body itself. It is not borrowed from or parasitic on some more primitive spatial manifold, as it is in the Newtonian system. This use is much more in keeping with the Aristotelian/scholastic view. There, extension is an "accident" falling under the category of quantity. As an accident, it inheres in a subject (in this case, a body) and the question of that body's gaining its extension by reference to some spatial container or manifold never arises. This view is vividly at work in a thought experiment, due to John Buridan, in which a person manages to sneak out to the last sphere in a finite cosmos and raises their hand, thereby creating *ex nihilo* some new extension (Grant 1981, 15). Thus Leibniz boldly proclaims to Clarke what must have sounded arcane and baffling to Newtonian ears: "a body can change space but cannot leave its extension" (Clarke, 5.37).

As to Leibniz's critique of extension: that involves at least three main arguments. One of them – the Divisibility Argument – I have just examined thoroughly. The other two are, respectively, what I call the "Conceptual Argument" and (following the terminology in 2.5) the "Reality Argument." While the Reality Argument was there examined briefly, I look at it in detail here because it bears directly on the issue of bodily extension.

Conceptual Argument. Leibniz often says the concept of extension is a derivative or relative one rather than a primitive or absolute one. He claims that extension can be analyzed into more primitive concepts: continuity (which entails homogeneity and indeterminacy), plurality, and coexistence (or "simultaneity"). C. D. Broad has asked whether this is true:

> ... there is something peculiar and unanalysable in the notion of extension, viz. the factor of *spatial* diffusion. This may be *analogous* to ... the discontinuous simultaneous repetition which is at the basis of number according to Leibniz. But it has its own unique character. It would be misleading to say simply that the notion of extension can

be analysed into the notions of plurality, continuity, and simultaneity ... What is peculiar to extension is the unique way in which an extensible quality constitutes a continuous diffused whole of coexistent adjoined parts.

Broad (1975, 55)

Leibniz's way with extension seems capricious. He finds some common-alities between extension and other concepts. He then claims that because these features are shared between them, the commonalities are more basic than the concepts with the commonalities. But his claim has no more plausibility than the following parody:

Time isn't fundamental because it brings to mind plurality and priority – which time shares with causation and numbers. So there's nothing metaphysically special about time; it is a derivative concept rather than a fundamental one.

Of course the priority in causation is often thought to be temporal priority, and plurality and priority in numbers seems something different in kind from temporal priority.

In the end, the question of conceptual priority comes down to determin-ing which concepts are primitive, which derivative. Nearly always one's pre-theoretical assumptions determine what is considered primitive. In fact, in the correspondence with the Cartesian De Volder, Leibniz makes little headway in convincing him on this point because De Volder comes at the matter with a thoroughly Cartesian stance on extension. Extension is pri-mary, the "common denominator" of what's physical, as it were. How could anything be more basic than that?

Leibniz knows he must furnish an answer. He casts about looking for features extension shares with other items. At one point he writes,

[T]he concept of extension ... may be analyzed into plurality, which it has in common with number; into continuity, which it has in common with time; and into coexistence, which it has in common even with things that are not extended.

(23 June 1699, to De Volder, G 2, 183/L 519)

Two years later he tells John Bernoulli (1667–1748) he can't understand why extension seems so important to De Volder and puts it down to a deep-seated prejudice:

Not the least of the prejudices of our friend, the brilliant De Volder, is that he sees extension as something primitive, constituting the nature of body. Whereas in fact extension brings to mind nothing other than a certain diffusion (or continuous repetition) of some common nature throughout a plurality of coexistents. He does not say what this nature might be, but he presupposes it. It follows that extension is something relative rather than absolute, and that the actual nature of corporeal substance (that is, the nature which is understood as being diffused) is something prior to extension.

(27 December 1701, to Bernoulli, GM 3, 689)

Both passages are more armchair psychology than serious conceptual analysis. Things extension "may be analyzed into" and which it "brings to mind" reveal more about Leibniz's assumptions than about the nature of extension. Leibniz himself would be most severe on another philosopher carrying on in that way. The truth is: he has already decided to reject extension as basic. Thus G. H. R. Parkinson rightly notes that "his reasons for defining extension as he does are not clear; he tends simply to assert the definition, without arguing for it" (Parkinson 1965, 166).

So Broad has a point. There is something primitive about spatial continuity. And that just is Descartes's original point. The Conceptual Argument has done nothing to challenge it.

Reality Argument. By contrast with the Conceptual Argument, this line of reasoning, like the Divisibility Argument, seems much more damaging to Descartes. Recall from 2.5 that the Reality Argument says extended things derive whatever reality they have from some other things that have more substantial "primitive reality" – i.e., from things that are not themselves merely derivatively real.

Descartes had found the common denominator for physical things. But precisely because it was so abstract and general, it was metaphysically vacuous – like Hegel's "being in general." As Broad says, Leibniz seems to win this round: "To talk of anything being *merely* extended, without any extensible quality which fills and marks out its area or volume is to talk nonsense" (Broad 1975, 55).

It is that "quality" that Leibniz's philosophy is devoted to establishing in extended things. The universe must contain some qualities – some things with qualities – else "out there" would be one big empty inert continuous undifferentiated indeterminate vacuum with nothing "spread out."

But note: this Reality Argument – like the Divisibility Argument – rests foursquare on the Realist aggregate thesis. Idealism hasn't the resources to put up a fight on this point, as its bodies are continuous and inert – and subjective to boot.[11] Idealism's extended bodies necessarily owe their reality, not to mind-independent, non-extended, indivisible, primitively real *substances*, but to the single primitively real *substance* doing the perceiving. Without Realism neither of the most convincing criticisms of Descartes can stand, and Leibniz's critique of extension falls flat.

Some interpreters suppose that the critique of extension depends directly on endorsing Idealism. The thought is that while Descartes's bodies are extended, Leibniz's are non-extended since they are states of purely spiritual minds.

That is indeed a safe escape from extension. But Leibniz has *no arguments* from within the sterile fortress of Idealism. Within the four walls of that spiritual haven, he is entitled to conclude the existence of only his own mind and – thanks to the grace of God – other minds.[12] He is completely defenseless against John Toland's quip that "M. Leibniz's *minds* are *all in his mind*, and entirely imaginary."[13] One Idealist commentator has claimed explicitly that aggregate thesis arguments are "defective and circular." His advice: Leibniz would have been better off if he "had instead postulated the existence of simple substances" and used that as a "basic doctrine of his system" (Anapolitanos 1999, 81). How easy it seems to dispense with Realist themes! One simply invokes the Ivory Tower Metaphysics of Idealism – where "postulations" are waved on without question – and away go the problems. And the arguments.

This comment points up a deep difference between Exclusive Idealism and my perspective. Such Idealists seem to want Leibniz to *assume* everything he needs to compose a pretty picture and then stand back and say "There, isn't that nice?" But Leibniz himself seldom does that. After the standing back and admiring is over, he *argues*, on non-theological grounds, that there are substances and then puts those substances to work granting bodies a measure of reality.

The arguments for substances and their employment in constituting material things seem to belong to his deepest thought. With these moves he is establishing a Realist foothold so he can argue that substances are mind-independent – can answer Toland's joke about the whole thing being a delusive dream. If he doesn't do that, he'll never get out of Idealism's solipsist prison house. And argumentatively he'll be completely dependent on utterly trusting readers who ask no questions.

3.4 "Divisible" and "Divided"

Leibniz has a tendency to work in the seams of analogies, to find connections between analogous concepts that have traditionally been viewed as disparate. In his mereology of body, he trades off between "divisible" and "divided."

As is clear by now, "divisible" is most at home in his discussions of ideal items like space, time, and geometrical bodies. "Divided," by contrast, indicates something already accomplished, something determinate and fixed and not in the least up to anyone's whim. In the "fertile passage" examined in 3.2 he said that matter is "actually infinitely divided" while space and time are granted divisions only as "made by the mind" (G 2, 278–9/R 245). That is, since space and time are ideal, they admit only of possible divisions – so are *divisible* rather than *divided*.

A look at the corpus shows there is little change on this topic during the entire mature period – evident strikingly in the fact that he is saying exactly the same things in the early "Specimen of Discoveries" and the late *Monadology*. First, from the early text:

[T]here are no atoms, but every part has other parts which are actually separate from it and excited by various motions; or, what follows from this, every body, however small, has parts which are actually infinite, and in every particle there is a world of innumerable creatures. ... [T]he mass is subdivided.

No body is so small that it is not actually divided into parts which are excited by different motions; and therefore in every body there is an actually infinite number of bodies.
(c. 1686, A Specimen of Discoveries, G 7, 315; 317: A VI 4 B, 1623; 1626 (N. 312)/PW 82; 85–6)

And from the *Monadology*:

[E]ach part of matter not only is infinitely divisible, as the ancients recognized, but also is actually subdivided without end, each part into parts, each of which has its own distinct movement. Otherwise it would be impossible that each part of matter could express the whole universe. It is clear from this that there is a world of creatures, living beings, animals, entelechies, souls, in the smallest particle of matter.
(1714, Mon 65 & 66, G 6, 618/L 649–50)

Though it is impossible to include here an exhaustive textual study of this contrast, the theme makes a non-trivial appearance in the mature writings. That is important because the actual division of bodies is devastating to Idealist interpretations. Idealist appearance-bodies are not the right sorts of things to be divided into substances. So when Leibniz persists in saying bodies are divided into an infinite number of monads, souls, or – as late as 1714 – animals, the Idealist's metaphysics seems in danger of shattering asunder. Two claims in particular from the *Monadology* passage above are threatening. (i) The Idealist's appearance-bodies cannot be divided into substances and (ii) some of the substances Leibniz here says they are divided into are not monads.

It must be noted, however, that while the divisible/divided contrast is well-represented in the mature writings, a few texts construe bodies so that what is in view is their status as homogeneous "extended masses" that contain infinitely *divisible* mass-parts. I will call bodies so construed "mass-aggregates." Mass-aggregates are extended bodies that do not "bottom out" on substances because they do not "bottom out" at all. They are endlessly divisible – thus divisible but not divided. In a text from 1690 he writes that while bodies can be viewed as divided – containing "an infinite multitude" of substances ("things that are one") – they also might be construed as "always further divisible, and any given part always has another part, to infinity" – in which case "every part of matter has parts" (March 1690, Notes on Fardella, A VI 4 B, 1668–9; 1671 (N. 329)/AG 103; 105).

This construal of bodies as divisible gives him the ability to play around a bit with his account of bodies, sometimes insisting they are actually divided, and other times admitting they are divisible – depending on which construal he needs. Indeed, in the *Monadology* passage just cited he says matter is "not only infinitely divisible, . . . but also actually subdivided."

I think this represents an unfortunate equivocation in Leibniz, since in light of it one cannot be sure which construal of body is "on tap" in any given discussion. Again around 1704 he mixes the two accounts together in a passage to De Volder:

> The true substance is not in the whole aggregate but in individual unities, just as in the ocean there is not one substance or one thing, but every drop contains other things, although every drop is assumed to be made of similar mass. However, even before it is formed into drops, the water is actually divided, as is the mass of ivory you proposed even before it is formed into statues; it is the same way in every mass.
>
> (G 2, 276/AG 182)

Here the more typical "actually divided" account, according to which the ocean's drops "contain other things," is compromised by the claim, "every drop is assumed to be made of similar mass" – in my terms, every drop could also be viewed as a mass-aggregate (see 3.6). The drops are divided into substances but, from another perspective, endlessly divisible.

Like all equivocations, this one is dangerous. It plays fast and loose with the doctrine of the continuum. The "actually divided" account points towards bodies' reality having a foundation in substances, to their *not* being endlessly divisible. The "endlessly divisible" theme cuts against this and would accord to bodies the sort of continuity and lack of reality supposedly reserved for space, time, mathematical bodies, and other continuous magnitudes.

While I recognize this use of 'divisible' is occasionally found in Leibniz, I will not invoke it much. In what follows I will consistently use the 'divided' account since it is in line with the thrust of the mature continuum doctrine.[14]

3.5 Some Definitions in Leibniz's Mereology of Body

I proceed now to a more formal presentation of Leibniz's rules governing parts and wholes. Particular attention will be paid to those terms that are crucial for understanding how matter is related to its parts.

These definitions are not meant to form a comprehensive list, and they are not consistent with every passage in the mature corpus. Derived principally from the "Metaphysical Foundations of Mathematics,"[15] they are fairly representative of the mature period[16] and will furnish enough structure to understand the various senses of 'divisible' and 'divided.'

IN: x is *in* (is an "ingredient" of) y iff: positing y entails positing x, but not conversely.[17]

QI: x is *qualitatively identical* with ("similar to") y iff: x and y are indistinguishable unless:

i) x and y are perceived together and differ either in quantity or position, or
ii) x is perceived after y, but before the memory of y is destroyed, or conversely, so that x and y are perceived to differ either in quantity or position.[18]

HM: x is *homogeneous* with y iff:

i) x is qualitatively identical with y; or
ii) x is transformable by continuous change into y; or
iii) x is equal to or transformable by continuous change into z, and y is equal to or transformable by continuous change into z' (where possibly z = z'), and z and z' are qualitatively identical.[19]

Comment: Homogeneous are: all lines, regions of space, and stretches of time (by (i)); 2 lines transformable into one another (by (ii)); and 2 lines each transformable into a third (by (iii)). Extended masses are homogeneous with extended masses (both are pluralities), but not substances (individuals); lines (pluralities) are homogeneous with lines but not (single) points; times (periods of duration, pluralities) are homogeneous with times but not (single) moments. Samples of water are homogeneous with other samples of water. Whatever is homogeneous must be of a certain kind, K, "all the way down" in its decomposition, or "all the way up" in its composition.

PART: x is a *part* of y iff: x is in, and homogeneous with, y.[20]

Comment: A smaller bit of extended mass is a part of a larger chunk of extended mass when and only when positing the chunk entails positing the bit. A smaller line segment is part of a larger line that it is in, a smaller region of space or stretch of time is part of a larger expanse of space or time that includes it. A smaller sample of water is part of a large vat of water that it is in. But a nose is not part of a face; it is *in* it but not *of* it. The nose isn't K ("is a face"), while the face is. And because homogeneity is violated, a point can be in but not part of a line or region of space; a moment can be in but not a part of a stretch of time.

Most crucially for this study, *a substance can be in but not apart of a body*. As points and moments can't be chained together to constitute a line or period of time, so partless substances can't be chained together to constitute a continuous extended body.

CW: y is a *composite whole* at t only if: y has at least two discrete, determinate, logically prior parts (e.g., x1 and x2) at t. (GM 7, 19–20/L 668)

IW: y is an *ideal, continuous whole* iff:

i) y is logically prior to any of its parts,
ii) y is given conceptually as a whole; and
iii) y is arbitrarily divisible into an infinite number of merely possible parts.

Comment: A composite whole is put together from logically prior parts. It is capable only of identity at a time because there are no persistence conditions for such wholes (though there are for the substances that are in them and well-found them). Identity at a time is determined by mereological essentialism – requiring that the composite have exactly the parts it has at any given time.[21] In the case of bodies, the "prior parts" are bits of infinitely divisible mass that add up to a larger mass by straightforward mereological agglomeration. (The "prior parts" cannot be substances, since homogeneity does not hold.) Also because homogeneity fails, a point or infinitesimal is not a part of the ideal whole, space, as a moment is not a part of the ideal whole, time. Instead, the parts of space or time are always arbitrarily small or large stretches of space or time.

Space and time, like mathematical lines, are ideal continuous wholes. "Ideal" because they are only concepts humans use to track bodies and events. "Continuous" because they have no determinate division-points. "Wholes" in the sense that they are given conceptually *en bloc*. They arrive in our thoughts as a whole manifold, and one can carve them up however one likes. Or leave them whole. Either way, they have possible parts. And, of course, the parts are all in that whole and homogeneous with it. (They meet the conditions laid down in *Part* above.)

3.6 The Perceptual Continuum

Though in strict terms, ideal notions are continuous, yet they are applicable to phenomena ...

Even though Leibniz held phenomenal change and extension to be discrete in character, the law of continuity applied. For the repetition of discrete but simultaneous states creates the perception of continuity.

McGuire (1976), 312

In the perceptual process, continuity from the mind/concept side is meshed with discontinuity emanating from the substance side. The result is that mass or secondary matter can, in light of the equivocation noted at the end of the last section, be taken in either of two ways: (1) as an infinitely divisible, continuous *Mass-Aggregate* or (2) as an actually divided, discrete *Aggregate of Substances*. Because of the logical barriers involved, these two ways of taking mass cannot be coalesced into a single account. Thus they are shown disjunctively in Figure 3.1, and "Mass-Aggregates" will soon be abandoned in my analyses.

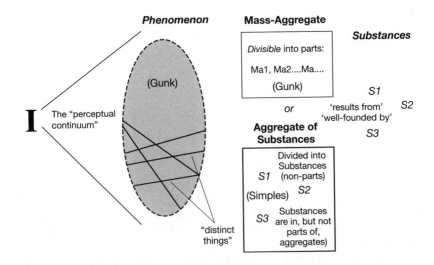

Here the incompatibility of the 2 construals matter on the right is clear: the top one is a Gunk metaphysic; the bottom one a Simples metaphysic.

Figure 3.1. The Perceptual Continuum

This diagram represents an effort to combine the various elements of Leibniz's theory, especially as regards the relationship between spatial continuity and body.

Spatial continuity has its home in the mind of the perceiver as an innate concept of a whole that is homogeneous and arbitrarily divisible into bits of the same kind. This conceptual structure is imposed on phenomena. As a result, phenomena have the nature of continua.

In light of the analyses of aggregates and animals that lie ahead, the importance of that claim can scarcely be overestimated. The reader is asked to note particularly these texts in which phenomena are said to be divisible or continuous: first,

> Phenomena can therefore always be divided into lesser phenomena which could be observed by other, more subtle, animals and we can never arrive at smallest phenomena. Substantial unities are in fact not parts but foundations of phenomena.
>
> (30 June 1704, to De Volder, G 2, 268/L 536)

And second,

> Matter appears to us to be a continuum, but it only appears so, just as does actual motion. It is rather as alabaster dust appears to form a

continuous fluid, when one boils it over the fire, or like a spoked wheel appears continuously translucent when it turns with great speed – without which one could tell the location where the spokes are from the empty spaces in between the spokes – our perception running together the separate places and times.

(31 October 1705, to Sophia, G 7, 564)

These claims make it clear that the appearance matter produces in us is continuous – or, to put the point another way, phenomena are continuous or endlessly divisible. Leibniz blames "our perception" for giving us the impression that matter itself is continuous, while it is actually discrete.

The reason this claim about the continuity of phenomena is so crucial is that, as one might expect, Idealists are going to be inclined to say bodies are continuous since bodies are, for them, phenomena. This will create major problems for understanding mature continuum doctrines and according them a place in Idealism.

Moving on in Figure 3.1, "distinct things" appear in phenomena given the "actual divisions" (G 4, 568/L 583) in nature (G 2, 2, 250/L 529). Such distinct things seem to be due ultimately to the presence of discrete substances in the body (construed as an "Aggregate of Substances") at the next, more fundamental, level. Such Aggregates have the discrete substances in them and are divided into substances (non-parts). The other, less well-represented construal at that level (again represented disjunctively) concerns a "Mass-Aggregate." That sort of Aggregate is divisible into always-further-divisible mass parts. Finally, the "Substances" are just the sheer substances themselves with no added structural constraints. From these the perceived bodies ultimately "result," and on them the bodies are "well-founded."

It is sometimes said that, despite his claim that he'd found a way out, Leibniz remained lost in the "labyrinth of the continuum" (e.g., R 117). To that charge: Yes and No. Yes: he is lost if one insists on taking body univocally as something that is either infinitely divisible (i.e., in Leibniz's sense, continuous) or not. He can't get out then, for he needs body to be something which can be taken in one or the other of two ways: as body-qua-infinitely-divisible-mass-aggregate or body-qua-actually-divided-aggregate-of-substances. In the first way it is infinitely divisible; in the second it is not. With that distinction in place, the answer is No: he is not lost. He has in fact found a way through.

But it is no trivial matter that these two concepts of body are inconsistent. Leibniz is doing little more than using "qua" to mask and legitimize a case of outright equivocation – in effect, breaking the rules by which the other participants in the debate are playing. Philosophers will have to decide how much equivocation they're willing to tolerate. In any case, the equivocation casts grave doubt on Leibniz's portrayal of himself as having emerged triumphant while everyone else is still groping about helplessly in the maze.

4   Introduction to Aggregates

The material covered up to now has been preparatory, in many ways, for what lies ahead. As I enter the topic of aggregates – or things made up of other "smaller" things – matters quickly become complicated. It will be helpful to pause and look at the general textual and conceptual situation.

The tension between the claims of the Idealist theory of aggregates and the Realist one emanates from Leibniz's writings. But the same tension exists in our ordinary thinking. Nearly everyone thinks a sand dune has no real integrity, with grains constantly blowing away and being replaced by others and yet the "same dune" remaining. Indeed, it seems that the singleness of "a dune" lies only in our minds. For convenience's sake, we simply summarize the grains as one big heap, but are not at all committing ourselves to the existence of a dune in nature. Thus a sand dune seems mind-dependent – in line with Idealism.

But Realism also asserts itself when we confront the question of whether the dune is merely an appearance in our minds – say, a dream image – as it would be on an exclusively Idealist analysis. The dune is composed of grains, and the grains themselves seem not to be mind-dependent. Thus the dune may borrow from them whatever measure of mind-independence it has so as to distinguish it from the "dream-image dune." In this sense the dune is mind-independent, or, in the terms I'm using here, "real."

If one substitutes "substances" for "grains" in that story, one is well on the way to understanding Leibniz's struggles with aggregates.

4.1 Aggregates: An Overview

Recall that the study in Chapter 3 revealed three main candidates for fulfilling the role of aggregate: (1) phenomena, (2) mass-aggregates, and (3) aggregates of substances.

Here (2) is set aside. Mass-aggregates were all along only of marginal interest, as they simply represented a way of viewing external bodies through the "lens of the continuum" as it were. Because mass-aggregates are gunk, Leibniz thinks they can't possess unities – hence can't have even the derivative, residual reality that is supposed to characterize aggregates.

I will devote my attention wholly to the conflict between the metaphysics of (1) phenomena (Idealism) and (3) aggregates of substances (Realism). Of course Theory-Pluralism enables me to view the "conflict" as benign in the end. It is not important that one emerge the victor, trampling the other into the dust. Still, quite often one does seem poised to strike the final blow. But before it can, the other rights itself and continues the battle.

Many passages argue, in line with the Idealist theory, that aggregates are phenomena, since the mind plays a crucial role in housing aggregates and bringing them into existence. In particular, the mind is said to portray aggregates as unified and extended – qualities they could not have without the mind's activity.

But other passages – often in the same texts – fall in with Realism. There aggregates are granted mind-independent status because they contain mind-independent substances, are "actually divided" into substances, and their qualities supervene on the qualities of the substances.

It would be premature to declare one theory more adequate than the other at this stage. Many factors – some historical, some philosophical – must be considered and carefully weighed before arriving at a verdict. Of course the beginnings of a philosophical case for the Realist theory have appeared in connection with Leibniz's arguments for substances (2.5) and his critique of extension (3.3). But the textual situation remains unclear at this point, and there is a possibility that Idealism has philosophical strengths that more than offset those of Realism.

The remainder of this chapter is devoted to clarifying, in a provisional way, the textual situation. I will not attempt an exhaustive survey of texts on aggregates. There are far too many to manage anything like that. I expound a few representative texts from each main camp. Many more passages are relevant, of course, and some will be used in the chapters that lie ahead to help extract the precise details of the several options within each main theory.

4.2 Idealist Texts

It is first necessary to provide a bit of textual evidence for what I called (in 1.7) the Canonical Metaphysics: (1) The only substances are monads. (2) Relations are either purely ideal or reducible to intrinsic states of the relata. (3) The "predicate in subject" doctrine holds universally. (4) Bodies are eliminatively reduced to phenomena. (5) Universal harmony and mirroring holds between all the perceptual states of all the monads. (6) "Parallelism" is denied. (7) The "aggregate thesis" is denied. (8) Animals are not true unities, but mere aggregates of monads. Add to these claims endorsements of "Phenomenalism" (which are counted separately in the Doctrine Tables) and one has the entire Idealist text-base. Indeed, in the five mainstream works canvassed in the Doctrine Tables, one can readily see where the Canonical and Phenomenalist endorsements are found. In all, they represent some 245 occurrences.

The *Discourse on Metaphysics* and Arnauld correspondence occupy a crucial position in Idealism. The Doctrine Tables show that DM and LA are replete with Canonical claims – containing, respectively, 32 and 62. Explicit endorsements of Phenomenalism are also relatively frequent here at 11 and 27. More impressive than the number of endorsements is the depth and explicitness of Phenomenalism in DM – as I'll illustrate in a moment. Indeed, it's no accident that it was the reading of these two works that the Idealist Russell found threw a "flood of light" on the "inmost recesses of Leibniz's philosophical edifice."

First is a passage from DM 14:

[E]ach substance is like a world apart, independent of any other thing save God; thus all our phenomena, that is to say all that can ever happen to us, are only consequences of our being. These phenomena maintain a certain order in conformity with our nature, or so to say with the world which is in us, and this enables us to make observations which are useful for regulating our conduct and are justified by the success of future phenomena, and thus often to judge the future by the past without making mistakes. This would therefore suffice for saying that these phenomena were true, without troubling ourselves about whether they are outside us and whether others perceive them also.

(A VI 4 B, 1550 (N. 306)/Leibniz 1953, 23)

And another sent to Arnauld in 1686 reads thus:

[A]lways, in every true affirmative proposition, necessary or contingent, universal or particular, the concept of the predicate is in a sense included in that of the subject. [T]he concept of the individual substance contains all its events and all its denominations, even those that one commonly calls extrinsic (that is to say, that belong to it only by virtue of the general connection of things and of the fact that it is an expression of the entire universe after its own manner), since *there must always be some basis for the connection between the terms of a proposition.* [E]very individual substance is an expression of the entire universe after its own manner and according to a certain relationship, or, so to speak, according to the point of view from which it looks at the universe; and ... its succeeding state is a sequel ... of its preceding state, as though only God and it existed in the world: thus each individual substance or complete entity is like a world apart, independent of everything except God. [A]s all created substances are a continual production of the same sovereign being in accordance with the same plans, and are an expression of the same universe or of the same phenomena, they harmonize exactly among themselves, and that causes us to say that one acts upon the other. ...

(LA 56–7)

The line of reasoning is perfectly clear in these stunning lines. The predicate is in the subject, explicitly or "virtually" (DM 8). Each substance must contain all the properties within itself – even those commonly called relational properties. For instance, when I see a sphere, it seems as if an "extrinsic" relation must hold between an external sphere and me. But actually, I already contain the sphere-appearance and its presence in me is guaranteed whether or not there is anything external. I get along perfectly fine with only God external to me. My whole mental life unfolds from within – each "frame" in the march-past of phenomena is due solely to my own "preceding state" – assuming of course that God has destined that state to give rise to a next one.

And robust phenomenalism is on display. The subject's own resources make all would-be external objects unnecessary – no need to "trouble ourselves" about whether they're there! The supposed relations between me and something not myself are explained away, leaving bodies nowhere to go but into the mind of the perceiving individual.

Another statement of phenomenalism is found later in the Arnauld letters:

> To be brief, I hold as an axiom this identical proposition which is diversified only by emphasis, namely that what is not truly *one* being is not truly a *being* either. It has always been believed that one and being are mutually convertible things. Entity is one thing, entities another; but the plural presupposes the singular, and where there is no entity, still less will there be many entities. What clearer statement can be made? I have believed therefore that I would be permitted to distinguish beings of aggregation from substances, since those beings have their unity only in our mind, which relies on the relations or modes of genuine substances.
>
> (LA 97)[1]

Thus, if being and one are convertible, then "beings of aggregation have their *unity* only in our mind" is equivalent to "beings of aggregation have their *being* only in our mind." And that simply is phenomenalism as understood here.

Later on, one gets a bit of help in understanding how the mind does the aggregating:

> [I] agree that there are degrees of accidental unity, that an ordered society has more unity than a chaotic mob ... that is to say, it is more appropriate to conceive of them as a single thing, because there are more connections between the constituents; but then all these unities are made complete only by thoughts and appearances, like colors and other phenomena, which one nevertheless calls real. The tangibility of a heap of stones or of a marble block does not constitute a better proof

than the visibility of a rainbow does of its substantial reality. [I]t can therefore be said of these composites and similar things what Demo-critus said very well about them, 'they exist by opinion, by convention'. ... Our mind notices or conceives some genuine sub-stances that have certain modes. These modes contain relations to other substances. From this the mind takes the occasion to join them together in thought and to put one name in the accounting for all these things together, which serves for convenience in reasoning.

(LA 100–1)

These texts are impeccable, their picture unmistakable. Aggregates are extended beings and so exist only as phenomena in perceiving minds. Those minds construct the aggregates as they notice modes possessed by indivi-duals around them. There is nothing more to an aggregate than a mental "thinking together" of the constituents. And underneath all the relatively superficial talk of the mind's "joining" and "naming" is the deep meta-physics of individual substance, according to which substances are just purring along on their own resources.

These themes are perhaps a bit less prominent in later works, but do surface from time to time – enough in any case to show that Leibniz did not abandon them. Thus, in 1695 he writes that God "created the soul ... in such a way that everything in it arises from its own nature" and that each substance is "as in a world apart" (NS 14). In 1703 he writes to De Volder: "For an aggregate is nothing other than all those things taken at the same time from which it results, which surely have their union from the mind alone on account of what they have in common, like a flock of sheep" (G 2, 256/Rd 234). And in 1714 (Mon 7, 11) he claims that "monads have no windows" and that their changes come wholly from an "internal principle."

Again, my goal in this section is not to present a comprehensive case for Idealism's canonical metaphysics and phenomenalism. This sample is suffi-cient to show that Leibniz advocated an Idealist theory. No other sense can be put on the words. Aggregates on this view get the back of his hand. They are "nothing but" things thought of in a certain way, and their exis-tence is only "in the head." That's just what we should expect given our usual thoughts about things like sand dunes: the "duneness" is not in nature, but foisted upon it by the conceiving mind.

4.3 Realist Texts

Other passages reveal a different picture. The Summary reveals that in the five major works there are 251 endorsements of Realist themes. (101 of those are references to Animals. A full-dress defense of the claim that they demand a Realist analysis is presented in Chapter 8.) These endorsements are not found outside the works cited above in favor of Idealism. For instance, the Arnauld Correspondence Doctrine Table reveals that while

Idealist themes maintain an almost exclusive grip on a large stretch of text (LA 39–58), the Realist theory *joins* the Idealist one after that. For instance, a look at some important phenomenalist claims – say, those quoted above from LA 97 – shows they are surrounded by Realist ones.

In the paragraph immediately *before* the one concerned with the convertibility of being and one, there is this:

> I believe that *where there are only entities through aggregation, there will not even be real entities*; for every being through aggregation presupposes entities endowed with a true unity, because it obtains its reality from nowhere but that of its constituents, so that it will have no reality at all if each constituent entity is still an entity through aggregation; or one must yet seek another basis to its reality, which in this way, if one must constantly go on searching, can never be found.
>
> (LA 96)

Again following the clear sense of the words leads to but one conclusion. Beings through aggregation have constituents that are real true unities. It is from these unities that beings through aggregation extract their reality, so that those beings themselves can retain a degree of reality. The true unities must be mind-independent. But since these beings are deriving their reality from the unities, those *beings* must also be mind-independent.

In the paragraph immediately *after* the phenomenalist passage concerning convertibility, one finds Leibniz apparently reversing his field, reverting back to the Realist picture:

> I do not say that there is nothing substantial or nothing except appearances in things devoid of true unity, for I grant that they always have as much reality or substantiality as there is true unity in what goes into their composition.
>
> (LA 97)

Again talk of "composition" is wholly out of place in phenomenalism. Phenomena cannot in any obvious way retain the reality of mind-independent constituents because they can contain at best mind-dependent constituents – smaller sense-data, perhaps (G 2, 268/L 536).

Outside the Arnauld exchange, this odd mixture of Idealist and Realist elements is the rule rather than the exception. Thus *New System* 14 is heavily Idealist, but three sections earlier he had written that "true substantial unities" are needed to compose "collections." He says that such unities are rightly regarded as "atoms of substance" acting as "the absolute first principles of the composition of things" – that is, such things as "masses of matter" (NS 11). These are all Realist claims, requiring that the things composed of "atoms of substance" be, like the "atoms," mind-independent.

A year after he sent De Volder the brief phenomenalist passage (G 2, 256/ Rd 234) cited at the end of the last section, he wrote: "Whatever things are aggregates of many, are not one except for the mind, nor have any other reality than what is borrowed, or what belongs to the things of which they are aggregated" (G 2, 261/R 249). He is claiming that an aggregate's *unity* is mind-dependent, but its *reality* is a different matter – it is derived from its constituents. As was evident in the Arnauld exchange, one seems to find a reluctance to endorse phenomenalism fully. He allows the unity, but *not* the being, of aggregates to be mind-dependent.

Finally, the *Monadology* also blows hot and cold. An Idealist passage was cited in the last section, but at the very outset unmistakable Realist themes emerge. He writes that "there must be simple substances, since there are composites; for a composite is nothing but a collection, or *aggregate*, of simples," adding that "what is in a composite can come only from its simple ingredients" (Mon 2, 8). It is impossible (i) that the "simples" here mentioned are mind-dependent or (ii) that the composites here mentioned are mind-dependent. Yet if all aggregates are mind-dependent, as they are in Idealism, (i) and (ii) are inevitable.

Even with these few passages in hand, it is easy to see why Leibniz's rationality is open to criticism. "Beings by aggregation" are handled in two ways that seem incompatible. Ideal sand dunes in minds are quite different from real sand dunes in nature, and the conditions under which they exist differ wildly.

It seems clear to me that, indeed, they can't both be True. I will continue to regard them as claims at home in separate and incompatible theories. This allows me unproblematically to divide the theories into Idealist (Chapter 5) and Realist (Chapter 6). Once the separate analyses have been presented, however, I will revisit the compatibility issue intensively in Chapter 7.

5   Idealist Analyses of Aggregates

I begin with the more familiar Idealist analyses of aggregates. They have their home in "Idealism" – which will in this chapter refer to the set of distinctively Idealist doctrines taken to be Truths rather than theory-relative truth-claims. I will try to capture all the possible ways of construing Leibnizian bodies as "ideas" or appearances in minds. Each one has a foothold in the texts, though some receive more attention than others. I don't need to try to narrow it down to one view he "really" held. Theory-Pluralism has plenty of room for all of them. He "plays the field" a bit even within the category of Idealism. Just as he withholds unqualified assent to Idealism or to Realism, the same provisional attitude seems evident towards sub-varieties of those broader doctrines.

After examining two such accounts – "Reductive Phenomenalism" and "Mental Constructions," – I conclude with a third: "Well-Founded Phenomena." The third one looks to be the best supported and most fleshed out view of this sort.

5.1 Reductive Phenomenalism

> There were indeed times when Leibniz toyed with phenomenalism, suggesting that to talk about physical things is only to talk about perceptions. The idea which he puts forward is that physical things might be 'true phenomena' – that is, that each physical thing is simply a coherent set of the appearances present to a soul or souls. However, the idea is put forward only to be rejected, Leibniz arguing that it can be proved that there exist physical things as well as souls.
>
> Parkinson (1965, 166)

The first broadly Idealist option is a full-blown eliminative reduction program aimed at bodies. As Parkinson says, Reductive Phenomenalism claims roughly that "to talk about physical things is only to talk about perceptions." The envisaged reduction tries to construe the entire universe as a vast series of perceptions of all the world's minds.

While this position does not have a large following, parts of it surface regularly in many interpretations.[1] Indeed, sometimes Leibniz says this is exactly what he has in mind.[2] In recent times it was "put on the map" as a viable interpretation by Montgomery Furth in his influential article, "Monadology" (1976). I will here devote my attention entirely to that article.

Furth claims Idealism and Realism are inconsistent. He notes that the phenomenalism, discernible in some of Leibniz's texts, that reduces bodies to harmonious perceptions is at odds with his other claim (which I've been calling the "aggregate thesis") that a body is an "*aggregate*' of monads that go to *make it up*," and that renders it "a 'being by accumulation' of simple substances" (Furth 1976, 121). This reveals, he claims, the "deepest ambivalence" in Leibniz's thought – one that does not allow phenomenalism to be "consistently maintained" (121, 119). Also, an example of "his notorious habit of writing in a *simpliste* fashion when he believes that the immediate occasion calls for popularization" can be found in "Leibniz's way of explaining the Harmony as a concomitance that holds between events that take place in the mind and events that take place *in the body* – as if the latter category had some independent, unreduced sense" (120).

Finally, Leibniz sometimes suggests that the Harmony is "the *result* of the monads' all perceiving the same independently existing physical universe, rather than that the Harmony is constitutive thereof. . . . " This latter suggestion "would greatly diminish the interest of his theory, shearing the Harmony of explanatory power" (120–1).

In my terms, Furth is an Exclusivist Idealist. He takes seriously harmony-of-perceptions texts and denigrates those that contradict it. Among the texts that remain acceptable are all those friendly to phenomenalism, in which bodies are reduced without "residue" to perceptions.

But, as argued in Chapter 2, the phenomenalism Furth takes to be definitive of monadology is, from an argumentative point of view, its most deadly poison. The monadological *picture* seems to align Leibniz with Idealism, but when one adopts that picture exclusively, all the non-theological arguments for substances – hence monads – fall away into the rejected part. A closer look shows that even Furth's envisaged monadology needs, in addition to himself, "an infinity of further monads, each experiencing ('expressing') some universe or other in the way I do that which is immediately present to me" (Furth 1976, 115).

How are such monads to be obtained? The only text Furth cites[3] contains a theological argument to the effect that an actual infinity of monads is established by its mere possibility "since it is manifest how very rich are the works of God." He can't cite any of the non-theological ones since they all depend on the rejected Realist theory.

Now basing a monadology on exclusively theological grounds is quite unsatisfactory. If that is done, the monadology will have its infinity of minds thanks only to the grace of God. This then throws one back on arguments for the existence of God – indeed a specifically Leibnizian sort of rationalist God, who is urged to create by "striving possibles," and is required by wisdom to make all possible gradations of minds, to leave no possible "spot" unfilled with being.

Of course someone might accept those terms. But Furth himself cannot so easily acquiesce to them because he is intent on showing that monadology is superior to Berkeley's idealism. Berkeley must rely on a "paltry population of observers" in arguing that physical objects are sense-data, while Leibniz puts similar sense-data in "every conceivable point of view of the universe" (Furth 1976, 118). This allows Leibniz to claim, more convincingly than Berkeley, that agreement across perceivers is sufficient for veridical perception because it allows a reduction of bodies, without "residue," to harmonious perceptions. But note that this advantage now depends on theological assumptions which, if simply granted to Berkeley (as they were to Leibniz), would make his idealism indistinguishable (in this respect) from monadology.

The other advantage over Berkeley – there being no need of "subjunctive conditionals" – is held hostage to the same theological assumptions. Berkeley has only analogies with other minds, and (at best) "notions," with which to purchase perceivers other than himself. If, *per impossibile*, he were simply to help himself to a rationalist God, he could get an infinity of them straightaway. Then he would no longer have the problem that "there are far too many gaps in the population's actual experience, too many unrepresented viewpoints and interrupted conscious histories" (Furth 1976, 118) to meet the no-residue condition.

Reductive Phenomenalism ends up impoverished because it must ignore so much of Leibniz's philosophy in trying to construct the account. And, while elements of Reductive Phenomenalism surface from time to time in Leibniz's writings, this view is not his principal account within the broader category of Idealism.

5.2 Aggregates as Mental Constructions

> Leibniz's claim is that aggregates have their unity, and therefore their being, only in the mind. [A]ggregates [are] logically or metaphysically constructed from the individual substances. This construction, in Leibniz's view, is a mental operation. ... They [such constructions] exist in the mind and are dependent on being thought of.
>
> Robert M. Adams (Ad 246–7)

> [A]ggregative beings – whose existence is dependent upon relations – can only exist for a mind. Only to the extent that a plurality of individuals is apprehended by a mind as forming a unitary being is an aggregate determined.
>
> Donald Rutherford (Rd 222)

Nowhere does Leibniz deny that matter is purely phenomenal. Leibniz agreed with Berkeley that only spirits and their perceptions existed.

George MacDonald Ross (1984, 176, 178)

The second of the broadly Idealist analyses assigns the mind a leading role in constructing and housing aggregates. The Reductive Phenomenalism just examined saw bodies as reducible to perceptions that existed in finite minds – where those perceptions did not require of the minds entertaining them any particular effort to "group" them together.

"Mental Constructions" grants the mind an active role very like that – one evident in Adams's quotation in the epigraph above. The Kantian tone of this position is unmistakable: aggregates arise when the mind constructs them – though, as in Kant, one can only assume that the "construction" typically goes on beneath the level of consciousness.

Texts that support Mental Constructions are found especially in some Idealist passages sent to Arnauld that I've already examined in 4.2. There, recall, Leibniz writes that aggregates "have their unity only in our mind" (LA 97) and that "our mind notices or conceives some genuine substances that have certain modes," whereupon "the mind takes the occasion to join them together in thought and enter into the account one name for all these things together" (LA 101). When Leibniz specifically says "one name" here, I take the linguistic point seriously. Thus only minds capable of language will be able to construct aggregates on this view. Such minds will be what Leibniz calls minds capable of "reflection," or as we might say, capable of having linguistic thoughts (G 3, 343–4/WF 221; also Mon 30). Thus a dog will not be among the possible perceivers of Mental-Construction-aggregates.

I will analyze the idea involved in Mental Constructions. But before doing so I must explain what might seem a suspicious-looking anachronism in the formulation. The analysis is put in terms of "monads," while in the Arnauld exchange animals, not monads, are the exemplary substances. (Monads would have to wait another decade to be invented.) I put this in terms of monads because many of the proponents of Mental Constructions are Idealists who want to preserve the Canonical Metaphysics, and in some cases see earlier substances as precursors to monads.

An analysis that seems to capture Leibniz's idea is this – where "the monads" is short for "an infinity of actual monads" and "$Monad_1$" is a mind endowed with reflection:

Men-AGG: Aggregate p exists and is (an) F at t iff: at t, "the monads" are represented (possibly unconsciously) in $Monad_1$'s intentional state as being so related that they are (possibly unconsciously) judged to form a unified object, p, that is (an) F.[4]

In terms of the mereological distinctions between phenomena, mass-aggregates, and aggregates of substances, Mental-Construction-aggregates are clearly *phenomena* (hence *p* is the subject of predication). *p* is judged to be a unity because of the meaning of 'F.' For instance, 'dune' means "a vast heap of sand grains": the concept of unity is built into the definition and is imposed by the mind on the separate grains (for Leibniz, ultimately substances) constituting the dune.

Unconscious representing and judging must be countenanced, for even in "higher" minds like ours, the "noticing" of modes and "joining" of substances is nearly always beneath the level of awareness. No persistence conditions are given because Leibniz seems to offer no hope that aggregates endure. Any persistence they have would be as conventional and "notional" or mind-dependent as their synchronic unity.

Here the predicate 'F' is made to play a crucial role because of the emphasis on linguistic conventions. Leibniz says societies[5] and mobs and dunes exist only by "convention" (LA 101). The very being of such things depends on a mind's decision about when to "put one name in the accounting for all these things together" (LA 101) or to bestow on them "the name of 'one'" (LA 119). Thus, without some term, 'F,' there wouldn't be aggregates. Without 'dune' there wouldn't be dunes.

Evaluation of the Mental Constructions Analysis

This analysis has several advantages:

1 As formulated here, it squares with the Canonical Metaphysics.
2 It represents many of the Arnauld texts and the story they tell about aggregates.
3 It allows us to know the "principles of aggregation" that are used to construct aggregates.[6] Because we are the ones responsible for grouping together various objects to form aggregates, the rules that are followed can, at least in principle, be discovered.

The disadvantages include:

a) It recognizes no mind-independent subject of predication for aggregates. Other than monads, the only subject in view here is *p* – a mind-dependent phenomenon. There is nothing of which one can predicate the properties Leibniz often elsewhere attributes to aggregates – especially reality, activity, and force.
b) The account seems inconsistent with Leibniz's doctrine of animals, since on that doctrine mind-independent animals have mind-independent aggregates as their bodies. This view would make all aggregates *p*s that depend on the mind's activity. This issue will be taken up in earnest in Chapter 8.

c) The number of monads that can perceive aggregates is pretty severely restricted on this view. For a mind needs a formidable conceptual apparatus in order to perceive the simplest aggregates. Non-reflective animals and lower monads can "catch" an aggregate as it reflects off a higher monad, but they cannot "initiate" a sequence of aggregate-mirrorings. This may or may not be viewed as a limitation. Indeed, it may seem a natural consequence of what Leibniz wrote to Arnauld and so is more a feature of the account than a demerit.

d) More seriously, the textual base is limited largely to the Arnauld correspondence. Now it is not completely unusual to find a philosopher's theory adumbrated in detail in one particular correspondence. But the case here is different. For, as I've argued in Chapter 4, those same letters contain many competing Realist themes that cast doubt on the claim that Leibniz – even within that correspondence – held unambiguously to "Mental Constructions."

An idea of the frequency with which Idealism and Realism are mixed together can be gleaned from the Doctrine Tables. Those Tables are a good guide to the overall mature corpus, and they show the writings do not contain only one view. This only compounds the puzzlement felt by commentators like Ross:

> But what could Leibniz have meant by saying that souls were *in* bodies? Obviously, if bodies are phenomenal, souls could not be literally *in* phenomena; nor, in Leibniz's philosophy, is there any third world of material bodies which souls could be *in* or related to in any other way. If he meant 'in' literally, the only remaining possibility is that the material world is a *compound*, of which souls or monads are the atomic *parts*. Leibniz himself did sometimes talk like this, particularly in his more public pronouncements. Perhaps the best known example is the opening of the *Monadology*.
>
> Ross (1984, 179)

Such commentators suggest that Leibniz only *occasionally* advances the aggregate thesis – and often in "public" pronouncements or what has been called his *simpliste* style found in "popular and pictorial" arguments in his "exoteric" works.

But as I've shown, he advances the aggregate thesis routinely and in the deepest, most esoteric works in the corpus. All of these deny that "matter is purely phenomenal."

For instance, consider the intermingling of phenomenalism and the aggregate thesis in this sent to Bayle around 1702:

> Moreover, there must be simple beings, otherwise there would be no compound beings, or beings by aggregation, which are phenomena

rather than substances, and exist (to use the language of Democritus) by convention rather than nature, that is, notionally, or conceptually, rather than physically. And if there was no change in simple things, there would be none in compound things either, for all their reality consists only in that of their simple things.

(G 3, 69/WF 129–30)

The Idealist-leaning language of "phenomena" and "convention" can't be stripped away – except by wilful blindness – from the Realist-leaning aggregate thesis claims of Presupposition, Composition, Supervenience, and Reality.

Catherine Wilson, in response to this vacillation between inconsistent accounts, is perplexed. She says Leibniz seems "confused" – thinking (at G 3, 622) that bodies can somehow be both perceptions (mental constructions) and the foundations of perceptions (aggregates of substances). She concludes that "it is impossible to read Leibniz as having a single theory of monadic perception" (Wilson 1989, 195) and, more recently, that his attempt to propound a system was a "failure" emanating from a "basic mistake" (1999, 373, 384).

It is possible he was confused. But the sheer number of times Idealism and Realism are found together makes it unlikely that his combining them was completely unintentional and overlooked. It is especially easy to avoid attributing confusion, failure, and mistakes to him if he was running two theories simultaneously rather than two Truths. Such is the power of Theory-Pluralism.

5.3 Aggregates as Well-Founded Phenomena: An Overview

[A] combination of non-extended simple substances becomes extended through our perception of it, which is confused. We see the Milky Way or a cloud of dust as *continua*, because our eye is not sharp enough to distinguish clearly the individual stars or particles of dust. Similarly, through our confused perception of a number of simple things, there arise within us … extended bodies, which must be called *entia semimentalia, phaenomena bene fundata*, because, like the rainbow, they have a real cause, though they only assume the form in which they appear to us …

J. E. Erdmann (1891, II:185)

[Leibniz] did not perceive that the denial of the reality of space compels us to admit that we know only phenomena, *i.e.* appearances to our minds. That Kant was able to assume even an unknowable thing-in-itself was only due to his extension of cause (or ground) beyond experience, by regarding something not ourselves as the source of our perceptions. This, which was an inconsistency in Kant, would have been a sheer impossibility to Leibniz, since he held perceptions to be wholly due to ourselves, and not in any sense caused by the objects perceived.

Bertrand Russell (R 74)

Leibniz often employs the idiom of well-foundedness, as when he calls a "mass of matter" a "well-founded phenomenon" (G 7, 564/Rd 222). The final Idealist option I'll present takes its cue from such passages and is probably the predominant way of construing Leibnizian aggregates. A comprehensive version of it will be considered the decisive Idealist option.

As in the Mental Constructions analysis, the subject of predication is p – an "in the head" appearance. This account uses quite a bit of the metaphysical machinery because other monads are called upon to play a role in the causation of p. It also conforms to the Canonical Metaphysics. This analysis, one might say, begins with epistemology ("phenomena" in a particular monad) and then adds the metaphysics ("well-founded" on some other monads). The Latin word order has it about right: *'phenomena bene fundata.'*

There are two main differences between Mental Constructions and this account.

(i) Unlike the Mental Constructions analysis, the Well-Founded Phenomena account is meant to dovetail with a specific metaphysical story – one that invokes other monads. However, the monads are not taken under some description by a reflective mind (as in Mental Constructions) and used to construct aggregates. The other monads are here remote causes (more accurately, "quasi-causes") of the aggregate (phenomenon) p. When it is well-founded, p is said to depend on the presence of the monads in a "monadic aggregate" in a way that pure, unsupported, free-floating ps do not.

The "dependence" mentioned here is weak. Genuine causation between Ss and p does not hold. The Canonical Metaphysics requires that all relations be "ideal" and not real connections. So *quasi-causation* must replace causation. As I'm using it here, "quasi-causation" refers to the fact that there is no genuine connection between the two objects typically seen as related causally – say, two colliding bodies A and B. To say A quasi-causes B is to say that A seems to move B, but the real story is that A and B would have done exactly what they did whether or not the other ever existed. Similarly, monads related quasi-causally act as if the others were there affecting them, but in fact each would do what it does without the others.

Relations like quasi-causation have generally been known as "cambridge relations."[7] The 'cambridge' part derives from some famous Cambridge University philosophers who tried to minimize the ontological commitments involved in some relations. Cambridge relations are often illustrated by the following analogy. God remains unmoved by changes going on in the world; his "ageing" is a mere cambridge change and affects him internally not in the least. Similarly, the relations between all the individual monads, and between the monads that quasi-cause or well-found p in *Monad$_1$* (the one doing the perceiving) are all cambridge relations.

Thus, against Erdmann's claim and in line with Russell's in the epigraph, the Well-Founded Phenomena account must deny that phenomena "have a real cause." Real causation is not possible if all relations are merely ideal.

(ii) The phenomena account drops 'F' altogether out of the picture, and along with it the requirement that only minds that can perform acts of reflection can perceive aggregates. While Mental Constructions involved the mind concocting aggregates by "noticing, joining and naming" by means of some 'F,' the Well-Founded Phenomena Account is concerned with bodies as mere representational contents of intentional states. These are available to all minds, however cognitively impoverished.

C. D. Broad championed this analysis in recent years:

> [C]ertain aggregates of these unextended substances present to us the delusive appearance of being extended, movable, massive substances, i.e. bodies. ... The monads are the real foundations of the partly delusive experiences in which we seem to ourselves to perceive bodies.[8]

Again, "present to us" and "real foundations" suggest genuine causation, but this view is entitled only to "quasi-present" and "apparent foundations."

Now the view under consideration is attractive in part because it can bring in the "perceptual continuum" (as does Erdmann) to explain the origin of extension. Indeed, it is not hard to see why commentators have, pace Russell, perennially flocked to this view. Given Leibniz's firm declaration that the realm of substance is not friendly to extension, there is little one can do with extension other than bury it in the mind – to construe it as a mere fabrication in the same way that colors are often chased out of the physical world and banished to the realm of mere "ideas."

The view is modeled on "representative realist" theories of perception familiar from the work of John Locke. On the one hand, there are the internal ideas or phenomena or sense-data; on the other are their remote (in this case, quasi-) causes. Like all such theories, this one is susceptible to a problem that corresponds to the "veil of perception"[9] that afflicts Locke's system. Just as Locke can never know material bodies directly, so here I am never acquainted directly with the substances. I know external bodies only indirectly through the internal ideas they cause, and I know Leibnizian substances only indirectly through what Broad calls the "delusive appearances" they quasi-induce in the mind.

The main differences between the Lockean and Leibnizian theories are:

1 Leibniz's "remote causes" are unextended substances rather than collocations of solid atoms.

2 Leibniz treats extension and the primary qualities in the same way Locke treats secondary qualities. That is, whereas Locke's atoms are not colored but are extended and have other primary qualities, Leibniz's substances have neither color nor extension nor any other primary quality.

3 Leibniz's "causes" are not, like Locke's, real "transeunt" causes, but mere cambridge relations that allow for only apparent "quasi-causation." This forces one to conclude that between p and what can be called the "monadic aggregate" there intervenes, not a traditional veil of perception, but a causal and epistemic *blockade*.

Now 1 seems no problem. As one never perceives Locke's atom clusters anyway, why not say instead that there are invisible, intangible substances over there? 2 gives one what was expected all along even of Lockean solidity and his other primary qualities: namely, that none of them as experienced matches up with physical qualities. 3 seems the most troubling. As Russell says, there seems to be no way for Leibniz to recognize mind-independent "sources" of perceptions. Being told that there is no real causation between items in the monadic aggregate and $Monad_1$ saps all the explanatory strength from the view, for now p's "well-foundedness" is more apparent than real – indeed, apparent *rather than* real.

Then why not simply scuttle 3? Because this account aspires to protect the Canonical Metaphysics, where there can be no "influx" from one substance to another. The cost of doing so, however, is that the uselessness of Leibniz's monads on the far side of his "blockade" is even more apparent than the futility of Locke's atom-clusters on the far side of his veil. Leibniz's complete concept doctrine assures one that each perception is born of the preceding perception and does not need anything other than that perception for its existence. By contrast, Locke is able to tie (veridical) perception to the genuine causal "powers" of individually "insensible" external atoms acting on the sense organs.

In formulating this account, I shall always distinguish between aggregates that are (as on Idealism) mind-dependent ps, and aggregates that are (on Realism) "aggregates of substances." There are a few places where Leibniz appears to equivocate on these two possible referents for 'aggregate,' but I will not follow them. A detailed discussion of the matter of equivocation will appear later in 7.1.3.

5.3.1 *"Real Phenomena"*

The first step is to lay out the directions for distinguishing "real phenomena" from non-real ones. One can thus tell "from the inside" which phenomena to single out as the well-founded ones.

In a brief text Leibniz lays down some epistemic constraints on phenomena, saying one can separate real phenomena from the others based on internal marks – which are strikingly similar to those later proposed by

Berkeley.[10] Some of the marks are solipsist — that is, refer only to the perceiver's own experiences; others are non-solipsist, referring to the testimony of other perceivers.

The solipsist marks include vividness, complexity, intensity, and internal coherence. When those marks are present, phenomena will be said to "cohere well with other phenomenal features of $Monad_1$'s experience."[11] The main non-solipsist constraint is also a coherence condition, requiring of phenomena "a consensus with the whole sequence of life, especially if many others affirm the same thing to be coherent with their phenomena also" (G 7, 320/L 364). Phenomena meeting that condition will be said to "cohere well with the testimony of others."

The rule of "mechanistic laws" is assumed in both coherence conditions so as to eliminate idiosyncratic perception. Such laws hold between bodies construed both as features of $Monad_1$'s own experience (thus assuring well-behaved sense-data for $Monad_1$) and as bodies whose existence and behavior is corroborated by others.

Finally, $Monad_1$ must be able to predict future phenomena on the basis of her experience of the real ones (G 7, 320/L 364). On the solipsist story this takes the form of requiring that phenomena be usable as guides to anticipating $Monad_1$'s own future experiences; in the other, that one's predictions are borne out by and cohere well with what others say.

In the following accounts, t ranges over all times, $Monad_1$ over all monads, c over all perceptual states, and {C} is the set {$c1, c2, \ldots, cn$} of states assigned to $Monad_1$ by God at creation. {C} is the embodiment of S's complete concept in the form of a "law of the series,"[12] according to which the unfolding of its perceptual states must follow a specific, determinate causal order.[13] Leibniz says those states are characterized by perception and appetite, using the appetitive side of the state to account for $Monad_1$'s striving to reach its next state. I streamline this by referring to these perceptual/appetitive states as "perceptual states." Here "representational content" is meant to contrast with the Cartesian "formal content" of mental states, and to pick out its intentional content — that is, what the state is of or about.[14] I include a diachronic account by making generous use of unconscious perception to fill in the "gaps" left by the sporadic activity of minds as they contemplate phenomena.

Real Phen-AGG

p is a real phenomenon at t iff: at t, $Monad_1$ is in some ci ε {C} such that: ci's (possibly unconsciously held) representational content includes a phenomenon, p, which coheres well with (i) other phenomenal features of $Monad_1$'s experience and (ii) the testimony of others.

p is a real phenomenon that persists from $t1$ to tn iff: at each ti between $t1$ and tn, $Monad_1$ is in some ci ε {C1} such that: the (possibly unconsciously held) representational content of each ci includes a phenomenon, p, which coheres well with (i) other phenomenal features of $Monad_1$'s experience and (ii) the testimony of others.

In the diachronic version of Real Phen-AGG, $Monad_1$'s set of career perceptual states is dubbed "{C1}." x's duration is underwritten by both solipsist and non-solipsist conditions. p persists in virtue of the continuity of $Monad_1$'s experience of it and its coherence with the testimony of others.

Applying this to the familiar case of sand dunes: A sand dune is a real phenomenon just in case there is some monad that is in a perceptual state dictated by its complete concept, where that state's representational content includes a phenomenon, p, of a dune which coheres well with that monad's other phenomena and with the testimony of others.

I will now fold in "monadic aggregates" to arrive at the comprehensive Well-Founded Phenomena account.

5.3.2 A Comprehensive Well-Founded Phenomena Analysis

Here the "monadic aggregate" is taken to refer to a specific, fixed infinity of non-extended substances, where necessarily the monad – again $Monad_1$ – that is in the perceptual states is not included in that infinity. These monads will be said to "quasi-cause" p because their relation to the perceiving $Monad_1$ can only be a cambridge affair. It is absolutely essential to bear in mind that, despite the beguiling connotations of "the monadic aggregate," there is no subject, "the aggregate" to which this refers. It is simply a way of picking out "the monads" *en masse*. Thus it is to be given a "purely extensional" reading – along the lines of David Lewis's "Composition as Identity" principle.[15] The phrase "monadic aggregate" is adapted from Nicholas Rescher's work on well-founded phenomena (Rescher 1967, 82–3) and he explicitly says that the substances in the monadic aggregate "do not unite at all."

Unity does, however, characterize the phenomenon p – which is why, I think, Leibniz says aggregates have unity only in the mind. The common mistake lies in *transferring* unity from p to the mind-independent monadic aggregate that is its remote quasi-cause.

Secondary qualities are also included among the properties of p that can't be transferred. A rainbow appears colored because the senses portray millions of colorless droplets as an arched color patch. Color and other secondary qualities are merely "apparent" and "relative to our senses."[16] (I will hereafter use 'color' as a brief way of referring to all the secondary qualities.)

Finally, the *primary qualities* are also non-transferable. Since such primary qualities as size, shape, and mobility presuppose extension (the inadequacies of solidity and mass have already been discussed in Chapter 2), it is sufficient to show that extension can't be transferred.

As was evident in Chapter 3, Leibniz explicitly blames the senses for running the parts of the aggregate together so as to make the collection appear to be a seamless, spatially continuous (i.e., extended) whole. It is just as much a mistake to attribute extension to the monadic aggregate as it is to attribute color or unity.[17] In what follows, when I say "*p* is considered to be an extended thing," "extended" is taken to represent all these primary qualities.

The Well-Founded Phenomena account incorporates "real phenomena" and the monadic aggregate as follows:

Well-Founded AGG:

p is a "phenomenon aggregate" at *t* iff: at *t*, $Monad_1$ is in some $ci \ \varepsilon \ \{C\}$ such that: ci's (possibly unconsciously held) representational content includes a real phenomenon, *p*, which is quasi-caused by the monadic aggregate; and $Monad_1$ considers *p* a unified, colored, and extended thing.

p is a "phenomenon aggregate" that persists from *t1* to *tn* iff: at each *ti* between *t1* and *tn*, $Monad_1$ is in some $ci \ \varepsilon \ \{C1\}$ such that: ci's (possibly unconsciously held) representational content includes a real phenomenon, *p*, which is quasi-caused by the monadic aggregate; and $Monad_1$ considers *p* the same unified, colored, and extended thing that it perceived at the other *ti*s.

A visual representation of these conditions is found in Figure 5.1. In particular, note that there are *two different aggregates* on this view: the phenomenon aggregate, *p*, and the monadic aggregate that quasi-causes *p*. So there is an ambiguity, explicitly acknowledged, in the meaning of 'aggregate.' It is harmless so long as one is clear about which aggregate is meant and so avoids equivocation.

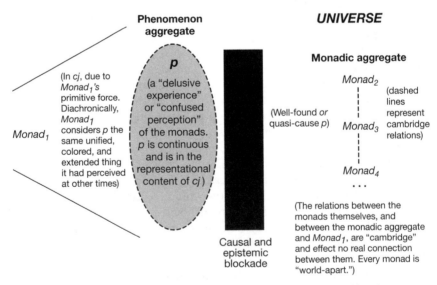

Everything to the right of the blockade is nonextended. Extension enters the picture only in *p*, which is extended because of the confused "considerings" of $Monad_1$ – due largely to the work of the "perceptual continuum."

Figure 5.1. Idealism: Aggregates as Well-Founded Phenomena

Again, applying this to sand dunes: a dune is a "phenomenon aggregate" just in case there is some monad that is in a perceptual state dictated by its complete concept, where (1) that state's representational content includes a "real phenomenon" (p) of a dune, which is quasi-caused by a group of monads (the "monadic aggregate"); and (2) the monad considers p a unified, colored, and extended dune.

As in the Mental Constructions account, here the mind is assigned rather a Kantian role. In the synchronic account, p gets to be the way it is because the mind reads unity, color, and extension into what is really a collection of many colorless, discrete, and only separately real things. Apart from the mind's work, there is literally nothing in the universe over and above the separate monads – that is, the monadic aggregate. This is quite clear in the diagram, which shows *Monad₂*, *Monad₃* etc. connected only by ideal, cambridge connections and not forming a composite object at all. That is why Rescher says:

> But how do monads unite into aggregates? The answer is that, in general, they do not unite at all. ... A monadic aggregate is a single "individual thing" only in a remote sense. The aggregate *appears* as one, as a unit, and is thus a phenomenon by virtue of some genuine similarity among its constituents, a feature which gives it some footing in the real, monadic world, and makes it a well founded phenomenon. ... The individuality of an aggregate is really "mental," i.e., perceptual: being apparent only to an internal or external observer, its monadic aggregates are mental entities (*entia mentalia*) which, having a genuine foundation in the monadic realm, are not (like a mirage) simply illusory or delusory phenomena, but *phaenomena bene fundata*.
>
> Rescher (1967, 82–3)

And Russell writes that Leibniz's position is reminiscent of Kant's "synthetic unity of apperception": "The mind, and the mind only, synthesizes the diversity of monads; each separate monad is real apart from the perception of it, but a collection, as such, acquires only a precarious and derived reality from simultaneous perception" (R 116). In the diachronic account, p's persistence is just as "precarious" as its synchronic unity, given the fact that it is an unreliable "in the head" affair. For it depends on *Monad₁*'s considering p to be the same thing as was perceived at other times in its career. There is no "outside the head" constraint on members of the monadic aggregate that could well-found p's persistence.

By contrast with Mental Constuctions, in this analysis language ('F') is notably absent: p is an appearance that can be "initiated" by any mind. The dog sees the stick just as Kirk sees the stick. Even the barest of naked monads can possess a p of the stick, and it needn't be gotten "second-hand," though of course the clarity of its perception will be relatively low.

5.3.3 *Evaluation of the Well-Founded Phenomena Analysis*

Among the advantages of this account are the following.

1 It preserves the Canonical Metaphysics. The complete concept can have aggregates encoded in it in the form of ps – which are, like all predicates, wholly contained "in the subject." Solipsist perception ensures that the march-past of phenomena is accomplished without the need for any other finite substances. Cambridge constraints are observed.
2 Insofar as common sense supports the "causal theory of perception"[18] – a belief even Kant couldn't shake off – this view supports common sense. Here, by contrast with Reductive Phenomenalism and Mental Constructions, appearances are appearances *of* something.
3 It has a significant textual base – comprising not only the passages that mention "well-founded phenomena" explicitly, but also many of those that may be used to support the other two views.
4 It allows every monad to perceive aggregates, which is an advantage because Leibniz explicitly mentions a dog's perceiving a stick (Mon 26), and that would be impossible on the Mental Constructions analysis.

Its weaknesses include the following:

(a) As in the Mental Constructions analysis, the Well-Founded Phenomena account has no mind-independent subject of predication for aggregates. In line with the Canonical Metaphysics, the only subjects here are monads. Aggregates, to the extent that they are subjects of predication, are mere ps. Thus Realist texts are left unmotivated and unexplained.
(b) Again as with Mental Constructions, this account conflicts with the mature doctrine of animals, since ps cannot provide bodies for beasts. A full treatment of this issue, however, must wait until Chapter 8.
(c) The "causal and epistemic blockade" completely sunders Reality from the knowing mind, and that puts a great deal of pressure on Leibniz's claim that nature is intelligible. It comes very close to the Kantian point that nature is "all in the mind" – a belief that runs counter to much of what Leibniz says.
(d) Quasi-causation makes the metaphysics of the monadic aggregate irrelevant to the nature of a phenomenon aggregate.
(e) As noted in Chapter 3, the "Aggregate of Substances" analysis predominates in the mature writings, and such aggregates demand a Simples metaphysic – with discrete true unities as constituents. But the Well-Founded Phenomena account's "monadic aggregate" is not an object at all. The only item that can be an aggregate in this theory is p. But p is continuous, not discrete. Moreover, it seems clear that p cannot contain unities – that is, p is not amenable to a Simples metaphysic. Thus, as long as it construes aggregates as ps, this account seems inconsistent with the mature doctrine of the continuum.

(f) In line with (e), Leibniz's critique of Descartes fails if *p* is the only available aggregate. For Leibniz often says Descartes's view of body is weak because on it bodies are inert and continuous. If this Well-Founded Phenomena account is right, however, Leibniz's bodies are as inert and continuous as Descartes's.

(g) This view is incompatible with Leibniz's philosophy of science. For there Leibniz proclaims that aggregates contain forces, or are reducible to forces. *p* is hardly able to accommodate such claims.

(h) In sum, *this theory turns the world into a "Realm of As If."* Reality (causation, constitution, relations) is replaced by Appearance (quasi-causation, a scattered monadic aggregate, cambridge relations). Here it seems that Leibniz's explaining something amounts often and routinely to his explaining it *away.* It is revisionary, but the payoff is seldom in view. One wants to know, What do we gain – except a "pretty picture" – by escaping always to a quasi-world?

I turn now to the Realist theory.

6   Realist Analyses of Aggregates

Now enter a new theory about the world – according to which there is a real, mind-independent universe whose denizens include, in addition to monads, aggregates and animals. There are various analyses offered here. Most have a foothold in the texts, though, as with the Idealist options, they vary in the frequency of their appearance there.

Leibniz seemed not to be much bothered by the redundancy involved in having multiple Realist alternatives. Still, in the end I develop a comprehensive Realist account which incorporates themes from several areas of his thought. It accommodates all the aggregate thesis doctrines, and sets the stage for the Realist analysis of animals in Chapter 8. It is the fit between the Realist construal of aggregates and the Realist analysis of animals that enables Leibniz's metaphysics to achieve a new sense of coherence and interest.

The Realist theory (sometimes abbreviated to "Realism") places new constraints on body. In particular, an aggregate must be composed of substances or contain substances and derive its reality and force from its constituent substances. At the most abstract level, the aggregate must be a *whole*, with substances serving as its components or constituents or parts.

I should note at the outset that the position taken here represents a departure from my earlier stance. I had written in 1992 that this world "contains exactly the substances it has, and no extra-mental aggregates" (1992, 542), saying that it was sufficient to "talk of aggregates as if they were mind-independent collections over and above their parts" and thus to indulge the "loose but useful" idiom of common sense (1992, 526). The sort of eliminative reduction I had in mind there for the aggregates of the Realist theory cannot work, as I now believe. For the only way to grant aggregates a strictly speaking, "not-just-as-if" mind-independent status is to make a decisive break with Idealism's eliminative reduction of aggregates to substances. Theory-Pluralism helps me now make that break, granting me freedom to recognize mind-independent aggregates at no cost to Leibniz's rationality.

6.1 How Leibnizian Substances can be Parts of a Body

The prospect of developing Realism depends on taking 'part' and 'whole' in what Robert Adams calls a "broader sense" (Ad 244) – broader, that is, than is available within the confines of Leibniz's strict mereological definitions. In those definitions, as we saw in Chapter 3, he restricts reference of these terms to items that are homogeneous. Thus, in that narrower sense, a part of a line must always be another line and never a point, and a part of a body always another body and never a substance.

But, as Adams rightly argues, Leibniz throughout the mature corpus helps himself to a more generous notion of 'part' than that, often claiming that bodies are composed of substances or have substances as their constituents or elements or – indeed – parts.

A striking text from the Arnauld correspondence addresses this matter:

[I]f one considers as matter of a corporeal substance not formless mass but a secondary matter which is the multiplicity of substances of which the mass is that of the total body, it may be said that these substances are parts of this matter, just as those which enter into our body form part of it, for as our body is the matter, and the soul is the form of our substance, it is the same with other corporeal substances. ... [T]he part ... basically is nothing else but an immediate requisite of the whole, and in a way homogeneous. Thus parts can constitute a whole, whether it has a genuine unity or not.

(LA 119)

Leibniz grants one permission to use part/whole terminology in regard to aggregates (here called "secondary matter," or a "multiplicity of substances" or "mass"), with substances as their parts. While homogeneity is mentioned, it is not insisted on for parthood as it is in the strict mereology. He even says explicitly that parts can constitute a whole *even if it has no true unity*. Aggregates are of course clearly among such non-unified wholes.

The permission is extended well into the mature period, as when he tells De Volder in 1699 that as soldiers are "parts of an army" that can be replaced by other men, so in extended bodies "some parts can be replaced by others" (G 2 193/L 521). That is, as armies have substances as their (in this broader sense) parts, so aggregates have substances as their parts.

Sometimes even in his more abstract, technical writings a similar permission is given. For instance, in 1686 Leibniz writes:

Besides 'entity' we shall also use 'entities,' from which there proceeds the whole and the part. In general, if A is not B and B is not A, and the proposition 'A is L and B is L is the same as C is L' is primitive, then C is called a 'whole' and A (or B) a 'part.' It can be doubted whether and how far C is one real entity; whether one entity does not always result from several, even if they are scattered; and when this results or does not result.

(C 377/Leibniz 1966, 66–7)

Again 'part' and 'whole' are applied generally to any "entities" that stand in the relation specified. In terms of this text, I will be taking A and B to be substances that compose the aggregate (whole), C. This application seems quite natural, since he says C's unity is dubious – which matches perfectly his oft-repeated claim that aggregates lack true unity. He also says it can be doubted whether each assemblage of parts yields a whole, and that it's unclear under what conditions this happens.[1]

And in a passage dated to 1689–90 he writes:

[F]or an aggregate it is sufficient that many beings, distinct from it, are understood to agree in a similar way with respect to it; namely if *A, B, C* are considered in the same way, and by that *L* is understood to be established, *A, B, C* will be the things aggregated and *L* the whole made by the aggregation.

(Inquirenda Logico-Metaphysica, A VI 4 A, 998 (N. 210)/Lodge 2001, 469–70)

A, B, and *C* are "the things aggregated" in the "whole," *L*. In terms of this text, the *L*s will be aggregates, while *A, B*, and *C* are substances. Leibniz's claim that *A, B*, and *C* are viewed as "agreeing in a similar way" with respect to the whole is fairly vague and admits of many applications. That's a good thing, for my purposes. For as the "agreement" relation is allowed to vary, several different Realist options become visible in Leibniz's later work. For instance, such relations as harmony, constitution, and supervenience will be said to hold between *A, B*, and *C* when they make up a whole.

6.2 Preliminary Comment on the Realist Analyses

The Realist theory "borrows" monads – and not much else – from the Idealist theory. But the monads so borrowed – though they still perceive and strive and have complete concepts – are transformed within the Realist theory. Monads here lose their "world-apart" or "windowless" status and are able to enter into fairly intimate "contact" (some non-spatial relation or other for which we have no name) with other monads and with substances and aggregates when the conditions are right. The "substances" of Realism comprise these altered monads *and animals*. (The reader who doubts that animals belong in this slot will have to await Chapter 8's full-dress defense of that claim.) Real rather than mere "cambridge" relations between the universe's objects are countenanced – real causation, real composition of an aggregate out of substances, and real supervenience relations between properties of aggregates and those of substances.

(It might seem that this change in the role of monads would signal a problem of equivocation on 'monad.' Analogously 'aggregate' would mean "phenomenon" in Idealism, while in Realism it means a collection of substances. These equivocations are innocuous, however, since the Realist or Idealist context can be used to disambiguate the use of this term on any given occasion. Leibniz himself seldom disambiguates the terms in this way – hoping, as I suppose, for a way of tying the two together – and hence sometimes embroils himself in equivocation. Viewing the term as having different meanings in different contexts is done in the spirit of charitable interpretation. So in this chapter, 'monad,' 'aggregate,' and their ilk will, unless otherwise noted, have their Realist meanings, while in the Idealist theory they retain the other.)

The analyses offered here are not intended to be the "last word" on Leibnizian Realism. Additional accounts will no doubt be forthcoming as scholars begin to focus on these themes intensively.

6.3 The Aggregate Thesis and Some of its Texts

As the doctrines grouped under this title together define what I am calling Realism (with Animals added later in Chapter 8), I will repeat them as they appeared in 1.8. Here I include in parentheses the number of endorsements these claims receive in the five major works canvassed in the Doctrine Tables:

Composition	Every body is composed of substances. (11)
Containment	Every body contains substances. (43)
Divided	Every body is actually divided into substances. (9)
Force	Every body has derivative active force that supervenes on the primitive active force of the substances it contains. (16)
Mass	Every body is a "mass" or aggregate of substances. (7)
Plurality	Every body is a plurality. (14)
Presupposition	Every plurality presupposes genuine unities. (11)
Reality	Every body has some residual derivative reality because of the presence in it of primitively real substances. (13)
The Ss	Every body *is* substances. (8)
Supervenience	Every derivative quality of a body must arise from the primitive qualities of the things it contains. (18)

In all, the Aggregate Thesis receives 150 affirmations in the five central texts.

In Chapter 4 I examined a few Realist passages in the Arnauld correspondence. Here I will concentrate on passages from the mature corpus that lie outside that exchange. First there is this endorsement of Reality and Composition in the "Notes on Fardella" of 1690: "Hence, unless there are certain indivisible substances, bodies would not be real, but would only be appearances or phenomena (like the rainbow), having eliminated every basis from which they can be composed" (March 1690, Notes on Fardella, A VI 4 B, 1668 (N. 329): Leibniz 1857, 320/AG 103). And about four years later a draft of NS mentions Plurality, Mass, Divided, Containment, and Presupposition:

> When I say 'me', I speak of a single substance; but an army, a herd of animals, a pond full of fish (even if it is frozen solid with all its fish) will always be a collection of several substances. That is why, leaving aside souls or other such principles of unity, we will never find a corporeal mass or portion of matter which is a true substance. It will always be a collection, since matter is actually divided *ad infinitum*, in such a way that the least particle encloses a truly infinite world of created things, and perhaps of animals. [I]t must necessarily be that true unities can be found in corporeal nature, for otherwise there could be neither multiplicity nor collections.
>
> (c. 1694, Draft of NS, G 4, 473/WF 23)

Four years after that he reiterates Containment, Divided, and Mass:

> You ask me to divide for you a portion of mass into the substances of which it is composed. I respond, there are as many individual substances in it as there are animals or living things or things analogous to them. And so, I divide it in the same way one divides a flock or fish pond, except that I think that the fluid that lies between the animals of the flock, or between the fishes, and also the fluid (indeed, any remaining mass) contained in any fish or animal, ought to be divided again as if it were a new fish pond, and so on to infinity.
>
> (20/30 September 1698, to Bernoulli, GM 3, 542/AG 167–8)

These three passages from the early and "middle" years say bodies will not be real pluralities unless there are, contained in them and composing them, substances. And the substances most prominently on display at this stage are, predictably, animals.

After 1698 or so, "monads" arrive on the scene. These are in some ways continuous with the old view, since they have the same qualities as the soul or substantial form in animals, though added to their qualities is an independence from all else usually not said to characterize such souls or forms. These monads *join* animals as objects possibly contained in or composing or lending reality and force to bodies. For instance, in 1703 he endorses Mass, The *S*s, Force, Supervenience, and Reality while expressing them in terms of the generic "substances" rather than distinguishing between simple and corporeal:

> [S]econdary matter, or a mass, is not a substance, but substances, like a flock of sheep or a lake full of fish.

There are two sorts of force in bodies, a primitive force which is essential to it (*the first actuality*), and derivative forces, which also depend on other bodies. And we have to realize that derivative or accidental force, which we cannot deny to moving bodies, must be a modification of primitive force, just as shape is a modification of extension. Accidental forces could have no place in a substance without essential force, because accidents are only modifications or limitations, and can never contain more perfection or reality than does the substance.

(22 March 1703, to Jaquelot, G 3, 457/WF 200–1)

A year later, still in the generic idiom, he gives expression to Plurality, Composition, Reality, Containment, Divided, Supervenience, and The *S*s in remarks to De Volder:

I had undertaken to prove these unities from the fact that there would otherwise be nothing in bodies. I gave the following argument: *first*, that which can be divided into many, is aggregated or constituted from many. Then *second*, things that are aggregated from many are not one thing except mentally, and they have no reality other than what is borrowed or from the things from which it is aggregated. Therefore, *third*, things that can be divided into parts have no reality unless there are things in them which cannot be divided into parts. Indeed, they have no other reality other than that which is from the unities that are in them. I do not see what you could get stuck on, especially since you concede that many things which are adjacent to each other or which are impelled against one another, do not constitute one real thing on account of that; so from where will you derive their unity, or that reality which you give the whole thing, except that which it derives from those things? For this reason I feel that bodies, which are commonly taken for substances, are nothing but real phenomena, and are no more substances than parhelia or rainbows. . . . The monad alone is a substance, a body is substances, not a substance.

(21 January 1704, to De Volder, G 2, 261–2)

And many of them are repeated six months later:

A thing which can be divided into many (already actually existing) is an aggregate of many, and a thing that is aggregated from many is not one except mentally, and has no reality but what is borrowed from the things contained in it. Hence I inferred therefore, there are in things indivisible unities, since otherwise there will be in things no true unity, and no reality not borrowed. Which is absurd. For where there is no true unity, there is no true multiplicity. And where there is no reality not borrowed, there will never be any reality, since this must in the end belong to some subject.

(30 June 1704, to De Volder, G 2, 267/R 242)

In 1706 monads are explicitly brought in when Containment and Plurality are endorsed: "[I]n actual things, there is only discrete quantity, namely a multitude of monads or simple substances, indeed, a multitude greater than any number you choose in every sensible aggregate, that is, in every aggregate corresponding to phenomena" (19 January 1706, to De Volder, G 2, 282/AG 185). Again, monads are featured in the composition-role in Mon 2: "there must be simple substances, since there are composites; for a composite is nothing but a collection, or *aggregate*, of simples."

The upshot of these later texts is largely the same as that of earlier ones. The aggregate thesis continues to be the claim that aggregates contain substances – corporeal or simple – and draw their force and reality from them.

6.4 Aggregates as "the Ss"

Of course, as there is nothing real except the monads, body must consist of them.

J. E. Erdmann (1891, II: 184)

Because the only true unities are monads, it follows that bodies must be pluralities of monads.

Donald Rutherford (Rd 220)

The first Realist construal of aggregates that has a foothold in Leibniz's text is absolutely minimalist. Call it "the Ss." It is the claim that an aggregate – which will in this chapter be considered a *whole* and abbreviated as "*w*" – is nothing but a certain particular infinity of substances. The brutally impoverished existence conditions are as follows:

Aggregate *w* exists at *t* iff at *t*, the Ss exist.

On this construal, Leibniz's aggregates are not "sets" or "pluralities" or "groups" or "multitudes" – or even (what would typically be called) "aggregates" – of substances.

Such a move can be motivated on purely conceptual grounds. Expressions for pluralities can quickly become problematic and confusing.[2] They beg for ontological commitment of their own, raising the question, What is the relation between the set/group/multitude/aggregate and its constituents? In light of this, Peter van Inwagen recommends referring to simples as "the xs."[3] Here I follow his lead, encouraged along by some remarkable passages in Leibniz, and changing 'x' to 'S' for obvious reasons. Even independently of those passages, it is clear Leibniz was fond of nominalism.[4] Eliminating unneeded ontological commitments is what nominalism does best, and that's certainly what "the *Ss*" does.

I will first examine some texts in which this account is arguably manifest.[5] Often Leibniz is drawing a stark contrast between substances and aggregates: an aggregate, he says, is not a substance, but substance*s*. (It is possible of course that in all these cases he is speaking cryptically – that full-fledged aggregatehood has necessary conditions in addition to the sheer existence of substances. Indeed, such additional conditions appear in the non-minimalist analyses that follow this one.)

1 [I]f we consider their extension alone, then bodies are not substances, but many substances. (c. 1689, Principia Logico-Metaphysica, or "Primary Truths," A VI 4 B 1648 (N. 325): C 523/AG 34/PW 92)

2 The body is an aggregate of substances, and is not a substance properly speaking. (23 March 1690, to Arnauld, LA 135)

3 [B]ody is not a substance, but substances or an aggregate of substances. (March 1690, Comments on Fardella, A VI 4 B, 1672 (N. 329): Leibniz 1857, 322/AG 105)

4 Secondary matter, or mass, is not a substance, but substances. (c. August-Sept. 1698, to Bernoulli, GM 3, 537/AG 167)

5 You ask how far one must proceed in order to have something that is a substance, and not substances. I respond that such things present themselves immediately and even without subdivision, and that every animal is such a thing. (20/30 September 1698, to Bernoulli, GM 3, 542/AG 168)

6 Man is a substance; his body or matter is substances. (17 December 1698, to Bernoulli, GM 3, 560/AG 170)

7 Extension is an attribute, that which is extended or matter is not a substance, but substances. (23 June 1699, to De Volder, G 2, 183/L 519)

8 [S]econdary matter, or a mass, is not a substance, but substances, like a flock of sheep or a lake full of fish. (22 March 1703, to Jaquelot, G 3, 457/WF 200–1)

9 For an aggregate is nothing other than all those things taken at the same time from which it results, which clearly have their union from the mind alone on account of what they have in common, like a flock of sheep. (10 November 1703, to De Volder, G 2, 256/Rd 234)

10 The monad alone is a substance, a body is substances, not a substance. (21 January 1704, to De Volder, G 2, 262)

11 In the *mass of extension*, or rather, of extended things, or, as I prefer, in the multitude of things, I say that there is no *unity*, but rather innumerable unities. (1704 or 1705, to De Volder, G 2, 276/AG 182)

12 And *secondary matter* (e.g. an organic body) is not a substance, but … a mass of many substances, like a pond full of fish, or a flock of sheep; and consequently it is what is called *unum per accidens* – in a word,

a phenomenon. (4 November 1715, to Remond, G 3, 657/R 226/Rd 287)

The *S*s analysis takes these words literally: "an aggregate is nothing other than all those things taken at the same time from which it results" (text 9). But he immediately goes on in this more expansive text to add in mental construction themes, saying the mind is responsible for an aggregate's unity. So it is unclear from this text whether "the *S*s" – "the totality of things it results from" – all by themselves are sufficient for an aggregate's existence. If not, then the mind's unifying role is an additional necessary condition that needs to be added to "the *S*s" before an aggregate is constituted.

This is counted a *Realist* analysis because the *S*s are themselves mind-independent, and so if a body simply is "the *S*s," that body must also be mind-independent.

Evaluation of "the Ss"

The advantages of this analysis lie in its ontological economy, as one would expect given its nominalist motivations. There is something beautiful about its simplicity. It has the same allure that eliminative reductions have in many areas of metaphysics. They all promise to get rid of something problematic, leaving behind the unproblematic things that all along one wanted to be the only things around – as when the mental is eliminated in favor of the physical.

But "the *S*s," like its fellow eliminative reductions, is implausible given its severity. ("Simplicity is the most deceitful mistress that ever betrayed man" Adams 1974, 441, ch. 30.) It's just asking too much for one to believe that there is nothing more to an aggregate than the *S*s. Surely their sheer existence is not nearly a sufficient condition for an aggregate. For instance, nothing whatever is said about what they need to *do* to become an aggregate. In the case of a physical aggregate, the mere simultaneous existence of two slices of bread and a slice of ham would not be sufficient to constitute a sandwich. Something further must be said about their arrangement and proximity – otherwise the bread could be in Luxembourg and the ham on the moon and, notwithstanding, the sandwich is constituted. Of course, someone might define 'sandwich' so loosely that it would apply to such scattered objects, but that would be a maverick, stipulative definition.

Quite apart from these counterintuitive features of "the *S*s," there is the decisive point that, in case of Leibnizian aggregates, it is plainly impossible that this be a sufficient condition. For Leibniz, while denying that substances are extended, explicitly says that aggregates are extended. The existence of non-extended substances can't entail the existence of extended objects.

Thus the texts must be seen as emphasizing – with a bit of hyperbole embodied in one of those quick turns-of-phrase Leibniz loves so much –

what he says elsewhere more expansively and carefully. Texts "elsewhere" I have already used as a basis for the Realist arguments for substances (2.5) and the analysis of "aggregates of substances" (3.6). The claim is that, in regard to their reality, activity, and force, aggregates are completely and utterly dependent on substances. The dependence is not so complete, however, as to render an identity (and with it, trivially, equivalence of necessary and sufficient conditions) between aggregate and substances, as a literal understanding of "a body is substances" would suggest.

Indeed, the original austere analysis showing the Ss as necessary and sufficient for an aggregate must be weakened. Their existence must be reckoned only a necessary condition. Leibniz argues that extended aggregates entail ("presuppose") the existence of non-extended substances in them. His arguments did not begin with substances and argue that they are sufficient for the existence of aggregates; they began with aggregates and argued that their existence is sufficient for the existence of substances. Outside the texts just examined, aggregates are said to be born of substances plus at least one further condition.

Sometimes the "further condition" involves the *supervenience* of an extended body on non-extended substances. Other times, the perceptual continuum story helps explain how the mind reads spatial continuity into an appearance caused by the Ss. Each of these stories in its own way helps clear away the air of paradox surrounding the claim that extended aggregates owe their existence to non-extended substances.

The weakened analysis is:

Ss-AGG: Aggregate w exists at t only if at t, the Ss exist.

This analysis can now be carried forward to appear in some of the more complex accounts below, where further necessary conditions will be added with the goal of arriving eventually at sufficient conditions.

6.5 Aggregates as Mereological Sums[6]

Mereological sums are perhaps most often what the man in the street has "under his hat" when he thinks of aggregates. Sums – also sometimes called "fusions" or "compounds" – come into existence when various objects ("parts") join together in some way roughly analogous to addition in mathematics.

Construed as a *plain sum* a sandwich is:

slice + ham + slice

But the question immediately arises: what exactly is the "+" function? In the case of the bread and ham, it's easy to see it as a spatial relation between the three parts. I could say that "+" requires that the components be" contiguous and added together in spatial order," with the ham between and in contact with the slices.

Following this model, Leibnizian aggregates construed as plain sums would be:

Aggregate w exists at t iff at t, S1 + S2 + S3 ...

One should then require an interpretation of "+" that is consonant with Leibniz's thought. Since substances aren't in space, I can't follow the example of the sandwich-maker and simply line up the ingredients so that they're in contact. Instead, "+" must signify some sort of "metaphysical glue" or "principle of aggregation" that bunches substances together into groups – something at least roughly analogous to addition. And the substances would have to do that all by themselves – would have to be so constituted internally that they "fit" (in some non-physical sense) into others.

Even within the Realist theory a glue or aggregating principle is hard to come by. The substances are most often presented as self-contained and sufficient in themselves. So simple sums seem unlikely candidates to capture what Leibniz is after.

There are ways to account for composition other than making the substances accomplish it all by themselves. I can avoid countenancing a "+" relation that requires some sort of structure in the intrinsic nature of the substances. *Something* must, according to the analysis eventually recommended here, reach down and effect a real connection between the substances in an aggregate, but it will be a relation that accomplishes it.

Trope sums take a step in the direction of specifying that relation. Tropes are relations between the parts in a sum, and are typically construed as universal or general properties that are instantiated in particular objects or sets of objects at a particular time and (if the objects are spatial) space.

As a trope sum, the sandwich is:

slice + ham + slice + r,

where r is a trope roughly characterized as "betweenness and contact instantiated in this ham with respect to these two slices of bread at t." r must be construed as a part of the sandwich – just as much as the bread and the ham are – if this is a mereological sum.[7]

And Leibniz's aggregates, as trope sums, would be:

Aggregate w exists at t iff at t, S1 + S2 + S3 ... , + r

where "r" is some composition-relation between the Ss – perhaps "composition instantiated in these Ss at t." (I ask the reader not to place much weight on "times" here. They are used for specificity and convenience, and ignore for the moment that Leibniz was skeptical about time and may have offered a "causal theory of time" which replaces temporal precedence with causal precedence. The details of that need not concern us now: on either theory, there is an ordering, and my "times" are just points in the ordering, whether it's genuinely temporal or merely causal.)

At this juncture my earlier decision to set aside the Canonical doctrines becomes crucial. For if I upheld it, I could simply rule out real relational tropes as non-Leibnizian, citing passages such as this:

> Since every extended body, as it is really found in the world, is in fact like an army of creatures, or a herd, or a place of confluence, like a cheese filled with worms, a connection between the parts of a body is no more necessary than is a connection between the parts of an army. And just as some soldiers can be replaced by others in an army, so some parts can be replaced by others in every extended body. Thus no part has a necessary connection with any other part, even though it is true of matter in general that when any part is removed, it must necessarily be replaced by some other part.
>
> (G 2, 193/L 521)

But I will follow Leibniz's lead in the Realist canon in countenancing real relations – the sort tropes must be. The trope *r* must be seen as a part of *w* in the same sense that the substances are. This is an adding together of substances and a trope – by the same operation, "+" – to arrive at a trope-sum. In Kit Fine's words, the trope must be a part of *w* "in the same way as the standard ingredients are" (Fine 1999, 64). Applied to Leibnizian trope sums: the trope must be on an ontological par with the substances.

I think something very like a trope is what's needed to give Leibniz's aggregates mind-independent status. While the trope is not a substance, it needs to be able to effect a "melding," in some sense, of substances in a collection. Even if the substances aren't premade to fit with the others, this aggregate-maker needs to effect a suitable accommodation.

Make no mistake: tropes of this sort, specifically tied to certain substances, would be like the ratio between two lines construed as "an accident in two subjects, with one leg in one and the other in the other" famously scorned and rejected in an Idealist passage (Clarke, 5.47). By comparison with a simple ratio, a trope envisioned for aggregates would sin infinitely more often against the rule that an accident can only be in one subject. It would be a monstrous "infinipede," with a foot in every one of an infinity of subjects! Here's more evidence that the Realist theory is inconsistent with the Idealist one.

I think the closest thing to a trope in Leibniz's corpus is the idea of a *vinculum substantiale*, or substantial bond, which binds substances together in aggregates and assists the dominant monad in unifying animals (See, e.g. G 2, 517/R 274 and Look 1999). That doctrine is wildly inconsistent with much in Leibniz, including the doctrine of the continuum. For this substance-like bond would effect a real continuity between the substances in a body, thus "melting their edges" so they can compose something extended. I think it's a non-starter.

I will be assigning a trope-like function to the relation I focus on as the chief "aggregate-maker" in the final Realist analysis below. This relation is more sophisticated and multidimensional than a simple trope, and can be used to make better sense of the texts.

One issue that tropes raise, and which may be handled now, is that they represent relations between specific infinities of substances rather than a general "harmony" or "resulting" relation. Theirs is a harmony between just these substances, S1, S2, etc., at this particular time. Now Leibniz has several general harmonies – between the substances, between their perceptual states, or between mind and body. Does he have specific harmonies too?

Some texts remove any doubt about that. For instance, Leibniz says that "whatever happens in the mass or aggregate of substances according to mechanical laws, the same thing is expressed in the soul or entelechy" (G 2, 205–6/Ad 283–88) and that mechanical causes are "concentrated in souls" (G 4, 562/WF 116). He seems to mean that, for each moving body, there is some sort of account of its movement – say, its path around a curve – in the Ss within it. Thus, in the analyses that follow, I will make good use of relations between the Ss in a given w.

It turns out that Fine proposes an aggregate-maker which can be used to develop an account that's more fruitful for understanding Leibniz's philosophy than one based on mere tropes. I turn to it now.

6.6 Aggregates as Rigid Embodiments: An Overview

Rigid embodiments – wholes invented by Fine as an alternative to standard mereological sums – provide yet another model for aggregates.[8] In fact, a version of this analysis is more accommodating of the aggregate thesis than any other I'll examine.

Rigid embodiments are unlike mereological sums because they incorporate an element – called "R" – that does not pretend to be a part on all fours with the components. Fine's R (which is not exactly the one I will settle on for my own analysis) is roughly analogous to an Aristotelian form, and the parts or components that it organizes are its "matter" (Fine 1999, 62, 65). R's most crucial role is predicative: it determines the general category under which the resulting whole is classed, as the form "statue" determines that this bronze is a statue rather than a cannon ball.

The ham sandwich, as one of Fine's rigid embodiments, would be:

at *t*, slice, ham, slice / R

where '/ R' abbreviates "standing in relation R to one another." R is the formal element, in this case (roughly) "betweenness and contact[9] as instantiated in this ham with respect to these slices of bread, so as to constitute a sandwich." R is the "sandwich-maker," ham and bread the "components." These embodiments are "rigid," as opposed to "variable,"[10] because R is a relation between fixed components – a specific ham slice and two particular slices of bread.

Fine explains the difference between the sandwich components and R:

> Intuitively, this new object is an amalgam or composite of the component objects a, b, c, ... and the relation R. But it is a composite of a very special sort. For the components and the relation do not come together as coequals, as in a regular mereological sum. Rather, the relation R preserves its predicative role and somehow serves to modify or qualify the components. However, the result of the modification is not a fact or state. It is a whole, whose components are linked by the relation, rather than the fact or state of the components being so linked.
>
> Fine (1999, 65)

Fine says rigid embodiments are "a new kind of whole"; they are "*sui generis*" – not to be understood on analogy with any other sort of whole (Fine 1999, 65–6).

As I said at the beginning of the chapter, at least once Leibniz developed the idea of a whole of this sort. Leibniz says A, B, and C are understood to "agree" with respect to the "whole L," and that agreement is very like Fine's relation "R" holding between a, b, and c so as to allow them jointly to constitute this "new object."

The Metaphysical Status of R

By comparison with the trope r, Fine's "R" is not a part of the whole in the same sense that the spatiotemporal bread and ham are. From the examples Fine gives, R would appear to effect its "modification" of the components without making them jointly take on some special "aggregative state." In a way, R does its work from afar – it doesn't "touch" the components at all.

An R like that would be most welcome in Idealism, where every substance is a "world apart" and all interaction is only apparent. Within the principal Realist analyses, however, R is going to need more punch than that. For it is going to have to effect aggregatehood between the substances – it will have to have a trope-like "side," so that by the time it's done its work the substances *have* been melded into a new thing. Leibniz's R will be more a "meddling" relation – a concept I'll develop in the next section – than a mere ideal relation.

The *other side* of my R is going to resemble more Fine's R. This has to do with R's "predicative function." That seems extremely Leibnizian in light of the "Mental Constructions" analysis (5.2) – according to which aggregates depend on linguistic conventions and the mind's unifying role. Fine says of R that it is "an intensional or conceptual element" that is "directly implicated in the identity of the embodiments" (Fine 1999, 73). He continues:

> The material world is standardly conceived in extensional terms. . . . the material things may have properties or enter into relations, but these properties or relations are not themselves taken to be constitutive of material things in the same kind of way that they are constitutive of the propositions concerning those things. But on the view I wish to advocate, properties and relations will be as much involved in the identity of the one as of the other. Thus, if I am right, we see yet another respect in which the divide between the concrete and the abstract realms is not as great as it is commonly taken to be.
>
> Fine (1999, 73)

The relevance to Leibniz is palpable. Leibniz's world is often conceived (by himself and his commentators) in purely extensional terms. There are the substances, but properties and relations (which help constitute aggregates) are altogether outside the world of substances – say, in minds perceiving them or thinking of "propositions" about how they are related. Running counter to this, Leibniz sometimes suggests that the concrete world of substances is brought into close association with abstract linguistic concepts. Indeed, Leibniz's claim that a whole is created when A, B, and C are "understood to agree" in some way with respect to the whole is naturally taken to assert that there is an abstract, broadly linguistic R that makes it appropriate to refer to A, B, and C, jointly, as a whole. (The "understanding" mentioned here need not be a conscious act; it is broadly linguistic and justifies one's predicating 'whole' of A-and-B-and-C.)

Rigid embodiments – with the Rs appropriately enriched so as to include a trope-like meddling side – can combine these mental construction themes with aggregate thesis doctrines. Meanwhile, the "intensional" side of R avoids the extreme "in the head" psychologism of mental constructions while yet preserving something linguistic and hence broadly psychological. Such rigid embodiments have their trope-like compositional roots in the substances, but also partake of the mental in the broad sense that they invoke abstract linguistic conventions.

There is a price to pay for this exciting prospect. I, like Fine, feel some unease at having such an "amalgam" on my hands. Still, Fine's R remains so completely aloof from the ingredients that he can only say R "somehow serves to modify or qualify the components." My R does much more than observe the components from afar – it "gets down in there with them" and effects composition and supervenience. Though no one could be expected to provide details about this, *how* the modification takes place is not as much of a mystery as it is on Fine's (or the Idealist's) account. Nevertheless, given that the R adopted here is also partly intensional, an aggregate composed of non-extended substances and (partly of) meanings seems mysterious – though not as mysterious as Fine's physical objects composed of matter and *only* meanings.

The word–world connection is somewhat easier to characterize given the trope-like character of my Rs. This makes them pretty determinate and not as vulnerable to the contingencies of linguistic convention. Indeed, as Leibniz says more than once, if there is an accommodation, it will have been made from the dawn of time and will come up naturally and automatically. So whether or not there is an aggregate – i.e., R is instantiated – is not (though it may appear to us to be) at the mercy of individual decisions or community practice.

What makes Leibniz's task so daunting – and refreshingly bold – is that he aspires to explain *all* aggregates on the same basic conceptual platform. Fine's project is more modest, limited as it is to familiar composites – suits and sandwiches, flower bunches and molecules. I think of *those* as aggregates because I know they are. I know in each case what their components are and which of Fine's Rs – embodied in linguistic conventions – are relevant to deciding when the components, so arranged, count as a suit or a molecule.

Leibniz, however, is taking on the whole realm of aggregates – familiar ones like piles of sand as well as unfamiliar ones like the sand granules themselves. Sand piles have familiar components and are governed by familiar Rs. But for a sand *grain* one has only a vague idea of its components, and even less of a grasp of what Rs might be relevant to one's properly predicating 'sand grain' of an array of such components. Thus it is quite natural that Leibniz talks about aggregative conventions only in relation to familiar everyday objects – rings and chains and flocks and rainbows and fish ponds.

6.6.1 Cambridge v. Meddler Relations

Idealism is keenly interested in Rs – like Fine's – that have no effect on the intrinsic nature of the components. Recall (from 5.3) that such relations are "cambridge relations," which I now define as follows:

> For any rigid embodiment a, b, c / R, R is a *cambridge relation* = $_{df}$ R's instantiation in a, b, and c makes no difference to the intrinsic nature of a, b, or c.

Fine's R seems clearly cambridge. A sandwich is plausibly taken to be located where at least one of the components is located when they stand in R to one another (Fine 1999, 66), and the "standing in R" seems not to bother any of the components. R can be a cambridge relation provided the "contact" is "gentle" and doesn't compress or deform the slices.[11] Fine's sandwich thus would be the rigid embodiment:

at *t*, slice, ham, slice / R (spatially between, contact so as to constitute a sandwich).

Note that we can imagine an R (though it may be rejected by Fine as an actual R) that effects such a change in the components that they cannot remain unscathed by its "modification." Fine's own examples leave one with the impression that R will never alter the intrinsic nature of the components. But if ham and bread – or flowers – were modified by the relation "being crushed in a vise," R will have gone beyond a mere relational change and will involve a thorough modifying of the components. The components will be smashed and distorted. They will undergo a change of state. And the components so altered could be used in an alternative analysis of the sandwich and the bunch that is arguably equally adequate yet does not include R at all. In a way, when the components are crushed, most of R's relational work shows up in the intrinsic nature of the components – and so, contrary to what Fine wants, the "result of the modification" seems to be a "fact or state."

There is indeed a limit on how much distortion the components can endure. If R were "minced together in a food processor," there would no longer be a sandwich or bunch of flowers for R to help constitute because the components will have been destroyed and the remains merged into an inchoate "mixture."[12]

So somewhere between cambridge and component-annihilating relations lie relations that disturb but stop shy of destroying the components. I call them *meddling relations*. They represent what I have been calling the "trope-like side" of Leibniz's R. Even though in the Idealist theory, Leibniz has no use for meddling relations, he does when constructing the Realist one.

6.6.2 Harmony Embodiments

"Harmony embodiments" are analyzed as follows (where "the *S*s" again abbreviates *S1*, *S2*, *S3* ... – that is, not just any *S*s, but a rigidly fixed, specific infinity of substances):

Harm-AGG: Aggregate *w* exists at *t* iff at *t*, the *S*s ... / R (harmonize so as to constitute an extended rigid embodiment whole, *w*).

According to this definition, a harmony between some *S*s is sufficient to justify predicating 'extension' of the whole ("aggregate *w*") they jointly compose. Of course a proper understanding of it depends on what is built into "harmonize."

Some passages lean explicitly in the direction of harmony embodiments, as does this one that gives expression to Idealism and upholds cambridge relations:

[I] show that corporeal mass, which is thought to have something over and above simple substances, is not a substance, but a phenomenon resulting from simple substances, which alone have unity and absolute reality. I relegate derivative forces to the phenomena, but I think that it is obvious that primitive forces can be nothing but the internal strivings of simple substances, strivings by means of which they pass from perception to perception in accordance with a certain law of their nature, and at the same time harmonize with one another, representing the same phenomena of the universe in different ways.

(G 2, 275/AG 181)

As the substances "harmonize with one another," aggregates "result from" them.

This passage is typical of those that concern the harmony in that it is vague. It indicates that when substances are aligned (in some sense) with one another, a body comes into existence. It tells me nothing about how the alignment of perceptions produces a body. But it probably is not meant to do that. The harmony is a relation between substances that, if we were privy to it, would make it seem quite natural that they – rather than some others – should be underpinning a particular body.

But such harmonies cannot be *informative* – that is, they can't tell me anything about what harmony comes to. We have the term and a few vague ideas of what it means, but nothing rich enough to call an account.

One might try to "beef up" harmony-Rs with a trope-like side which somehow ensures that the harmonized substances and *w* really "feel" the effect of the harmonization. I don't know whether this can be done successfully, and I won't try it here. I will just say that it seems to cut against Leibniz's whole point about harmonies – which is that they hold even when the individual bits are completely unaware of the others. To illustrate the point, he once uses the example of a symphony playing in harmony even if no member ever hears any other member playing their part (LA 95).

Evaluation of Harmony Embodiments

On the whole, harmony embodiments are explanatorily hollow. R seems to constitute an extended body by metaphysical alchemy. How can sheer cambridge harmony between super-isolated non-extended substances bring an extended body into existence? There is no explanation here. All one has is a word, and it can't help bridge the explanatory gap between extended and non-extended. Emergence is not just a threat; it is annihilating.[13]

In metaphysics generally this sort of problem is common. For instance, contemporary physicalists say claims about the world couched in psychological or "intentional" vocabulary are made true by ones couched in physical vocabulary. But, as Frank Jackson notes, such theorists had better have to hand an account of how accounts in the two vocabularies are interconnected. For instance, physicalists who are not eliminativists about intentional states have to say *something* about how the physical story about our world makes true the intentional story about it. Otherwise their realism about intentional states will be more an act of faith than anything else.

Jackson (1998, 29)

With harmony embodiments, one is told that claims about the world couched in the vocabulary of extended bodies are made true by claims couched in the vocabulary of harmonizing substances.

But nothing whatever is said about how the two vocabularies are interconnected. As became apparent in the last chapter, the pressures applied by the Idealist Leibniz are against saying they are related at all. In light of this, one's belief that there is an explanation of one in terms of the other can be nothing more than an "act of faith." Indeed, it makes the belief that there are after all extended bodies an act of faith. What could they add to the serious ontology of the world if they are eliminatively reduced to substances? Aren't they merely putative? And if they are, Idealist phenomenalism is inevitable.

Probably that line of reasoning is what lies behind the frequent dismissals of extended bodies in Leibniz's writings and among the commentators. Idealism neatly avoids extended bodies and invokes the harmony and "quasi-everything" so that what seems Reality is actually Appearance. And again, interpreting these as Truths makes it impossible for both to hold. If they are theories both are taken to be possible accounts, with neither designated as Appearance or Reality.

There are interpreters who see in the harmony a wealth of explanatory power and promise. I do not. Harmony seems to me a surrogate for a type of more informative explanation that can't be found. As Catherine Wilson writes,

[The metaphysics of phenomenalism implies] that each substance is dreaming up a world of other substances – producing them from its own depths – and that these dreams are congruent, there being after all many substances, and form together a harmonic system.

Now, if each substance is only dreaming up its own world, then the postulated harmony is apparent only to God and explains nothing about the experiences of any particular substance.

Wilson (1989, 107)

Right. Harmony "explains nothing." It is an empty name, a placeholder for a rich explanation that is merely postulated by rationalist optimism.

Of course "harmony" fails to explain only in the sense that I take explanatory adequacy to attend relations that apply distinctively only to a limited number of things and in fairly specific circumstances. Thus chemical bonds can explain fragility because they apply to only a very definite set of objects and circumstances. But harmony applies to every object, and under all circumstances. A beautiful sunset is as much an instance of harmony as the grisly torture and murder of a young child in Chicago at the hands of his own parents. Harmony of this sort "explains" everything, and so explains, actually, nothing – rather as in Hobbes's state of nature, everyone "owns" everything, so no one owns anything.

I must press on to other, more full-blooded embodiments that find a place in Leibniz's metaphysic.

6.6.3 *Plain Supervenience Embodiments*

Plain supervenience embodiments take R's trope-like side quite seriously, explicitly giving it the job of (possibly non-spatially) arranging the components in order to (i) *constitute the rigid embodiment w* and (ii) ensure *property supervenience* between *w*'s properties and the native properties of its components. I follow Leibniz (see 1.9) in combining "mereological supervenience" with "property supervenience." "Plain" is used to distinguish this sort of supervenience from a more specific sort – explored in the next section – that lays down conditions in addition to (i) and (ii). Often 'rigid embodiment, *w*' will be simplified in these analyses to '*w*.'

A preliminary abstract analysis of plain supervenience embodiments is:

Aggregate *w* exists at *t* iff: at *t*, *a*, *b*, *c* / R (are so related that they:

i) constitute *w*; and
ii) provide a base for the supervening properties of *w*).

a, *b*, and *c* must be related appropriately in order for there to be an object of which R is properly predicated – i.e., when R's linguistic side is invoked. A "base" is provided by R's trope-like side when the relations needed for a given case of property supervenience are instantiated. In many cases this will require the constituents to be closely grouped together and, for physical objects composed of atoms or molecules, to be bonded in definite ways.

The sandwich would be analyzed as:

Sandwich *w* exists at *t* iff: at *t*, slice, ham, slice / R (are so related that they

i) constitute a sandwich, *w*; and
ii) provide a base for the supervening properties of *w*).

But what are some examples of "supervening properties" of the sandwich that need a "base" in the bread and ham "so related"? The property of "weighing 5 ounces"[14] is probably a borderline, somewhat degenerative supervening property, since it seems more due to mereological agglomeration than supervenience of properties. One wants to say: "It's because I've added two bread slices of 2 ounces each to a 1-ounce ham slice that the sandwich weighs 5 ounces." Nevertheless, weight counts as a supervening property because it remains true that, as the analysis states, the sandwich's being 5 ounces is owing to the fact that ham and bread are "so related."

More typical examples of supervenience can be brought out in the analysis of a window – roughly, molecules / R. The window's fragility finds its base in the molecules' being "so related." Again, the "so related" constraint has real teeth in it, requiring that the molecules be in a tightly delimited spatial region, there to be linked together chemically in a specific way. It does not allow the molecules to be in, say, sand granules, even if the granules are placed edge to edge so as to accommodate spatial arrangement and contiguity requirements.

When one turns to Leibnizian aggregates, non-spatial substances replace ham, bread, and molecules. "R" will have to be understood as some non-spatial principle of order among substances. The general "plain supervenience analysis" of Leibnizian aggregates is:

Plain Sv-AGG: Aggregate w exists at t iff at t, the Ss / R (are so related that they

i) constitute an extended w; and
ii) provide a base for the supervening properties of w).

(i) and (ii) represent the activity of the trope-like side of the Rs to effect mereological and property supervenience.

If there are such Rs for *every* aggregate, most are known only to God. I am only guessing at the R most of the time. Especially the trope-like side of R will remain elusive – at least until true total science arrives. Things are a bit more hopeful for the "linguistic side" of R, though even here I must stumble along with makeshift concepts of R – R in the guise of 'F' as one might say. 'F' will depend radically on conventions, limited information, and fallible methods of reckoning. This point is similar to Locke's claim (*Essay* III, vi, 6–9) that our knowledge of objects is always filtered through a "nominal essence"[15] (which corresponds to R's linguistic side, or 'F'). I never know the "real essence" (R's trope-like side).

Behind my 'if' in "if there are Rs for every aggregate" is uncertainty as to whether Leibniz actually thought there are, for all aggregates one can name (sand dunes, all the world's hub caps, trout-turkeys), mind-independent Rs that determine precisely when they exist and what their supervening properties shall be. Understandably he writes next to nothing about such Rs. He often is skeptical about the claim that every assemblage constitutes a being – as he is here: "It can be doubted whether and how far C is one real entity; whether one entity does not always result from several, even if they are scattered; and when this results or does not result" (C 377/Leibniz 1966, 66–7), and here:

> Shall we say … the substance of the composite of these things [e.g., rings interwoven so as to make a chain] is as it were in suspense and depends on the future skill of the man who will wish to separate them? Fictions of the mind on all sides.
>
> (LA 102)

Still, because he never draws a line between the true aggregates and those that "don't make it," I won't (at the moment, at least) draw a line. Later on I will stipulate that a "threshold" for genuine aggregatehood must be met.

Plain Sv-AGG underscores the point that it is the substances' properties alone that can provide a base for a composite's supervening properties. Leibniz shows that tight connection when he writes in the *Monadology* that simples must have qualities because, as to the qualities of a composite, "what is in a composite can come only from its simple ingredients" (Mon 8).

Evaluation of Plain Supervenience Embodiments

I don't know what is built into the "so related" constraint on R's trope-like activity so that the Ss together constitute w and ensure property supervenience between it and its Ss. I know w must be mind-independent, and that the Ss will need no help from perception to pull this off. When "no one's about in the quad," any "plain-supervening" oaks, benches and stones should remain unperturbed by darkness and desertion. Still, nothing is offered as a model for how this happens.

And precisely because "so related" remains amorphous, plain supervenience embodiments are explanatorily sterile. Nothing short of emergence-defying magic will allow non-extended substances to constitute and provide a subvenient base for these extended ws. In particular, as regards property supervenience, the analysis does not require there to be anything in the subvening substances that corresponds even remotely to what's found in w.[16]

Indeed, typical contemporary examples of supervenience – molecules/fragility or physical/moral – show clearly that even when "strong supervenience" is in force, there is no requirement of resemblance between supervening features and base properties. Supervenience in its very origin is a response to emergence worries. It's precisely because supervening objects and subvening components are so utterly unalike that I look to be rescued from my puzzlement by law-like relations between them, assuring myself, as it were, that if "cucumber smell" is always in this world correlated with "trans-2-cis-6-nonadienal,"[17] it can't be all that strange.

In Leibniz's system, there are broad anti-emergence pressures to keep supervenience from becoming a totally incomprehensible relation.[18] But Plain Supervenience Embodiments have no requirement that the components and supervening object have any specific property in common. That extra requirement is added in "direct supervenience."

6.6.4 Direct Supervenience Embodiments

There is a richer, more specific sort of supervenience required by many of Leibniz's texts. It remedies some of the explanatory deficiencies of plain supervenience.

Direct supervenience maintains that at least one property of the supervening object has a close analogue (usually bearing the same general name as the supervening property) among the components. When it does, I will assume that this analogue property is wholly responsible for the supervening property's presence in the whole, in which case the whole's quality will be said to *supervene directly on* the components' analogue-property. Where "*w*" designates some whole in Leibniz's rigid embodiments,

> *Direct Supervenience*: w's property G supervenes directly on property F of the Ss (where possibly G = F) iff:

i) G and F are close analogues; and
ii) w's being G is explained wholly by the fact that each of the Ss is F.

"Close analogues" will include identity as a limiting case. Thus, the sandwich's weight is not merely a plain supervening quality, but a direct (in this case, identical) one as well. The sandwich's weight supervenes directly on the native weight of the components. Similarly for location. By contrast, fragility and goodness cannot supervene directly, as there is no close analogue for them among the components.

I know that Leibniz wants an aggregate's derivative reality, activity, and force to supervene directly on the Ss' primitive reality, activity and force. Thus, the "direct supervenience analysis," with "**R**" now in bold font, is:

> Direct Sv-AGG: Aggregate w exists at t iff at t, the Ss / **R** (are so related that they

 i) constitute an extended w; and
 ii) provide a base for the supervening properties of w; and
 iii) ensure that w's derivative reality, activity, and force supervene directly on the primitive reality, activity, and force of each of the Ss).

By contrast with the other Rs I've encountered, this one relates the *components' qualities* to the *qualities of the whole*. Plain supervenience Rs entailed only a relationship "horizontally" between the components so that the whole could be constituted and its properties supervene. In addition to this horizontal liaison, the direct supervenience **R** establishes a "vertical" link between components and whole, allows them to pass along something of their nature to the whole.

Direct supervenience **R**s are particularly important for fulfilling Leibniz's explanatory goals. Since they allow substances to enrich body with reality, activity, and force, they play a crucial role in the aggregate thesis doctrines and the arguments for substances that depend on them. *There is at last an interesting explanatory connection between the realms of body and substance*, and this upholds rationalist constraints on nature.

Direct supervenience is needed to sustain such aggregate thesis doctrines as the following. On *reality*, Leibniz writes:

1 An aggregate "obtains its reality from nowhere but that of its constituents." (LA 96)
2 Aggregates retain "as much reality or substantiality as there is true unity in what goes into their composition." (LA 97)
3 The "reality remaining to [a body] comes from its constituent parts." (LA 100)
4 "A multiplicity can derive its reality only from true unities." (G 4, 478/ WF 11)
5 "[I]f there were no true substantial unities there would be nothing substantial or real in such a collection." (G 4, 482/WF 16)
6 An aggregate has "no reality other than what is borrowed or from the things from which it is aggregated." (G 2, 261)
7 "So from where will you derive their unity, or that reality which you give the whole thing, except that which it derives from those things?" (G 2, 262)
8 An aggregate "has no reality but what is borrowed from the things contained in it." (G 2, 267/R 242/Ad 260)
9 In the case of compound things, "all their reality consists only in that of their simple things." (G 3, 69/WF 129–30)
10 "{A}ll the reality of aggregates resides in their simple elements." (GM 3, 756)

On *activity and force*, Leibniz claims:

1 "[I]n corporeal things ... there is something prior to extension, namely, a natural force everywhere implanted by the Author of nature ... [I]t must constitute the inmost nature of the body, since it is the character of substance to act." (GM 6, 235/L 435)
2 "[F]orce and action cannot be modifications of a thing which is in itself merely passive." (GM 3, 756)
3 "[T]here must be force and perception in these unities themselves, for otherwise there would be no force or perception in all that is formed of them." (G 7, 552/R 248)

Elsewhere he says the world of created things would be quite dead without the injection of activity and force by the substances that retain a "subsistent effect" of God's creative act:

> For since this command in the past no longer exists at present, it can accomplish nothing unless it has left some subsistent effect behind which has lasted and operated until now ...

> This inherent force can indeed be understood distinctly, though it cannot be explained by sense perception. It is no more to be thus explained than is the nature of the soul, for this force belongs among those things which are grasped, not by the imagination but by the understanding. ... But if some advocate of the new philosophy which maintains the inertness and deadness of things should go so far as to deprive God's commands of all lasting effect and efficiency in the future ... we cannot excuse him from giving us a reason why things themselves can have an enduring permanence while the attributes of things, which we designate as their 'nature', cannot have this permanence. [T]he substance of things itself consists in the force of acting and being acted upon; hence it follows that no enduring thing can be produced if no force that long endures can be impressed upon it by the divine power.

> [A] modification ... of something essentially passive cannot make it something active.
>
> (G 4, 507–8, 512/L 500–2, 504)

In the context of this passage, Leibniz is concerned to distinguish his own position from (among others) that of Newton and occasionalists. And he can't do that without direct supervenience **Rs**. For he needs something that will instil activity in nature so that the obvious blooming, buzzing activity of bodies won't have to be explained by appeal to emergency tinkering by God (Newton's "active principles") or routine occasionalist interventions. If his substances don't "lend" activity and force to bodies, he's stuck in the same predicament as everyone else. So again, argumentatively, direct supervenience is critical – not just for the positive arguments for substances, but also for these negative critiques of competing systems.

The strong connection between forces in bodies and those in substances is reiterated here: "derivative or accidental force, which we cannot deny to moving bodies, must be a modification of primitive force, just as shape is a modification of extension" (G 3, 457/WF 201); and "derivative and variable forms of force are modifications of a substantial and permanent thing" (GM 3, 720).

Looking back: Harmony-Rs had no trope-like side, while plain supervenience R's trope-like side was simply stipulated and no guidance was provided concerning how it worked.

By contrast, direct supervenience **R**s have a clear mission. They establish a real metaphysical liaison between substances and whole – a connection strong enough to sustain transference of (analogous) properties from the constituents to their whole. Such **R**s can arrange a "loan" between the Ss and w – a transfusion of S's reality, activity, and force to w.

An Objection to Direct Supervenience

An objector might say, "Yes of course he says things that suggest that picture of loans and transfusions, but they're all just metaphors, don't you see? By taking them literally, you end up in quite a morass." Reply: they *are* all metaphors in the Idealist theory. But on the Realist side, his arguments for substances, his dynamics, his critique of Descartes and atomism depend on their *not* being metaphorical.

The Idealist theory is not being developed in these texts. "They don't fit in and if we include them Leibniz will be guilty of incoherence" Idealists seem to say.[19] Indeed, if Idealism were True, there would be incoherence aplenty. For, to mention a few high points, first, in direct supervenience it is blindingly clear that w *must be a mind-independent object*. The envisioned "transfusion" conducts reality, activity, and force from the substances to the body. So the body, like the substances, must be mind-independent. If it were mind-dependent, the substances would be, so to say, too "far away" to do the body any good. If w were a mere appearance in someone's mind, any reality, activity, and force it had would be due solely to her *thinking of* the Ss as real, active, and possessing force.

Second, this **R**, in light of its role in establishing liaisons, is a real relation, as promised in 6.2. It has two mind-independent, real relata: S and w. Thus "**R**" in SRw is a relation with one foot in S and another in w – in the Idealist Leibniz's words, "contrary to the doctrine of accidents." Moreover, since there are *lots* of Ss, the "infinipede" looms again (see 6.5).

Third, liaison-establishing direct supervenience **R**s are *irreducible relations*. I cannot invoke the Canonical Metaphysics and perform either of Leibniz's favorite operations on them to get rid of their relationality. That is, I can't (i) declare SRw is equivalent to "S is H" and "w is J," for some monadic qualities, H and J. Nor can I (ii) claim they are "mere ideal things" superimposed on S and w by the mind. There must be more to them than either of these accounts would allow, else the transfer of reality, activity, and force would fail.

In relation to this third point about **R**'s irreducible relationality, a powerful response is available from the corpus generally considered. For, despite Leibniz's talk about God leaving an inherent force in matter as a "subsistent effect," he often says it's a *continually renewed* effect. That is, some passages convey a healthy doctrine of divine conservation – never healthier than at Mon 47: "all created or derivative monads are products, and have their birth, so to speak, through continual fulgurations of the divinity from moment to moment." Now consider the relation GRS for some creature, S, conserved by God. What is the status of R? *It has the very same status as a direct supervenience* **R**. It is a real relation with real relata. Indeed, Leibniz explicitly allows for this one exception to his usual "no influx" rule: "with the exception of the dependence of creatures on God, no real influx from one [individual substance] to the other is intelligible" (G 7, 312/PW 79). These "divine-conservation Rs" had better not be reducible to the intrinsic natures of God and S – otherwise they could not effect any real dependence of S on God. (Ideal or cambridge or "quasi-dependence" in this case would be clearly heretical, since it involves allowing that creatures are ontologically independent of the Creator.) And direct supervenience **R**s are neither merely ideal nor are they reducible to the intrinsic natures of the body and the substance.

Since there already is one relation with the same credentials as direct supervenience **R**s recognized by Leibniz, there is no *a priori* or conceptual problem with such relations.

Anyone who wants to eliminate direct supervenience **R**s faces a dilemma. He must (i) eliminate divine conservation from the canon; or else (ii) recognize that the canon already contains a clear commitment to non-cambridge relations. This is a genuine interpretive choice, and the stakes are very high.

Since the Realist theory need not abide by Idealist strictures – and also because it is implausible to eliminate divine conservation from Leibniz's philosophy – I will include these **R**s in the summary analysis of Leibnizian bodies.[20]

Evaluation of Direct Supervenience Embodiments

Direct supervenience **R**s are overall more satisfactory than their harmony or plain supervenience cousins. For I now am told something fairly specific about the explanatory intercourse between w and its Ss.

However, I still have no real guidance about the details of the trope-like constitution and supervenience functions. It remains a complete mystery how non-extended Ss generate an extended w, or how non-mobile Ss can provide a base for a mobile body's properties. On these two matters, I've reached the end of the line: no standard, unenriched rigid embodiment analysis will give me the details I seek.

But hope for such details is not altogether lost. I can reach back to the "Mental Constructions" analysis and the "perceptual continuum" story and fold some of their themes in with the rigid embodiment analysis. In the end, this will yield a richer, more satisfying account than any rigid embodiment analysis can provide on its own.

6.6.5 *Epistemic Access to Rigid Embodiments through 'F'*

Note: **R** is now dividing into two parts. "**R**" will henceforward designate only what I've been calling **R**'s "trope-like side," and F will take on the role of what I've been calling **R**'s "linguistic side."

With the rigid embodiment analysis now in hand, the metaphysics of direct supervenience **R**s (construed now as trope-like relations only) is nailed down. It remains for me to address epistemic access to them. This will take the form of conditions on judgments about aggregates – judgments that involve the concept of "F." Thus this section is largely devoted to developing an account of what I have been calling the "linguistic side" of **R**s.

The role of extension also needs an explanation, and for that I will look to the perceptual continuum story. The conditions developed here will be the final ones needed to provide sufficient conditions for Leibnizian aggregates construed as mind-independent embodiments.

Recall that every other Rigid Embodiment analysis – harmony and both kinds of supervenience – left unresolved the issue of how extended ws can emerge from non-extended Ss. Simply saying this is due to "supervenience" helped little. But if 'extended body' (and roughly equivalent predicative phrases) were simply one of the Fs in terms of which w is conceived, the appearance of "extension" in the picture would be explained. The details are already familiar from the perceptual continuum story in Chapter 3.

In the direct supervenience embodiments which will serve as the heart of the final analysis, **R** will be construed as largely independent of shifts of meaning in natural languages. While the meanings of Fs are set by "baptisms" and traditions of actual usage, there seems to be a permanent, abstract meaning of 'sandwich' (representing what needs to happen – given **R**'s work – so that 'F' can rightly apply to it) that could intelligibly be said to have been there in "logical space" long before the Earl of Sandwich began slicing up bread. (The English term 'sandwich' does, however, depend on such concrete social happenings.)

Indeed, Leibniz accords "historical or geographical contingencies" (say, something in the environment acquires an onomatopoeic name) a role in shaping natural languages (Dascal 1998, 11–12). But he also recognizes invariant elements across such languages – which he calls "roots" – saying "almost all natural languages are but variations, often quite mixed up, of the same roots."[21]

Despite Leibniz's own leaning towards a distinction between terms and "roots," one may wonder whether one should make the **R** in rigid embodiments *wholly* independent of linguistic conventions. The direct argument for doing so is that real bodies of the sort demanded by direct supervenience should not be vulnerable to the vagaries that linguistic expressions are subject to. As the last student leaves the quad on a dark and dreamless night, the extended benches and stones should remain there, serenely pulling their reality from the Ss "beneath them" – just as they do when someone is there, considering those Ss under the 'F,' 'real.' And if, during that night, some sort of lexical conspiracy succeeded in changing the meaning of 'reality' to something radically different from its accepted meaning, the world's furniture should remain unaltered. Moreover, if Julius Caesar were to have picked up two slices of bread and put a piece of beef between them, he should be able thereby to create a sandwich whether or not a natural language has or ever will have a term with the appropriate meaning affixed to it.

So **R** is no more dependent on language than Platonic forms are dependent on languages that can refer to *them*. Long before the term 'dinosaur' (or some natural language equivalent) was invented, there was (in logical space, awaiting assignment as it were) the "form of dinosaur" or, in terms of the present analysis – the **R**s which, if activated, would bring a dinosaur into existence. In general these **R**s might be viewed as sets of possible composition and supervenience relations between components. Some of them, like H_2O, are at least in part discovered and used to define 'F' ('water') in natural languages, while others are not. This allows the *whole*, *w*, to be constituted whenever the components are in **R** – all that without dependence on any sort of F.

As Leibniz says, the very existence of some nameable aggregates – in terms of the current account, the direct supervenience **R**s that permit their existence – is dubious. As I said above, he doubts that a single entity always results from several – that is, he's skeptical of "universalism" in mereology (Lewis 1991). Especially in the case of such things as sand dunes, the world's hubcaps, and trout-turkeys, probably there is nothing there except the "scattered" (C 377/Leibniz 1966, 67) sand grains/hubcaps/fish-and-fowl and (of course) 'Fs' – the phrases and their concepts. It seems implausible *in excelsis* to hold that some **R** really, independently of any finite mind,[22] makes some *S*s into a dune, a scattered "collection" of this sort, or an ugly bird-fish amalgam. Indeed, since Leibniz thinks there are "degrees of accidental unity" (LA 100), it wouldn't be surprising if there were some "threshold of unity" that aggregates must attain in order to be considered real.[23]

So I will not assume there is an **R** for any consistently describable body. Only certain *w*s actually meet or exceed that threshold – namely, those that are mind-independent wholes deriving reality, activity, and force from their *S*s. Since I have no guidance about how to draw a crisp line between aggregates that "make it" and those that don't, I must leave the stipulation in this unsatisfyingly vague form.

Judgments about the persistence and reidentification of a particular *w* also need to be included in the final analysis. That might seem strange, as I have supposed that Leibnizian aggregates do not persist. But I am here concerned with epistemic access to the metaphysics, where fallible persistence and reidentification judgments are crucial. In particular, they must be brought in to accommodate Leibniz's claim that mobility, resistance, and impenetrability characterize *w* (G 4, 510–11/L 503). For surely *w* can't be judged to move or resist penetration except on the assumption that *w* is an F that persists through a period of time.

Leibniz is on record as holding that, as to the metaphysics of aggregates, mereological essentialism holds.[24] That is, a necessary condition for "same *w*" is "same *S*s." That is why I have tied the identity of rigid embodiments to a fixed set of *S*s at a time. Epistemic access to **R** seems fairly limited; I will consider it negligible. Instead, the epistemic *entrée* is found in the Fs predicated of *w* – as it were, after the metaphysics has already handed one a *w*.

Given that F is thus central in judgments about aggregates, I will step in on Leibniz's behalf and add another necessary condition for persistence-judgments. That is, the relevant F must be of the same general kind at the two times – otherwise some *S*s that had earlier been deemed a cannon ball might now be adjudged a statue and yet the theory would direct us (implausibly) to reckon the statue identical with the cannon ball.

So the relevant "judgments" about persistence and reidentification will have to do with (a) whether the same *S*s are present at a later time, *t1*, as were present at *t*, and (b) whether F characterizes *w* at the two times. Such judgments are, of course, open to error.[25] Lapses of memory could undermine (a), and so could the fact that, unbeknownst to the judger, between *t* and *t1* some of the invisible *S*s might have "leaked out" – or others "bled in." An incomplete grasp of F's meaning could compromise (b). Other conditions would of course be added, depending on the nature of F. For instance, motion will be predicated when some *S* judges, at *t1*, that (a) the very same *S*s that had constituted a *w* at *t* are now again constituting a *w*; (b) both *w*s are mobile bodies – and, in this case, *w* now occupies a different position than it had occupied at *t*.

Leibniz's overall doctrine of perception allows for a generous amount of unconscious perception. I will exploit that in the analysis of the role of F. The predication of 'F', and "judgments" about the *S*s and *w*'s position and resistance will often be unconscious mental acts. I know in dealing with physical aggregates that I seldom consciously apply to them a "dictionary definition" of some F, and that I almost never think about (let alone check to see) whether precisely the same parts are present when I say "this body moved." How much less likely that I will do that when I have no idea what the constituents are!

To minds altogether lacking a capacity for "reflection," I cannot attribute even unconscious thoughts of *w*.[26] As was evident in the study of "mental constructions," Leibniz's doctrine of animal thought allows a dog to recognize a stick, though not to know it through the concept of "stick." That is, the dog has "the means for recognizing the thing represented," but "cannot enumerate one by one marks sufficient for differentiating a thing from others" (G 4, 422–3/AG 24). Since Leibniz clearly recognizes that such minds "have no reflection" (G 3, 343–4/WF 221), I will count the capacity for reflection as necessary for epistemic access to *w*.

This restriction may seem to conflict with "universal mirroring" – embodied in Leibniz's claim that each simple substance is "a perpetual living mirror of the universe" (Mon 56). But it does not. Every substance can mirror a reflective mind's stick, though of course only a reflective mind can *initiate* a series of mirrorings of a stick.

I am now ready to blend these epistemic constraints in with the metaphysical ones in order to specify sufficient conditions for aggregates.

6.6.6 The Final Rigid Embodiment Analysis

The proposed final Rigid Embodiment analysis of aggregates incorporates direct supervenience and makes w knowable through some 'F.' An English term used for 'F' is understood to designate equivalents in all possible[27] natural languages.[28] When 'F' is 'extended body,' all equivalent predicates and predicative phrases (e.g., 'spatially continuous physical object,' 'spatially continuous mass') are intended. The scope of "finite minds" is limited to those minds capable of reflection. "w" is restricted to those aggregates that meet or exceed the "threshold of unity."

Rigid-AGG: Aggregate w exists at t iff: at t,

1   The Ss exist; and
2   The Ss / **R** (are so related that they
   i)   constitute an object, w; and
   ii)   provide a base for the supervening properties of w; and
   iii) ensure that w's derivative reality, activity, and force supervene directly on the primitive reality, activity, and force of each of the Ss); and

3   If some finite mind, S_1, is thinking (possibly unconsciously) of w, they are (possibly unconsciously) judging that 'F' is properly predicated of w, where
   i)   F is an accurate guide to the true nature of w when it

      a) characterizes w as real, active, or possessing force, or[29]
      b) characterizes w as a direct supervenience rigid embodiment; and

   ii)   F is not an accurate guide to the true nature of w when it characterizes w as a true unity; and
   iii) The perceptual continuum explains why 'extended body' is often predicated of w; and
   iv)   If S_1 is judging (possibly unconsciously), "w is the same F as the one I perceived before," the judgment will be open to error due to factors that include an inadequate knowledge of:

   a) precisely which Ss are present at the two times; and
   b) whether w is an F at the two times.

A visual representation of these conditions is found in Figure 6.1.
The explanatory power inherent in this combination of metaphysics – the Ss / **R** – with epistemology and language and the continuum doctrine is

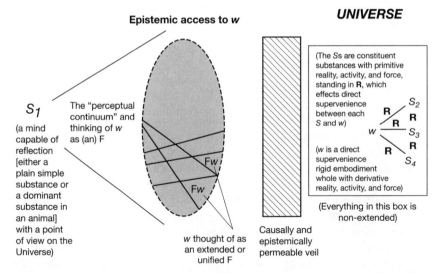

A different veil would intervene between non-reflective minds and *w*. Lucky minds could know *w* itself without any guise – as God does.

Figure 6.1. Realism: Aggregates as Rigid Embodiments

nothing short of breathtaking. It is a tribute to Leibniz's genius – to the range and depth of his synthetic powers – that he had prepared all the ingredients, as it were, for such a grand philosophical feast.

To illustrate the analysis, take the familiar case of the ocean to express the conditions in terms more colloquial.[30] An ocean exists at a given moment just in case any real, active substances are related in such a way that a whole, *w* is thereby constituted and *w*'s qualities supervene on the substances' qualities. In particular, *w*'s reality, activity, and force supervene directly on the substances' reality, activity, and force. When finite minds think of *w*, they do so through the concept of some predicate – say, 'ocean.' The meaning of 'ocean' ("a vast body of salt water") explains why *w* is thought of as a unity. The perceptual continuum story explains why it is considered extended. A reflective chap's judgment, "this is the same ocean as the one I saw yesterday," is open to error given inadequate information about whether the same substances are present now as were present yesterday, and whether in fact those substances constitute an ocean at the two times.

Melville provides the perfect poetic touch: "There is, one knows not what sweet mystery about this sea, whose gently awful stirrings seem to speak of some hidden soul beneath" (Melville 1950, 478 – Chapter 111).[31]

6.6.7 *Evaluation of the Rigid Embodiment Analysis*

This analysis accomplishes many things at once.

(1) *It provides a mind-independent subject of predication – w.* w can have the many properties Leibniz attributes to aggregates – most importantly, reality, activity, and force. This is the most far-reaching advantage this analysis holds over the Well-Founded Phenomena account, which could recognize no mind-independent subject to take the properties. Many of the advantages below depend on this one.

(2) *The Aggregate Thesis is accommodated.*

(3) *It captures many elements from the mental constructions analysis and Leibniz's philosophy of language as well as the perceptual continuum story (to explain the role of extension).* Thus it has significant explanatory power and renders compatible a large number of Leibniz's metaphysical doctrines.

(4) *All of Leibniz's arguments for substances (2.5) work for w.* w presupposes Ss; w's reality, activity, and force are derived from the primitive qualities of the Ss; w is (apart from **R**) "nothing but" the Ss and derives all its qualities solely from them; and of course the Ss are in w.

(5) *It squares with the mature doctrine of the continuum.* w is composed of discrete simples. Thus, by making w (in 2 (i)) only an "object," I allow that extension does not characterize w itself. According to (3) (iii), extension enters the picture only when w is *considered* an "extended body." The perceptual continuum allows me to invoke Leibniz's claim that I mistakenly regard bodies as continuous (G 7, 563) – that I regard w as falling under some F that characterizes it as extended. This leaves the rigid embodiment itself – w – free to be an "actually divided" aggregate of discrete, nonextended substances. Since w is actually divided, it is not a true unity – which is why any concept of 'F' that characterizes w as a unity is not an accurate portrayal of w. In addition, recalling the definition of 'in' from 3.5, one can see that the Ss are in w in the appropriate sense – that is, positing w entails positing the Ss.

(6) *The perceptual continuum solves the puzzle about how non-extended Ss can result in an extended w.* That is, w is not extended; it is only thought (through the concept of 'F') to be so. This puzzle, recall, remained insoluble in the harmony analysis and in all the Rigid Embodiment analyses – where the **R**s were supposed, somehow, to constitute an extended w from the Ss. Even with supervenience invoked, no details were provided about how w gets to be extended when the Ss are so very unextended.

(7) *A sturdy epistemic bridge is erected between mind and world* – a bridge that makes what's *metaphysically most fundamental* also what's *epistemically most reliable.* Pillars sunk deep into the bedrock metaphysics of direct supervenience support that span. Indeed, it is no accident that the mind can wander out of Idealism's solipsist prison house to make reliable epistemic contact with reality. It does so based on causal and epistemic "meddler" relations – allowing commerce through the "causally and epistemically permeable veil" – that guarantee a close resemblance between key features of the Ss and "the knowable." What is knowable is that w is a real, active, direct supervenience rigid embodiment that has force. The per-

ceptual continuum and concepts of various 'Fs' conspire to color w with all manner of further properties – some better indicators of the true nature of w than others.

This "permeable veil" permits a genuine connection between w and S_1. Indeed, that is what makes the Rigid Embodiment metaphysic a version of Realism. It is possible, on this view, to know what is in Reality. Reality is something mind-independent and waiting to be known. How that occurs is as much a mystery in this system as in any other.[32] But only with such a picture can one make sense of Leibniz's frequent claim that substances view the universe from their own point of view – which is why S_1 is said here to have a point of view on the universe. That picture requires a universe outside the perceiver, waiting to be known.

Those who are not content to have a mystery at the heart of their metaphysic are in good company: Leibniz didn't like it either. That's why he continually invokes cambridge relations and the other competing Idealist picture when he gets close to endorsing this one. He does not want to pay the dues Realism exacts, to face the full fury of objections lying in wait for anyone who would declare a meaningful connection between knower and reality. A nice example of Leibniz's sliding from one set of commitments to another is in the Arnauld exchange. After giving a pretty clear endorsement to Idealism, declaring that the unity of entities through aggregation "exists only in our mind" (LA 97), he immediately – in the very next paragraph – denies a logical implication of this and endorses the other, Realist conception: things "devoid of true unity" nevertheless "have as much reality or substantiality as there is true unity in what goes into their composition."

As soon as he gets the gist of sailing under Idealism, he senses instinctively its explanatory limitations and so launches Realism, doing his best to navigate in what are sure to be rough waters as the two crafts pull in opposite directions. Things are easier for us with Pluralism invoked, since the two crafts need not pull in the same direction as they are theories rather than Truths.

Looking at this result – seeing the perfect fit this analysis effects between knower and known – Leibniz probably could not forbear to exclaim that this is compelling evidence of God's wisdom. Indeed, I think Leibniz's system culminates in such a close fit largely because the theoretical unity inherent in divine sagacity was all along one of his guiding principles.

(8) *w is not an unknown substratum or an unknowable "thing-in-itself" stranded on the other side of a causal and epistemic blockade.*[33] The "sturdy epistemic bridge," spanning the permeable veil, gives us an insight into the nature of bodies that is not available for Lockean "solidity," Kantian noumena, and similar programs that have objects hidden from perceivers.[34] As I said in the chapter on substance, all explanation comes back to I. In this case, I know from the inside what reality, activity, and force are. They provide me a strong analogous knowledge of the nature of external objects, whose

derivative reality, activity, and force bears a close resemblance to the primitive versions of those traits I experience directly.

Indeed, the strength of Leibniz's version of "inside-out" metaphysics can be appreciated from this vantage point. For *Leibniz gets out*. He does so by endorsing panpsychism about the physical. Some would see the price as too steep. He does not. Instead, the high price actually is exacted from those who unwittingly back into a solipsist corner. Descartes never gets out because body is completely different from mind. And Locke, with his "real essences" back behind the veil, tries in vain to claim experienced solidity reveals matter's solidity.

Again, the importance of intelligibility in Leibniz's panpsychist picture is clear. He insists that the nature of body must be intelligible. It must also be occurrent and categorical, as it can't be a causal agent in the world if it is a mere disposition.[35] Body's inherent nature must also be monadic and occurrent. He finds some "inner" qualities that meet all these criteria and makes them the nature of matter!

Leibniz knew well that a choice for intelligibility and the inner was a choice against reliance on the deliverances of the senses. He says that force can be explained to the understanding, but not the imagination, else one would be asking "for sounds to be painted or colors heard" (G 4, 508/L 501). And he asks De Volder, who complains that he "perceives nothing" of the forces, "would you seek to sense things which can only be understood, to see sounds, to hear colors?" (G 2, 270/L 537).

Before leaving the discussion of panpsychism, it is interesting to note that Idealism and panpsychism are, by all accounts, incompatible. An Idealist rendering of physical objects will make them appearances; a panpsychist one will underpin them with something mental. So again it seems plain that the Realism which leads Leibniz straight to panpsychism, is inconsistent with Idealism.

(9)   *Properties that presuppose that aggregates persist have been accommodated without attributing persistence to w itself.* This is possible because such properties as mobility and resistance depend essentially on judgments about *w* rather than on *w* itself. That puts these features in their proper (mind-dependent) place, allowing the metaphysics of non-persisting *w*s to remain intact despite the attribution of those features to *w*.

(10)   *It avoids equivocation on 'body,' 'aggregate,' 'phenomenon,' and cognate terms.* On this analysis, *w* is the aggregate. Indeed, *w* is the *only* aggregate. And *w*'s metaphysical nature is explicitly demarcated. When someone has an idea of *w*, this is not an additional "aggregate in the head" – say a phenomenon or mental construction – but a bit of thinking about the aggregate *w*. In the language of "well-founded phenomena," the aggregate here is the "well-founding part."

(11)   *It explains why there are no knowable "principles of aggregation" for Leibnizian aggregates.* The topic of principles of aggregation has been raised by

Adams, and is discussed in detail below in 6.7.1. The important point here is that on the Mental Constructions picture Adams favors, it is natural to suppose I could discover the relations I use as I construct aggregates. But in Rigid Embodiments I don't construct aggregates at all. Thus it is no mystery that "Leibniz does not give much explanation on this point" (Ad 249) – there is nothing to say. An aggregate w is formed by virtue of the liaisons established by R. The establishing of such liaisons between substances is something I *never* have access to. I only conceive of R through some F and through the work of the mind as it inflicts the "perceptual continuum" on w.

(12) *It makes it clear in what sense aggregates and animals are on a metaphysical par, so that a bug can unproblematically crawl on a rock.* Catherine Wilson has raised an interesting puzzle emanating from an Idealist construal of aggregates as appearances in light of Leibniz's commitment to animals as real substances. There is, she says, a "certain absurdity" in saying that a real bug can crawl around on an unreal appearance-rock (Wilson 1993, 667).

On the Realist proposals offered here, the absurdity disappears. The rock is a mind-independent whole, w, that derives its reality from its constituent substances and is thought of as an extended F. The bug is a more complicated mind-independent whole – an animal (the full analysis of which awaits us in Chapter 8) – whose mind-independent organic body is an aggregate with the same status as the rock. Its real organic body is what is crawling about on the real rock.

(13) *It makes sense of Leibniz's critique of Cartesian extension.* While the Well-Founded Phenomena account construed aggregates as continuous, inert ps in minds, w is discrete and active. Thus it bears out what Leibniz says repeatedly: his view of body is radically different from Descartes's in just these ways.[36]

(14) *It makes sense of Leibniz's physics,* which is largely devoted to studying the forces in bodies and laying the foundations for field theory by claiming that force is more fundamental than matter. Unlike ps, ws can have force-bearing substances in them, and thus explain the connection between physics and metaphysics.

(15) *Mind-Body Parallelism is explained.* Idealists see this doctrine as problematic. Benson Mates illustrates the dilemma nicely:

Since bodies are only phenomena, whereas minds are real, one would suppose that the mind–body problem, the problem of how the mind can act causally on the body, would simply disappear. But Leibniz does not seem to be content to leave it at that.

Since phenomena do not really exist, all such statements [about bodies] should be analyzable into statements about the perceptions of monads. But Leibniz gives no clues as to how such reductions should be accomplished; we can only conjecture that he would have followed a phenomenalistic line. ... At any rate, when he considers the mind-body problem explicitly, he goes off in another direction.

Mates (1986, 206–7)

There follows the quotation of a little-known text (Leibniz 1889, IV vi 12f 15), with one other cited (Leibniz 1948, 266), in which Leibniz conducts a thought experiment. He considers a scenario where, *per impossibile*, all minds (not substances, as that would do in Realism as well) are destroyed yet bodies remain intact. And Mates finds it "puzzling and unsatisfactory" because Leibniz "ignores" the fact that "bodies are only phenomena" and treats bodies as if they had some other status.

The reason Mates is astonished is that he takes Leibniz's mind-body parallelism to be True rather than as a doctrine belonging to a separate theory. He tries to keep the doctrines attributed to Leibniz consistent to protect Leibniz's rationality. But when passages like this appear, all the cover comes undone, the project of protection backfires. What Leibniz says so betrays Idealism that Mates can only look on in disbelief, as if to say "There he goes – off in a different direction – ignoring the right path!"

From what Mates writes, there would appear to be not too many places where Idealism is betrayed in this way. Two lesser-known passages were cited, but, as I've argued, hundreds could have been – all places where Leibniz seems to lose track of his easy phenomenalist way out of problems and to take on – by Mates's lights, inexplicably – all the baggage of mind-independent bodies. In particular, NS (14) and Mon (78–81) contain clear endorsements of parallelism, and the Arnauld exchange presents a perfectly clear thought experiment similar to the one cited:

> I admit that the body apart, without the soul, has only a unity of aggregation, but the reality remaining to it comes from its constituent parts which retain their substantial unity because of the living bodies which are included in them without number.
>
> (LA 100)

An exemplary Realist text, right in the midst of a mainstream correspondence, and (to make matters worse for Exclusivist Idealists) in the same letter typically used to clinch the case for Idealism. Selected out and hidden. To protect Leibniz from incoherence charges. "For his own good."

But anyone who needs *that* much help isn't a great philosopher. Indeed, "damage-control" of this sort is as unnecessary as it is futile. So long as mind-body parallelism belongs to a different theory of Reality, rather than the same Reality, its appearance in Leibniz's writings is not puzzling at all.

(16) *The monads finally do something!* Idealists say things like "body must consist of [monads]" (Erdmann 1891, II: 184), or "bodies must be pluralities of monads" (Rd 220). But they can never really deliver on that. The reason is that in Idealism each monad just – well – *exists*. If no other things do – the cost of eliminative reductions – then "bodies" (since there are none) can't consist of them or be pluralities of them. The Idealist theory holds that each monad carries on with its solipsist-like perceptions and doesn't worry much about what else there is – except that it's pretty sure there are others like it "out there." In light of the Realism developed here, it is clear Leibniz never intended to leave the monads on a shelf – so pretty! – and have them perceive and strive their way through a lonesome eternity. He had work – explanatory work – for them to do. Only in the Realist theory *are* there things that can consist of them; only there is it even intelligible to say aggregates are pluralities of monads.

In sum: it was a long time coming, but the reward is finally before us: *in Realism, substances can play the role they are assigned in Leibniz's final system.*

As to the weaknesses of the Rigid Embodiment analysis, there are a few:

(a) It yields no account of w's constitution or how supervenience is carried out. There is here no explanation of exactly how Ss constitute w, or how the Ss' properties provide a base for w's properties.

Reply: This objection expresses a worry aired all along: how does **R** work? How does it modify the components so as to produce w? I have suggested that w is a mind-independent whole that comes into existence whenever **R** is in force. Since the components in this case are nonspatial and invisible, it is little wonder that details about constitution or supervenience are not forthcoming. I will go so far as to say this: no account of Leibnizian aggregates will ever explain these things. Perhaps they belong to the "utopian"or "ultramundane" (G 2, 281/AG 184/L 538). In any case, the reticence of this analysis simply reflects Leibniz's.

(b) It violates the Canonical Metaphysics.

Reply: Yes it does. But that is no longer an objection to the Realist theory.

(c) A residual substratum issue remains. That is, what exactly is w? It seems to be a "something I know not what." Arguably, one can't even call it an "object," since that falsely attributes unity to it.

Reply: w is a rigid embodiment whole, composed of Ss in relation **R**. It is not a substratum – a Kantian thing-in-itself, say – since it is real, active, and has force. w provides a basic subject of predication which, given the work of the perceptual continuum and Fs, gets conceived of as extended and unified and possessing various physical forces. It's very hard to see what aggregates could be other than something very like rigid embodiments, given the aggregate thesis.

An objector who remains unmoved by this, yet hasn't any novel proposal, would be thrown back on some analysis already examined and rejected. She then faces a dilemma. If she wants something *weaker* than these rigid embodiments with direct supervenience, she will have to accept mereological sums – with or without tropes – or harmony or plain supervenience embodiments. If she wants something *stronger*, she will be shown the distasteful prospect of substantial bonds. But apart from all that, when one strips objects of all their qualities, one ends up with a mere placeholder subject that defies description. That is trivial and uninteresting.

(d) This analysis says the stick the dog sees is not an aggregate, as non-reflective minds can't perceive them. By making 'F' such an integral part of aggregatehood, you have limited the perceiving of aggregates to the linguistically-endowed. The best the dog can do is to mirror the stick some reflective mind perceives.

Reply: This "objection" is not so much a demerit of the analysis as it is a comment upon it. Yes, as in "Mental Constructions," restrictions are placed on the kinds of minds that can handle thoughts of aggregates – can initiate mirrorings of sticks, as it were. In this regard it follows Leibniz's philosophy of language.

(e) This analysis makes the Ss spatial, for it assigns them a place in w.

Reply: I have already addressed this somewhat in the list of advantages. But again: w is non-spatial. The Ss have not been granted spatiality by this analysis. When Leibniz says bodies "contain" substances he must be taken to mean that the body is actually a nonspatial aggregation of nonspatial substances, despite the fact that it appears to be extended. Thus, saying the Ss are in w is analogous to saying 1 is in the set $\{1, 2, 3\}$. Indeed, as Donald Rutherford notes, "there are many types of collective entities that are not spatial aggregates of parts (e.g., sets of numbers)" (Rd 219). In 2.5 Leibniz's struggles with this problem were explored a bit. He sometimes says that the monads have a "position in extension." This analysis does better than that misleading characterization by assigning substances a place in nonspatial wholes that appear extended, thus removing the threat of spatiality for the Ss. (This issue will be treated more fully in 6.7 below.)

Looking back at the comprehensive analysis, one could weaken it by removing certain conditions. Eliminating (2) (iii) would transform it into a plain supervenience analysis; if (2) and (3) are eliminated altogether one is left with "the Ss." Take away (1) and (2) and one has an enriched version of the Mental Constructions account. But then, given that last move, substances become metaphysically and epistemically otiose. Needless to say, there is a significant cost to any redactions.

(3)(i) and (ii) recognize "the true nature of *w*" in line with *w*'s mind-independent status. Those who like a more "Kantian" Leibniz will no doubt want to weaken this to something like, "the most adequate possible human conception of *w*."[37] That reading is encouraged by the fact that there are so many ways for aggregate-judgments to go wrong that one may finally despair of ever making an accurate judgment about them. Indeed, Leibniz himself often declares them unfit for metaphysics and relegates them to his favorite wastebasket, the "phenomena."

But more often he realizes that there can be no wholesale dismissal of the external world. "[I]t is not necessary to say that matter is nothing," he says scoldingly of Berkeley's *Principles*.[38] Indeed, Leibniz's struggles with aggregates, manifest in his many conflicting pronouncements on the subject, are due in large measure to his deep appreciation of their virtues *and* their vices. He knows only too well that they are indispensable denizens of the world, yet are, metaphysically and epistemically, on very thin ice.

6.7 Two Problems for Accounts of Aggregates

Now I pause to examine closely two persistent problems that have been raised for such accounts. Some have been touched on along the way, but it is time to ask the main two analyses – the Well-Founded Phenomena and Rigid Embodiment theories – to respond explicitly to them. Along the way I will evaluate some proposals in the literature that fall outside the bounds of those views.

6.7.1 "Principles of Aggregation"

It is natural to wonder what binds an aggregate's parts together into a whole. In the case of physical aggregates, it is often supposed to be "spatiotemporal position" that determines how the parts will be arranged into a whole. At a common sense level, take material parts A and B at time *t*. Let them be spatial neighbors at *t* and they might form a composite, AB. In the case of entities like letters, their being joined together is not really a spatiotemporal affair, but out of their joining emerges a new object – a syllable – with properties all its own. Numbers join together to form a new composite number, and members a set, though once again the joining is neither spatial nor temporal.

In Leibniz's universe of aggregates one seems clearly to be dealing with nonspatial constituents. Yet the analogy with letters, numbers, and members seems incomplete. While Leibniz's constituents, like all of these, are nonspatial, what is composed of them is a *body* – which, unlike syllables, composite numbers, and sets, is arguably spatial. So the initial mystery is: How can nonspatial substances jointly compose something spatial? Some of the other analyses used supervenience to answer that question, but the two main accounts answered it as follows.

The Rigid Embodiment Account

On this analysis, **R** is the principle of aggregation for a body. It determines how the Ss are arranged, and when its job is done the result is a whole, w, which is not spatial. The perceptual continuum and the concept of 'F' conspire to make humans construe w as spatial. This analysis clearly maintains "realism" about aggregates without encumbering the Ss in them with extension.

The Well-Founded Phenomena Account

This analysis aspired to preserve cambridge relations between the monads in the "monadic aggregate", and between the monads and the p (phenomenon aggregate) they "well-found." Given these commitments, it is impossible for the monads in an aggregate to form a whole in any meaningful sense. Thus the account maintains "nihilism" about aggregates: two or more things never add up to a third thing. Those fond of the canonical metaphysics will see this as the superior account, but it permits only a tenuous connection between the monadic aggregate and p.

Now in addition to those rather stark alternatives, a third one has been advanced in recent discussion. Robert M. Adams writes,

> What, then, are the relations among substances, on the basis of which they are aggregated to form a body? Although Leibniz does not give much explanation on this point, I think it is fairly clear that a body will be an aggregate of all or most of the substances whose positions are within some continuous three-dimensional portion of space. This is the natural assumption, and, so far as I know, Leibniz never suggests any alternative to it. What portion of space the body occupies, and which substances are members of the aggregate, may change over time, of course. Spatial togetherness is a necessary condition for any corporeal aggregation, but it is presumably not a sufficient condition for even the accidental unity that Leibniz ascribes to a stone. For such unity, additional, quasi-causal conditions on the way in which the members of the aggregate change their positions relative to each other will be necessary. ... The organic body is itself an aggregate, and hence a phenomenon; and spatial position is surely as merely phenomenal a property as size, shape, and motion. ... We can assign to each simple substance the spatial position of its organic body, for, according to Leibniz, each simple substance has an organic body. ... [M]onads "have some kind of position in extension" which they get through their relation to "their" organic bodies.
>
> (Ad 249–50)

Note that the proposal is in some respects akin to the Well-Founded Phenomena account. For instance, Adams maintains cambridge relations ("quasi-causation") and refers to the aggregate as a "phenomenon" (in my terms, p). But it goes against that analysis by putting the monads themselves into p. And there is where the trouble begins.

(a) Strictures emanating from the continuum doctrine forbid any meaningful mixture of discrete monads with continuous space. This consideration alone is weighty save for that text (G 2 253/L 531), invoked here, that maintains that monads have a kind of position in extension. There one can see a bit of textual support for the claim. Still, there are better ways of understanding it than the one offered. On the Rigid Embodiment account, Leibniz is to be understood as saying that monads are in w – which due to the work of the mind comes to be thought of and perceived as an extended body.

(b) The proposal seems inconsistent with Adams's overall position. Given that these "organic bodies" are aggregates, and that on Adams's "Mental Constructions" analysis (as on the Well-Founded Phenomena account) aggregates are mind-dependent ps, they cannot provide a body (and thereby spatial position) for mind-independent monads. It is a mind-independent monad that needs location, but the body that is to provide that location is in the mind of the perceiving monad rather than in the world attending to the needs of a monad outside the perceiving one.

6.7.2 Spatial Position for Substances

A related issue concerns spatial position for the substances in an aggregate. Indeed, in the course of addressing principles of aggregation above, I have already furnished the verdicts on this topic yielded by the two main analyses of aggregates, and my answer to Adams's proposal.

A look at the literature shows that this is the most oft-invoked reason for rejecting a straightforward understanding of the aggregate thesis. That is, if one allows that substances (especially non-spatial monads!) are literally in bodies, the game is up. A vestigial residue of extension will spoil the precious spiritual monadology.

Robert Latta writes, as a footnote to Mon 2's claim that there are composites, "Does not an aggregate always imply elements which are quantities, however small?" (Latta 1898, 217–18). The answer to that question is: No. In the case of syllables, numbers, sets, and rigid embodiments, the elements are not quantities. What is bothering Latta is that Leibniz seems here to commit himself to something other than the monads' existence – worse yet to use that something to prove monads exist – and that threatens the purity of Idealism and its Canonical Metaphysics.

Earlier G. M. Ross also expressed this worry, saying the claim that souls are literally in bodies makes no sense on phenomenalism and that Leibniz has no "third world of material bodies" that could house souls (Ross 1984, 179).

Donald Rutherford, whose alliance with Idealism is tempered somewhat by an attempt to combine it with the Realist aggregate thesis, uses a memorable image to make the point:

> To say that monads "are in" bodies is not to say that they are literally distributed throughout extended things like raisins in a pudding; rather, it is to say that a distinct understanding of anything as matter requires that we conceive of it as a plurality of unextended simple substances – something very different from what appears to us.
>
> Rutherford (1990, 549)

One is advised that monads are not spatially in bodies, but are merely needed to understand bodies. But the aggregate thesis seems to require more than monads as a means of understanding body. It requires that bodies siphon off their reality, activity, and force from the monads. If the monads are mere conceptual props, they would be ontologically too "far away" from an aggregate to permit this. Without the presence (yes, *presence*) of monads, the bodies would be reduced to nothing.

The Rigid Embodiment analysis can make perfect sense of the claim that S is in w without attributing to S spatial position and also without making it merely a conceptual tool needed to understand w. A nonspatial sense of 'in' is what Leibniz gives us anyway in his mereology: it is simply an entailment relation between container and contained. As a letter is in a syllable, a number in a larger number, or a member in a set, S is in w. And in that analysis **R** provides what Rutherford asks for a few lines later:

> When we say with Leibniz that a body is an aggregate of monads, we assert that its appearance is grounded in some specific plurality of monads. Implicit in this is the claim that these monads are related to one another in ways which determine the identity of a particular *ens per aggregationem*, and that as a result of the relations among these monads and their collective relation to some other monad, the latter is presented with the perception of an extended body. ... [W]hat exactly is the nature of the relations which unify individual monads in an aggregate?
>
> Rutherford (1990, 549–50)

In his book Rutherford develops an answer of his own, to which I now turn. He writes,

> To assert the relation of two things is, in effect, to recognize each as possessing certain intrinsic characteristics and to state something that is true of the way these characteristics stand with respect to each other.

[R]ecognizing their relatedness does not amount to recognizing a third thing in the world over and above the individuals and their intrinsic properties.

[T]he intrinsic properties of substances are limited to their perceptual states (and the tendencies of these states to change); and ... these perceptions are fully determined by a substance's own nature. ...

If we assume that aggregates depend for their existence on relations grounded in the harmonious perceptions of monads, these relations will be known in detail only to God. This, however, is sufficient for the aggregation of monads. Consistent with Leibniz's definition of the term, we can say that aggregates result from individual monads insofar as the divine mind apprehends certain objective correlations among those monads' phenomenal representations of the world.

(Rd 184, 184–5, 223)

Note that this account is similar to the Well-Founded Phenomena analysis, since he maintains cambridge relations and the existence of only monads and their perceptions and appetitions. It differs, however, in making God an essential player in the construction of an aggregate. From afar, and in such a way as to leave the monads wholly untouched, God notes harmonious relations between monadic perceptions and his doing so is "sufficient" for aggregation.

There are several problems with this proposal.

(a) As I have claimed all along, *quasi-causation amounts to quasi-explanation*. It is well and good to be told that this is going on in the heavenly realms, but Leibniz risks – and gains – nothing by saying it is. God's noticing or not noticing the relations is causally and epistemically irrelevant for finite perceivers. Leibniz himself seems to acknowledge as much when he writes, in the principal text cited by Rutherford, that through the relations God sees between monads, "things seem to be made one for us" (G 2, 438/AG 199). "Seem to be" – the explanatory thread between God-noticed relations and appearances in finite minds is vanishingly thin.

(b) The proposal is not clearly consistent with Rutherford's larger program. One is told that God apprehends objective correlations between the monads' "phenomenal representations of the world." But when Rutherford advocates what is equivalent to reductive phenomenalism for bodies – reducing them to coordinated perceptions of monads – he leaves us with no "world" monads could perceive.[39] The world, on that view, is reduced to coordinated perceptions and all talk of monads representing a world is out of place.

(c) Textual support is sparse. The first and main text cited (G 2, 438/AG 199: Rd 235) is found in some remarks intended for Des Bosses. It is only a draft not sent to him – which, because one has no idea why it was withheld, makes it unclear that it can serve as a guide to his thought. The second text is somewhat better, though again is from unpublished notes. In it Leibniz says of "relational truths" in general that their "reality comes from the divine understanding." This is part of a defense of a platonism (of sorts) about relations against those who would make them mere modifications of finite minds. Leibniz writes "Two things therefore acquire reality through the divine understanding alone" (Leibniz 1889, IV 8 Bl. 60, VE 1083 (N. 242)/Rd 235). While Leibniz is here concerned with relations generally and not specifically with those between substances constituting an aggregate, Rutherford is certainly entitled to use the position for that purpose.

(d) The desire to preserve cambridge relations in the overall interpretation is especially peculiar here, since "substantial bonds," as described in the Des Bosses exchange, would deny them. The set of notes relied upon (in part) to confirm that aggregates arise from God-noticed perceptions derives from a correspondence that undermines cambridge relations.

In the end Idealism's Canonical claims make most of Leibniz's mature metaphysics otiose. There the monads – metaphysically emasculated and epistemically pallid – are quite as useless as "things in themselves" were destined to become in Kant's philosophy.

7 Is Realism Compatible with Idealism?

There is only one move left in the grand dialectic of argumentation about aggregates. One might try to construct a philosophical reconciliation of Realism and Idealism. After all, what could be more Leibnizian in spirit than bringing together warring factions, reconciling the estranged, assimilating the alien?

I will call attempts to do that *Compatibilism* – with the noted restriction that this title will designate "Idealist Compatibilists," as only Idealists have offered detailed defenses of this claim.

Consider an analogy – which, while not perfect, serves as a point of departure.

A famous cosmologist seems to adhere to both the Ptolemaic and Copernican theories of the universe. She is very often found endorsing one and the other in the same texts. It is thought that this means she considers both True and consistent with one another – that they are, perhaps in some hidden way, compatible after all. "Why else would she feel free to endorse both simultaneously?" A new theory – "Ptolernicanism" – is devised to reconcile the inconsistencies and thus defend her rationality. That theory holds that "the earth is the center of the cosmos" and "the sun is the center of the cosmos" are both True and fully compatible.

A famous philosopher seems to adhere to both Idealism and Realism. He is very often found endorsing one and the other in the same texts. It is thought that this means he considers both True and consistent with one another – that they are, perhaps in some hidden way, compatible after all. "Why else would he feel free to endorse both simultaneously?" A Compatibilist theory is devised to reconcile the inconsistencies and thus to defend his rationality. That theory holds that "bodies are mind-dependent" and "bodies are mind-independent" are both True and fully compatible.

It seems these famous people are mad.

Unless, perhaps, a creative approach is taken in the reconciliation-projects represented in the new "hybrid" theories. That is, in Ptolernicanism, the two theories of planetary motion are not taken to be on an equal footing and their claims combined in a wholesale sort of way. Instead, the reconciliation is accomplished by giving Copernicanism the upper hand, and working in as much of the Ptolemaic theory as will fit. Similarly with Compatibilism: it is not an across-the-board joining of Idealism and Realism. Instead, Idealism is granted the upper hand and one works in as much of Realism as will fit.

Indeed, it is this latter project that Idealist Compatibilists take on. Of course they hope to capture *all* of Realism in this way – thus to construct a complete Compatibilism in which no inconsistencies remain.

I will proceed by laying out adequacy conditions for Compatibilism, and then examine how existing theories fare in regard to those conditions.

7.1 Six Adequacy Conditions for Compatibilisms

7.1.1 *Textually Inclusive*

Unless there is some overriding reason, one should not pick and choose among passages in the texts – on historical or philosophical grounds. As Compatibilisms are motivated by a desire to take the whole corpus seriously, they would seem to pass this test easily.

However, there are ways of being textually inclusive in one's overall work, but selective in highlighting texts that support one's interpretation. I call this "selective display." In Leibniz's case, every commentator must make use of this since almost always there are too many texts to consider at once. But selective display becomes problematic when texts which do not jibe with the interpretation offered are not taken seriously enough to qualify its claims. I will discuss selective display in relation to Robert M. Adams's version of Compatibilism.

Recall the discussion in 4.2. There I examined LA 97 and its strong case for Idealist phenomenalism. Indeed, Adams's Compatibilism depends crucially on the claim in that text that being and unity are convertible. In Adams's words, "Leibniz's claim is that aggregates have their unity, and therefore their being, only in the mind, and that this is true even of aggregates of real things" (Ad 246). Thus aggregates are "logically or metaphysically constructed from the individual substances. This construction, in Leibniz's view, is a mental operation. ... They [such constructions] exist in the mind and are dependent on being thought of" (Ad 246–7). These unqualified claims are attributed quite generally to the mature Leibniz.

However, as noted in 4.3, the preceding paragraph of this letter (LA 96) contains one of Leibniz's strongest Realist arguments, according to which "every being through aggregation" gains its "reality from nowhere but that of its constituents." LA 96 is not discussed in the same context as LA 97. It is handled in a later chapter, where Adams notes its contrast with the LA 97 argument and says LA 96 "does not presuppose the equivalence of being and unity" (Ad 336). Indeed, it not only does not presuppose it; it presupposes that the equivalence does *not* apply to aggregates.[1] Moreover, that same favored phenomenalist passage (LA 97) is followed immediately by one that reinstates Realism. As far as I can tell, Adams does not comment on the latter Realist passage in his book.

Adams's "Leibnizian Idealism" appears to be pure and unadulterated because of selective display. Many mature texts outside the Arnauld letters could have been cited to qualify the Idealist view, but even in this *one letter*, qualifications abound and cry out for recognition. If Compatibilism is sustained by ignoring Realist texts, it concedes defeat straightaway.

7.1.2 *Provides an Explicit Non-metaphorical Explanation of the Compatibility*

There must be a fully explicit account of what Realism and Idealism mean, else it will remain unclear how the theory manages to render them compatible and free of inconsistency.

Recalling the analogy I began with, the Compatibilist might cry foul at being asked to fulfill this requirement. For I said that the Idealist-Compatibilist avoids a "wholesale" reconciliation of Realism and Idealism, offering instead a theory which rescues as much of Realism as will accord with Idealism. But to my mind there is a limit on how much of Realism can be left behind or changed so as to accommodate Idealist strictures. If enough central Realist claims are handled in this way, the Compatibilist project of removing inconsistencies won't meet its goal, because the inconsistencies will be avoided simply by changing the meaning of some central Realist claims. And that would sidestep the problem rather than confront it.

In this section I will examine a few Compatibilist construals of Realist claims to see whether, in the Compatibilism, those claims retain their intended meaning.

On Idealism – the view Adams considers Leibniz to have "really" endorsed – things are pretty clear:

> The first thing to be said about phenomena, as Leibniz conceives of them, is that they are *intentional objects*. In this respect ... I believe that Leibniz's phenomenalism is a forerunner of the phenomenalism of Kant. ... [B]odies, as phenomena, may be thought of as the objects of a story – a story told or approximated by perception, common sense, and science. In calling them phenomena Leibniz means that they have their being in perceptions that represent this story to perceiving beings.
>
> (Ad 219)

And he says that substances are present in bodies as aspects of the representative content of these intentional states (Ad 222–3).

But there is ambiguity on the Realist side of things. Since substances and the phenomena they're represented in are so different, the question arises:

Doesn't this violate "the assumption that an aggregate of *F*s must have the same ontological status as the *F*s" (Ad 244)? Adams says in response,

> This is at best a controversial assumption. There is nothing at all odd about Leibniz's rejecting it. Aggregates are presumably close ontological kin to sets, and ... the assumption that a set of pencils must have the same ontological status as the pencils is highly controversial.
>
> (Ad 244–5)

Now the most important aspect of this reply is that it never addresses the question of how an "in-the-head" phenomenon could be an aggregate of substances. Certainly in-the-head phenomena are not close ontological kin to sets – except on a most radical mathematical psychologism. So likening aggregates to sets only sidesteps the most pressing issue. One is not told how an appearance in a mind (that is, "the aggregate of *F*s") could be so completely different from the *F*s themselves. That is much more difficult to explain than why sets have a different ontological status from *their F*s.

That unanswered question infects the immediately following discussion with unclarity – an unclarity compounded by Adams's claim that "presumably" aggregates are "close ontological kin to sets." This leaves the precise character of aggregates in limbo, stranded, in this context, somewhere between sethood and aggregatehood.[2] And that is a non-trivial ambiguity, since Adams later says Leibniz needs a "principle of aggregation" for aggregates (Ad 247–55). If aggregates were sets, no such principle would be needed. (1, 2, 3) and (2, 1, 3) are different *aggregates* but only one *set*, since sets place no structural constraints on their members. For instance, a plastic chip *set* is all the pieces, however arranged; a plastic chip *aggregate* is all the pieces arranged so as to form, say, a toy pirate ship. Indeed, Adams himself later favors the aggregate model over the set model, since a Leibnizian aggregate "depends on relations among its members in a way that the existence of a mathematical set does not" (Ad 248).

But the quotation from Adams leaves open the possibility that aggregates and sets are of the same ilk – thus that the features of sets might help one understand Leibnizian aggregates.

So for the nonce suppose Leibniz's aggregates are *sets*. Isn't there some limit on how different from its *F*s a set of *F*s can be? For instance, it would be odd to say that the pencils are wholly located within spatial region R1, while, at the same time, the set of those pencils is wholly located in non-overlapping region R2. Some sort of overlapping or collocation constraint governs sets and their members when the members are physical objects – as is evident in recent work that construes aggregates as sets.[3] It would be stranger still if the pencils were wholly in region R1 but the pencil set is located nowhere – is nonspatial. Surely that is too much of an ontological difference between a set and its *F*s. Yet such a fantastic theory of sets seems to be promulgated on Leibniz's behalf by this Compatibilism. For it supposes that a set (the aggregate of *F*s) can be a nonspatial mental content, while its *F*s are substances[4] which, while arguably not spatial, certainly have mind-independent status.

On the other hand, suppose Leibniz's aggregates are (as ordinarily understood) *aggregates*. A physical-object aggregate requires its parts to be "lined up" in a particular order – typically a spatial order. Here the ontological status of aggregate and parts must be fairly close.[5] But of course the aggregates Adams envisions are not physical. They are a different, perfectly legitimate, (sometimes) perfectly Leibnizian, type of aggregate – mental-construction-aggregates. Here a mind is putting together various items into a whole of its own making. With such aggregates, Adams is right: the assumption must be rejected – there the substances (*F*s) have a very different ontological status from the (mental construction) aggregate of them.

Notice, however, that coming down clearly on the side of mental-construction-aggregates will undermine the Compatibilism insofar as it would accurately represent Realist claims. For the items in such mental-construction-aggregates will be represented substances, not substances themselves. In the case of a flock, they will be thought-of-sheep, not sheep. And that makes it impossible to accommodate the aggregate thesis – which requires real substances in its aggregates, real sheep in its flocks.

So a dilemma arises. The theory needs simultaneously to affirm (a), (b), and (c):

a) the aggregate thesis (with substances as the *F*s),
b) mental-construction-aggregates, and
c) the denial of the same-ontological-status assumption for *F*s and *F*-aggregates.

If Leibnizian aggregates are sets, one can have (a) but not (b) or (c). If Leibnizian aggregates are mental-construction-aggregates, one can have (b) and (c) but not (a). The root of the problem is what it has been all along: (a) and (b) are incompatible.

In relation to the status of an aggregate of *F*s, Adams goes on to address what I earlier (in 2.5) called the Reality Argument. He says identifying aggregates with phenomena may seem "strange" because "Leibniz thinks reality in some sense accrues to corporeal aggregates from the substances of which they are aggregates" (Ad 245). The verdict:

> Again, I think there is nothing really odd here. An aggregate of substances is for Leibniz a sort of logical or metaphysical construction out of substances, and thus out of ultimately real things. Such a construction has more reality than a construction out of things that are not real, but it is still not ultimately real in its own right. The "reality" of the constructed aggregate is not the same ontological status as the ultimate or original reality of the substances that are elements of

the aggregate. Leibniz's theory of bodies is reductionist, and in a reductionist philosophy, being a logical or metaphysical construction out of ultimately real things is a different ontological status from that of the ultimately real things.

(Ad 245)

The phrase "a sort of logical or metaphysical construction" is vague. Recall that according to the Rigid Embodiment analysis, bodies (aggregates of *F*s, as one would say in this context) have derivative reality because they contain and supervene on primitively real *F*s. But here, 'reality' is put in quotation marks. Why? I suppose it is so-adorned because it is now unclear what this reality amounts to given that what is "real" (in this sense) is a "constructed aggregate." The status of this "reality" is held hostage to the vagueness in "a sort of logical or metaphysical construction."

Indeed, the move from reality to "reality" illustrates a tendency in Compatibilisms generally to substitute a metaphorical for a literal understanding of the Realist aggregate thesis. (It is always Realism that must compromise and make room for Idealism; an Idealist accommodation to Realism is never considered.)

The move to metaphor also appears in Rutherford's work. In a chapter section devoted to "The Nature of Matter," Rutherford says Leibniz's claim that bodies are aggregates of monads should not be understood to entail that "bodies are *spatial* aggregates of monads, that monads are spatial parts of bodies or spatially located within bodies" (Rd 219).[6] Very well. But now something must be done with passages that say monads are *contained in* bodies.

Indeed, in the next chapter, "Dynamics and the Reality of Matter," Rutherford quotes just such a passage from *Specimen Dynamicum* (GM 6, 235/L 435). There a "natural force everywhere implanted by the Author of nature" is said to be "present everywhere in matter" and to "constitute the inmost nature of the body." Of this text Rutherford writes:

> According to Leibniz, the demand for intelligibility requires that we conceive of body not simply as an extended being endowed with force, but as a being constituted from dynamical principles. The force that belongs to the essence of body is ascribed to the fact that the matter of bodies is constituted from substances that are by nature principles of action. This passage is typical of the way Leibniz describes his conception of body in the post-1695 period. His principal claim is that there is something else "in" body besides extension: a force introduced or implanted (*indita*) by God. [W]e are told that it is not sense but reason which assures us that the force is "present everywhere in matter." Once more, the significant point is that the force associated with body – what is required in order to render intelligible its action – is referred back to the force or power that is an essential property of substance.

(Rd 242–3)

Leibniz's literal 'in' is here transformed into a metaphorical "in." Rutherford says the substances are required for our "conception" of body. So that Leibniz's point about the contents of bodies is transformed into one about concepts. And that puts bodies safely into minds, as they are in Idealism.

Rutherford tells us it is the "essence of body," not body itself, that has force. That mysterious "essence" keeps us one step removed from what Russell called "the real world outside us" (R 107). "Essence" is vague enough to be, quite possibly (if one only knew what it was), something in our intelligible conception of matter rather than matter itself. And while Leibniz says this force "sometimes appears to the senses," Rutherford says "it is not sense but reason" that reveals force – again construing Leibniz's point as one establishing that matter must be *thought of* as having force.

This interpretation goes against the intended meaning of the passage. If God is said to establish force as the "inmost nature of body," one is simply bypassing the plain sense of the passage – and substituting for it a Kantian one – by construing it as a claim about conceptions of matter. The intended meaning is clear in light of his remark to Bernoulli several years later: "[T]hese forces are coeval with matter itself, since I think that matter *per se* cannot persist without forces" (GM 3, 552/AG 169).

The fact that Compatibilism can't let Realist claims mean what they mean – can't let the Realist theory alone in its own province – illustrates its bankrupting influence on Leibniz interpretation. Thus when Rutherford discusses the claim that an aggregate, as a multitude of monads, presupposes true unities, he says that this is an argument that has "centrality in Leibniz's philosophy," adding that it would be "no exaggeration" to claim it is one of the "key moments in his thought" (Rd 220). That is absolutely right. The Presupposition Argument is a key moment in his thought, a cause for celebration – a conceptual triumph. But Rutherford construes it as meaning that matter can only be "understood" via the "supersensible reality of monads" (Rd 220). So Leibniz's redeemable point is not one about the literal constitution of an aggregate by some monads, but, again, the more Kantian notion that we can *understand* the aggregate only by *understanding* monads (see also Rd 226).

The reason the presupposition point is transformed into a Kantian one is that it then becomes more amenable to Idealism. Rutherford needs the aggregates that presuppose monads *also* to be phenomena, or monads-related-by-a-mind. As long as the presupposition point is just about relating monads to matter in the understanding, it seems to fit in well with the Idealist point about aggregates being well-founded phenomena. The net result is that the true significance of the Presupposition Argument – and many other Realist themes – is overlooked.

In the end, Rutherford's Compatibilism, like Adams's, is committed to inconsistent claims. Aggregates on the "first part" of Rutherford's analysis are "pluralities of monads" (Rd 218–21) that are "immediate requisites" for bodies but are not "spatial aggregates of monads" (Rd 221). In the "second part,"

> [A]ggregative beings – whose existence is dependent upon relations – can only exist for a mind. Only to the extent that a plurality of individuals is apprehended by a mind as forming a unitary being is an aggregate determined. . . . The existence of any aggregate is necessarily mind-dependent; yet this does not mean that aggregates are merely mental things. Aggregates are instead "well-founded phenomena" . . . : They are pluralities of individuals which together determine a single complex being insofar as they are apprehended as having a certain sameness or connection with respect to one another.
>
> (Rd 222)

What object can be "necessarily mind-dependent" yet also be a plurality of monads which are necessarily not mind-dependent? It is said that the plurality of individuals determine an aggregate "insofar as they are apprehended as having a certain sameness." How far is "insofar?" One would think the "insofar" constraint would mean that without the apprehending mind, the aggregative being wouldn't exist. Indeed, this is what is entailed by Rutherford's claim, "the existence of any aggregate is necessarily mind-dependent." Yet if that is true, the "first part" of the analysis cannot stand, since that requires only the sheer presence of a plurality of substances, and no apprehended relations. In brief, for monads a and b, the aggregate would have to be identical with both (a, b) and (Rab). Since the presence of "R" in the second is mind-dependent, while a and b themselves are not, there must be two things here, not one.

It does not matter that the "mind" in Rutherford's analysis turns out to be God's (Rd 223). If an aggregative being is a "divine phenomenon," it can have no substances in it in the way the aggregate thesis requires. The substances can be *represented* in the phenomenon as God "apprehends" them, but they can't be *present* in it – composing it and lending it reality as required by the Reality Argument. One has only Rutherford's assurances that there are two "complementary" views of aggregates here rather than two inconsistent ones.[7]

As in the case of Adams, the effort to rescue Leibniz's rationality is well-intentioned, and certainly understandable as a response to Russell's all-too-eager attributions of inconsistency and the threat of Truth-pluralism. But the salvage operation fails if the Compatibilism itself proves inconsistent.

7.1.3 No Equivocation

Appealing to equivocation to solve inconsistencies is as effective as paying off debts with bad checks. Equivocation, or using a single term to designate two or more distinct things, is a fallacy because it represents an inconsistent use of terms. That is, use of equivocations is itself an inconsistency.

Note how easy it would be to effect "Ptolernicanism" with a little equivocation. One would simply allow certain crucial terms to have two meanings. Thus 'earth' might mean earth or sun; 'spherical' might mean spherical or elliptical; 'moving' might mean moving or at rest. Thus a Ptolernican might assert "The earth is the immobile center of the cosmos" and actually be claiming that the moving earth is the center or that the sun (moving or at rest) is the center.

Leibniz warns against the dangers of equivocation in DM 27:

> [I]t would be well to choose terms proper to the one and the other sense in order to avoid equivocation. Thus those expressions which are in our soul whether they are conceived or not can be called *ideas*, but those which are conceived or formed can be called *notions, conceptus*.
> (A VI 4 B, 1572 (N. 306)/Leibniz 1953, 46)

So the idea/notion distinction helps clarify what is being said when talking about the contents of the understanding – just as the aggregate of substances/phenomenon distinction helps clarify what is being said about the contents of Reality.

In the last section it became clear that Compatibilists are forced to stretch the meaning of 'aggregate' so far that an aggregate can perform logically inconsistent roles. Thus they encourage equivocations on 'aggregate.'

Sometimes Leibniz doesn't need any encouragement. He exploits ambiguities in 'aggregate,' 'body,' and 'phenomenon' and gives one the impression that he himself is a Compatibilist. A particularly striking case is found in some remarks to Remond, where he says (1) that a body is both a phenomenon and the foundation of appearances (G 3, 622) and (2) that a body is an aggregate of substances – i.e., a phenomenon (G 3, 657).[8] In pursuing a coherent interpretation of his philosophy, I am suggesting ways to improve it.

Here is one way to improve it: *don't follow Leibniz down that treacherous road*. Many an interpretation has lost its way on it.

A look at Adams's proposal is instructive. In one place he admits there might remain "doubts" about "the consistency of the view that bodies are aggregates and *therefore* phenomena" (Ad 247):

> If bodies as phenomena are the objects of stories told by perception, by common sense, and especially by science, as I suggested in section 1, can they also be aggregates of substances? Certainly they can also be aggregates, for, according to Leibniz, it is part of the story told by science, and less distinctly also by common sense and perception, that every extended thing is composed of actual parts, and that is enough to make extended things aggregates in Leibniz's book. On the other hand, it does not seem to be part of the story told by perception, common sense, or science that extended things are composed of *monads*, nor perhaps even that they are composed of *substances* at all. To this I think Leibniz might say that those stories do not *exclude* the

thesis that bodies are aggregates of substances. It is at least vaguely part of the stories told by common sense and science that the appearances of bodies have or may have some further foundation in reality. But no hypothesis of the nature of that foundation is part of the stories of Leibnizian science and common sense; it is left to metaphysics to consider what the foundation might be.

(Ad 247)

On this view, bodies appear as phenomena when science tells its story about objects in the world. Phenomena are mental constructions that play a role in that story, and so far there is no more reason to suppose that "phenomena" of this sort have mind-independent reality. It is a story, after all, and there are no guarantees that the story is accurate even if it takes itself to be an account of the external world.

But here things get tricky. Adams asks, "can they also be aggregates of substances?" He says "certainly." It is hard to see how. "They" must refer to those mental constructions that play a role in the story science tells. Could the mental constructions that play a role in the story science tells be aggregates of substances? No. His claim that they can be requires a shift of reference. Suddenly "they" – the things that can be aggregates of substances – are, not the mental constructions, but the "extended things" that those constructions purport to refer to in the external world. Of course such *things* might (with luck) be aggregates of substances. Things are mind-independent, just as the substances aggregated in them must be mind-independent. The mental constructions themselves, however, cannot be aggregates of substances.

Again, consider Adams's famous "glass fibers" case:

Suppose through a cleverly contrived network of glass fibers the images of a thousand different people walking, talking, and gesturing on a thousand different streets of a hundred different cities were combined to give you an image of an angry mob. This "mob," we might say, is an aggregate of real human beings, but the reality of the individual persons does not keep the mob as such from being a mere phenomenon.

(Ad 248)

There is a shift in meaning here – from 'mob' taken to designate a mind-dependent image to 'mob' taken to pick out a mind-independent "aggregate of real human beings." Speaking of her "image of an angry mob," someone might *say* "the mob is an aggregate of real human beings," but if she did, she would be speaking metaphorically. Anyone who understands the case would never consider real people as among the possible denizens of *that* mob. The "reality of the individual persons" can't affect the status of the mob-image because they belong to a different mob altogether. So equivocation spoils the proposed Compatibilism.

Equivocation also undermines Adams's proposed understanding of the Realist "Containment" claim – as reported by Paul Hoffman (1996, 113–15). Adams suggests that Leibniz's saying a substance is in a body might be akin to the claim that the historical Napoleon is in Tolstoy's *War and Peace*. Adams says it's not clear how to evaluate the "real person in a novel point," though he leans towards saying it is possible. He then writes, " . . . if you do think the actual Napoleon can be a character in a novel, why couldn't a real substance be an element of an intentional object?"

But 'in' in "real person in a novel" has a radically different meaning from 'in' in Leibniz's claim that there are "substances in a body." The hope that there might be some illuminating tie between the two "ins" is driven by Idealism. Adam's thought seems to be this. A novel is a mental, idea-like item. And if it can nevertheless have people in it, a mental phenomenon might also have real objects in *it*. But there is no need to search through ontological esoterica for some other meaning of 'in.' Doing so only takes one away from Leibniz's point.

Adams rightly notes that Leibniz himself sometimes advances Realist and Idealist accounts in the "same document." Indeed, in *nearly every* document. Adams takes such passages as evidence that "Leibniz seems to have regarded the two accounts as consistent" (Ad 260). He might have. Sometimes he appears to say so. But he certainly didn't have to. Theory-Pluralism holds that the appearance of the two accounts together is perfectly in order even if Leibniz deemed them inconsistent.

On another front, Rutherford offers, as evidence for his Compatibilism, this text sent to Princess Sophia in 1705:

> We can therefore conclude that a mass of matter is not truly a substance, that its unity is only ideal and that (leaving the understanding aside) it is only an aggregate, a collection, a multitude of an infinity of true substances, a well-founded phenomenon.
>
> (G 7, 564/Rd 222)

This fairly rare equivocation encourages Rutherford to assign Leibnizian bodies the two incompatible roles expounded in the last section. By exalting such texts, he is choosing in favor of the few equivocations and against many claims that would proscribe them. As noted in the detailed studies of Idealism and Realism, bodies that are "multitudes of an infinity of true substances" are almost always said to be real because they contain discrete unities, while a "well-founded phenomenon" is continuous and mind-dependent.

More recently, Paul Lodge (2001, 473) has advanced a less fully developed Compatibilism that is relevant here. He says Leibniz believes (based on G 2, 304) an aggregate "exists *only* if a mind exists and apprehends the relation that constitutes the essence of that aggregate." But, since that is not all that is required, Leibniz also believes (based on LA 96–7) "the being of an aggregate also depends on the being of the things from which it is aggregated." Lodge styles this a "univocal account of aggregates" (Lodge 2001 481) and claims for it "parsimony."

But, as 'aggregate' is given these two different meanings, the account is "univocal" in name only. In Lodge's words, "Leibniz's aggregates have a complex kind of being that is dependent upon the mind that aggregates and those things that are aggregated" (ibid. 483). This "complex kind of being" involves equivocation on 'aggregate.' For nothing could be so "complex" that it is two logically distinct things yet all the while is merely one thing – except through equivocation. As long as *that* is the kind of univocity this account has, it is, so to say, "univocally equivocal" and so *actually equivocal*. (An "absolutely relative" claim is, I suppose, relative.) Any gains in parsimony are more than lost in obfuscation, because each time 'aggregate' is used it is ambiguous and could mean a mind-dependent "apprehension-of-relations body" or a mind-independent "being-of-the-things-from-which-it-is-aggregated body."

In these texts Leibniz is talking about two different things – developing two different theories – despite his desire sometimes to appear to be talking about only one Truth. Lodge calls my reading "equivocal" (ibid. 484). But it is just clear and candid about the different meanings conveyed by 'aggregate' in the different theories. In the end *it* is more parsimonious because it explicitly disambiguates what is left ambiguous on Lodge's account.

In general on equivocation: allowing a fallacy would mean relinquishing one's philosophical resolve at the very point where it must be most unwaveringly firm. It would be equivalent to turning one's back on logic itself. Logic must be taken whole and entire, or not at all. One equivocation is one too many. Once allowed into the system, it spreads like a cancer and quickly ends up in the "lymph nodes" of argumentation. Thus if 'aggregate' can have two meanings, so can 'true': true and false!

With equivocation on board, it is hard to see how there could be any legitimate worry about inconsistency in Leibniz's thought, since that can arise only if logic remains fixed. Yet inconsistency is the worry Compatibilism tries to address.

7.1.4 No Leibniz's Law or Material Equivalence Problems

Compatibilism faces a severe uphill battle if it is committed to numerical identity between two objects that fail to share all their properties, or if it declares material equivalence between two items that have logically incompatible properties.

Leibniz's Law issues hound Rutherford's Compatibilism precisely because he takes the aggregate thesis literally when he writes,

> [B]odies are themselves pluralities of monads. For Leibniz, the term "body" does not refer merely to an appearance or phenomenal object.

Instead, a body *is* a plurality of monads, which happens to give the appearance of being an extended object when apprehended by other finite monads.

(Rd 218)

As Rutherford has confirmed in correspondence, this 'is' is the "'is' of identity." So the following objection applies. If extended bodies are "phenomenal objects" that are identical with pluralities of monads, an extended object will *per impossibile* be identical with a colony of unextended monads. Rutherford attributes this objection to a "confusion," but never says why it bespeaks confusion. The 'is' of identity demands that qualities on "each side" be identical. If the "appearance or phenomenal object" has a quality not possessable by "a plurality of monads," the identity claim must be abandoned. Nicholas Jolley (1995a, 19–20) and others (Hartz 1996, 76–8) have raised the objection and it remains unanswered.

To be sure, Compatibilism need not saddle itself with an identity between phenomena and aggregates of substances. It can settle for something weaker – say, material equivalence. Indeed, Adams takes that option.

Now I had pointed out that the Compatibilism in Adams's earlier article (1983, 246–7) could not defend its claim of material equivalence for phenomena and aggregates (Hartz 1992, 530–1). Adams's book withdraws the part of that claim that has to do with genuine continuity for bodies (Ad 233),[9] but reiterates the rest of the material equivalence without a reply (Ad 260). In particular, Adams is still claiming that x is a "coherent, harmonious phenomenon" iff x is an "aggregate of real things" (Ad 260).[10]

But a "coherent, harmonious phenomenon" is wholly mind-dependent, while an "aggregate of substances" whose reality (quoting Adams, 260) "consists at least partly in the reality of the substances that are aggregated in them" is (at least partly) mind-independent. Similarly, if phenomena and "aggregates of Fs" are materially equivalent, they would have to share the same ontological status – which is clearly impossible given that the Fs are here supposed to be giving some of their reality to the aggregates of Fs, while the phenomenon, in its little mental home, is necessarily isolated from all of the Fs and can't receive any reality from them. On two counts, then, the material equivalence fails.

Those two gloves are still on the ground.

7.1.5 Consistent with the Continuum Doctrine

Another glove thrown down in 1992 is still there. This concerns the continuum doctrine, according to which phenomena are continuous (divisible) but bodies are discrete (actually divided into substances). A Compatibilist is committed to identifying or declaring a material equivalence between phenomena and bodies, and that seems a direct violation of the doctrine.

In his earlier article, Adams said that "the aggregate as such can have the mathematical structure of continuity" (1983, 242). He mentions a passage (G 2, 282/L 539) in which Leibniz says an aggregate of substances cannot be continuous, noting that it is problematic because Leibniz there "appears to have forgotten his doctrine that aggregates, even aggregates of real things, are phenomena" (1983, 242). I criticized this by arguing that the passage is exemplary in its defense of the continuum doctrine. It declares that "in actual bodies there is only a discrete quantity" while "continuous quantity is something ideal" involving "indeterminate parts" while, by contrast, "there is nothing indefinite in actual things, in which every division is made that can be made" (Hartz 1992, 535–6). This is one of the many passages where Leibniz is *not* equivocating on 'aggregate.' Again, relying on equivocations to effect the Compatibilism makes Adams pay a high textual cost. Indeed, Adams's argument should go the other way round. In the few equivocation passages he "appears to have forgotten" his doctrine of the continuum, and that is a reason to doubt them rather than the many continuum texts.

In his later book, Adams changes his position in light of such texts. He writes that just as shape is only an apparent property of bodies, "I think Leibniz probably ought to hold that bodies only *appear* to be continuous" (Ad 233). That seems at first glance to solve the problem. But the "bodies" mentioned here are, within Adams's Compatibilism, phenomena. And it is unclear that there can be an appearance/reality distinction for phenomena. Could a phenomenon – in Adams's distinctive terms, the representational content of some idea – merely appear some way, but not actually be that way?[11]

If not, the distinction collapses, and the claim that "bodies only appear to be continuous" is equivalent to the original offender: "bodies are continuous." The old problem remains.

7.1.6 *Fully Integrated with the Doctrine of Animals*

There must be a good fit between one's metaphysic of aggregates and one's story about animals. In general, when one phenomenalizes aggregates, one severely handicaps the doctrine of animals.[12] Reducing substances of any sort – simple or corporeal – to mere mental contents is anathema on any reading of Leibniz. But if one element of corporeal substances is their organic bodies – which are just fancy aggregates – a real problem arises concerning how one is going to keep animals from taking up residence only in the mind. They too will become well-founded phenomena or appearances or mental constructions. And that is precisely the wrong story about animals, according to a multitude of texts – see 8.3.

One is rightly bewildered at this metaphysic. It has labored to show aggregates are appearances in minds, only to discover that Leibniz assigns those aggregates a key compositional role in animals – a role they cannot perform if they are appearances in minds.

I will postpone detailed discussion of "Compatibilist animals" until after I have expounded the mature doctrine of animals in Chapter 8. But even at first glance one can see plenty of trouble brewing on the horizon.

7.2 Compatibilism as an Interpretation

Compatibilism will never be a successful interpretation. That two of the best Leibniz commentators of recent times have failed to articulate a coherent version is more than suggestive. The logical barriers are simply too formidable. Since it can't be done, I suggest we stop trying.

It is hard to overestimate the effect of a Compatibilist collapse on Leibniz scholarship generally. Before it had been given a serious try, Compatibilism of this Idealist sort remained a viable alternative as a way of salvaging Leibniz's rationality while remaining textually inclusive. Now its failure closes the door irrevocably on that option. Since any "Realist Compatibilism" would likely meet a similar fate – making a hash of Idealism in pursuit of defending Realism – we seem thrown back on despair. "Is there then no coherent interpretation of Leibniz's philosophy?"

Theory-Pluralism rescues us from this precipice. For, unlike any of the other remaining Incompatibilist options, it explains how inconsistency is not a threat to coherence. Let the theories be as incompatible as the Ptolemaic and Copernican ones are: both can be held rationally so long as they are regarded as mere hypotheses.

Still, having seen their stories on aggregates, it will be well to see how Idealism and Realism fare on the question of animals.

8 Animals

The doctrine of animals (also called "corporeal substances" or "composite substances") in Leibniz has not attracted as much scholarly attention as that of aggregates. Commentators have tended to be dismissive of animals for various reasons.[1] But a main reason for their unpopularity is that they would compete with monads for the premier privilege of being substances. From the beginning to the end of Leibniz's mature period, substancehood is supposed to be reserved for indivisible things, and it seems the only such things, in a post-Cartesian universe, are purely spiritual.[2] Thus, even when Leibniz was operating without monads explicitly in mind, there is an attempt on the part of some commentators to see the monads in embryo form all the way back in the early DM and LA.

Thus, R. C. Sleigh, Jr. suggests that the "theory at which Leibniz ultimately arrived" is "the monadological theory." Here "the only substances in concreto are soul-like entities – the monads." Moreover, according to Sleigh, in that theory "corporeal substances are substances by courtesy. In the end, they must yield to phenomenalistic analysis of some sort" (1990, 100). He adds, "[A]ll things considered, the account of extension offered in the *Discourse* [DM] and the correspondence [with Arnauld] is closer to the monadological theory than any version of the corporeal substance theory" (1990, 101).[3]

Despite Idealist attempts to find the monadology hidden in earlier works, many of Leibniz's references to animals cannot be transformed into proto-monadological meditations. Since that is a minority opinion at the moment, more time than usual will be spent here establishing the textual base for the claim.

A look at the Doctrine Tables gives one an initial idea of the situation. Animals receive 7 endorsements in *Discourse on Metaphysics*, and 44 in the Arnauld letters. Further along in the mature period animals make a significant appearance – 13 times in the *New System*, 14 in the De Volder exchange selections, and 23 in the *Monadology* of 1714.

Those numbers alone cry out for explanation. First, while DM says very little about animals and probably best approximates an Idealist "manifesto," LA is saturated with explicit references to them. Yet both works are supposed, as Sleigh says, to be "closer" to the monadological theory than any animals-theory. If that is so, there are a *lot* of texts in LA to explain away. Second, if, as Sleigh says, Leibniz ultimately ended up at the "monadological theory" where animals have mere "courtesy appointments," why does he never seem to *arrive* there? 1714 is nearly the end of his life. And there is no hope of a "deathbed conversion" to pure monadology, since passages written after that upholds non-courtesy substancehood for animals just as does the *Monadology* itself.

A few of the texts not covered in the Tables are the following.

In 1698 Leibniz responds to Bernoulli's question about when, in dividing an aggregate, one arrives at a substance instead of simply another smaller aggregate. He writes, "I respond that such things present themselves immediately and even without subdivision, and that every animal is such a thing" (GM 3, 542/AG 168). Idealism predicts he would say, "every soul is such a thing," but that's not what is there. Instead he unblushingly says animals are indivisible – that is, have the marks of full substancehood – despite their apparent divisibility. This is more than suggestive since indivisible substances are most often in the spotlight in DM and LA.

Evidence of the full substantial status of brutes is evident again in a passage from 1712: "A substance is either simple, such as a soul, which has no parts, or it is composite, such as an animal, which consists of a soul and an organic body" (C 13/PW 175). In 1714 he adds that "Each monad, together with a particular body, makes up a living substance" (PNG 4). And a few sections later there is this: "[N]ot only souls, but also animals cannot be generated and cannot perish" (PNG 6). In these texts, souls and animals are equally substances, fully and unproblematically on a par.

I will leave the matter there for now. In this chapter I will look in detail at the texts and try to find a place for animals in the mature metaphysic – all the while preserving the critique of extension. It is a tall order, but it can be done.

8.1 A Look Back at Aggregates

And *secondary matter* (e.g. an organic body) is not a substance, but ... a mass of many substances, like a pond full of fish, or a flock of sheep; and consequently it is what is called an *unum per accidens* – in a word, a phenomenon. A true substance (such as an animal) is composed of an immaterial soul and an organic body, and it is the compound of these two that is called an *unum per se* ... [T]he metaphysical union of the soul and its body ... makes them compose an *unum per se*, an animal, a living being.

G. W. Leibniz, 4 November 1715, to Remond (G 3, 657–8/R 226/Rd 287)

This quotation is remarkable because it shows that, as interesting and important as it is in its own right, the account of aggregates is all along intended to be on its way to something further. That "something further" is the doctrine of animals. And it is only a Realist construal of aggregates that can capture what is intended in these references to "secondary matter" or "a mass of many substances." Since the aggregates it envisages are real and mind-independent, they can take on the task assigned them in the next step – namely, constituting animals when fancy ones ("organic bodies") combine with souls (also called "dominant monads" "substantial forms," or "entelechies").

This quotation is not unusual. There is no doubt that this dovetailing of the Realist theory of aggregates with the account of animals was his principal vision. Indeed, my earlier efforts to combine the theories of aggregates and animals was made possible only by Realist themes (Hartz 1992).[4]

The Idealist way with aggregates is a non-starter in this scheme. For it pins aggregates in minds, and that makes nonsense of the claim that aggregates will provide bodies for animals. Indeed, *the doctrine of animals is the Idealist's most unforgiving nemesis.* Everything in it is threatening to Idealism, which is typically forced into a rather extreme Exclusivism as a result. One sees evidence of this narrowness in the Well-Founded Phenomena account, which features only monads. By contrast, Realism's more generous and inclusive category of "Substances" takes it that a substance might be (i) a monad *or* (ii) an animal which, while itself composed of monads, re-enters the picture to help compose "higher-order" animals. In this scheme, animals play a key role – in the end nearly overshadowing the monads because of their pervasive presence in it.

Throughout the chapters on aggregates Idealist analyses struggled for explanatory adequacy when compared with the Realist accounts. Now the Idealist theory must endure the final crushing blow: it presents an impassible roadblock to understanding Leibniz's own vision of the universe.

In completing that vision, I will carry forward only the accounts of aggregates that can function within the doctrine of animals.

Somewhat surprisingly, one of the Idealist analyses will, with some work, serve that purpose. Recall that the mainstream "Comprehensive Well-Founded Phenomena" account had the luxury of recognizing two different aggregates: p (the mind-dependent phenomenon) and the "monadic aggregate" – a mind-independent collection of monads that quasi-causes or well-founds p. The monadic aggregate can provide a mind-independent body (of sorts) for mind-independent animals.

Among the Realist analyses, the Comprehensive Rigid Embodiment analysis will serve nicely here because its conditions can easily be adapted to accommodate Leibniz's requirements for organic bodyhood. It helps explain how mind-independent animals have mind-independent aggregates as their bodies.

I turn now to Leibniz's doctrine of animals and the texts on which it is based. After that, the two analyses will be applied to it.

8.2 The Mature Doctrine and its Critics

Leibnitz's theory certainly appears more comprehensive and more consistent if we leave out of account all the statements that affirm the substantial nature of a composite body or the possibility of a *substantia corporea*, i.e., of a *substance composée*.

J. E. Erdmann (1891, 2: 189)

Though everything in the [simple theory] ... is to be found in Leibniz, there are many other passages which lead to a totally different theory. This theory is to be rejected, I think, because it is wholly inconsistent with Leibniz's general philosophy. In this other theory, mind and body together make one substance, having a true unity. The mind makes the body into a *unum per se*, instead of a mere aggregate. ... My theory is substantially that of Erdmann. ...

Bertrand Russell (R 149–50, 154)

While the simple substances alone are real they appear as phenomena in groups or aggregates, which we call compound substances. The Monads are not *really* grouped or combined; the aggregation is purely phenomenal. We must not forget the essential difference between simple and compound substance. The former alone is really substance: the latter, in so far as it differs from the former, is merely substance by courtesy or common usage. Strictly speaking 'compound substance,' according to Leibniz, is not 'substance' at all.

Robert Latta (1898, 109–10; 406)

I]t is clear enough that for Leibniz the only substances are the monads. ... [H]e uses the term "composite substance" to apply to [aggregates of individuals].

Benson Mates (1986, 194–5)

Leibniz's deep metaphysics ... is the metaphysics of monads, in which all other beings, including living creatures, are no more than "phenomena" and "results."

Donald Rutherford (Rd 282)

That is a formidable battery of quotations. They underscore the depth and pervasiveness of Idealism and its dismissal of animals.

Despite such interpretations, I want to accept animals into Leibniz's system. I accord animals a fundamental, rigorous, serious status. They are viewed as substances on all fours with, but distinct from, monads. That makes them mind-independent – hence not "phenomena." There will be a sustained attempt to understand the complex conditions that must hold for an animal to exist. In particular, I aspire to clarify the relationship between monads and animals. As noted in the last section, I will be applying the "Well-Founded Phenomena" and "Rigid Embodiment" analyses to them.

While much has been written about animals over the years and a welcome resurgence of interest is apparent today, there are few detailed attempts to say how they fit into the mature metaphysics. Idealist dismissals have only encouraged people to avoid them. The work of Robert M. Adams – 1983 and Ad – is a welcome exception. He has tried very hard to spell out exactly where and how, if at all, animals fit in. My own study of animals owes much to his pioneering studies.

Stated abstractly, Leibniz's view of animals is that they are composites of a very special sort. The formulations vary widely, as a survey of the texts in the next section reveals. But the principal theme is that two things combine to form an animal (also referred to as a "living thing," "corporeal substance," "composite substance," or "one machine"):

1 A dominant substance (also "dominant monad," "soul," "entelechy," or "substantial form"); and
2 Some subordinate substances (also "subordinate monads," "secondary matter," an "organic body," "organic machine," a "mass" or "natural machine").

Dr. Frankenstein's "monster body," while it is still a mere collection of organs harvested from charnel-houses, is a vivid example of a natural machine. Each organ and cell is itself a separate, lesser machine. Those machines also have their own constituent machines – at the limit bottoming out on monadic machines. Until the "dull yellow eye of the creature opens" (Shelley 1969, 57: chapter 5), the body remains a fancy aggregate, all ready to go but not yet knighted.

In terms of current discussion, the position as described here is a "two substance theory" (Ad 265–9).[5] That is, animals – "corporeal substances" – are a second, different kind of substance in addition to monads, or "simple substances." Thus, in order to create Adam, God performs two logically separate acts: "first" he makes the monads, "then" he combines some of them with a special dominant rational monad to form the animal, Adam.

One standard way of keeping animals from adding a "second substance" to the metaphysics and thus interfering with a broadly Idealist "one substance monadology" is to relegate beasts to a particular time period.[6] For instance, in 1989 Catherine Wilson wrote that "around 1703 he stopped actively trying to reconcile monads and corporeal substance" because, as he told Des Bosses in 1712, corporeal substances could be safely "rejected" in a "fundamental investigation of things" [G 2, 450/L 604[7]] (Wilson 1989, 192–94; her position has since changed – see Hartz and Wilson, forthcoming). Sleigh also leans heavily on the same text to turn back Leibniz's claims elsewhere – he mentions two places[8] – that animals are genuine substances.

Of the favored 1712 passage Sleigh claims, "Leibniz had put his metaphysical cards on the table" (1990, 110).

But the entire weight of this position rests on a single isolated text, and it's not clear it can bear it. Indeed, the degree of isolation is accentuated by a careful reading of the texts in the next section (8.3). It (appearing there as text 31) is the only spot in the corpus I've been able to find where Leibniz says he is going to set aside or reject animals. In regard to this text, it is perhaps most telling that, as Sleigh recognizes, Leibniz ends up reinstating animals when he later (in 1715) sends a chart to Des Bosses (see text 35). So it is at best a standoff within this single exchange. If Leibniz was "putting his metaphysical cards on the table," he was quick to pick them up again.

Of course, even if the text was accepted, it would do little to show Leibniz rejected corporeal substances altogether, for he often said that "ultimate explanations" require only simple substances. Yet he does not, like the commentators, take these statements as endorsements of *Exclusive* Idealism. Working from G 7, 502, Massimo Mugnai writes, "*In the last analysis*, it is quite correct to say that everything is resoluble into simple substances and aggregates." Still, corporeal substances "play a significant role" within the system because they are themselves "combinations of pre-existing elements" – that is, of monads and aggregates (Mugnai, forthcoming, 6). Comparison with other texts confirms this practice. For instance, text 32 in 8.3 shows Leibniz saying that while he recognizes simple and composite substances, "in the end there are simple substances alone" (C 14/PW 175). Also, in the famous passage to De Volder written in 1704 (G 2, 270/L 537) he says "considering the matter carefully," one can say there is "nothing in things except simple substances." Apparently Leibniz takes this to be compatible with a commitment to animals, since a year earlier he had sent to De Volder an explicit statement about animals, distinguishing them clearly from monads (the text appears as number 22 in 8.3 – G 2, 252/L 530–1).

It is important to see how much of a Theory-Pluralist Leibniz proves himself to be. The endorsements of animals are casually – with no apparent hand-wringing – placed alongside endorsements of monads. He does not choose between them, but does drop a few hints about how animals might be seen as in the end composed of monads.

The search for a specific "date of passage" away from animals has continued among commentators intent on cleaning up the mature thought. J. A. Cover and John Hawthorne[9] have recently set the date at 1706. For it was then that Leibniz gave up the idea that harmony between substances can "ground *per se* unity" (Cover and O'Leary-Hawthorne 1999, 53). They also mention, in this connection, the notorious "substantial bond" doctrine, discussed only with Des Bosses.[10] This bond – likened by these authors to what unifies animals – was at best tentatively endorsed. By implication, animals should also have received a tentative endorsement. In the end, they write, "the introduction of composite corporeal substances seems to us rather a botch" (ibid. 53) which "we choose to ignore" (ibid. 55). It is an "affair" which "represents an ill-considered and not especially serious meta-physical commitment" or "some wayward thinking on Leibniz's part" (ibid. 54), while the monads-only ontology is "what Leibniz ought to have thought and what from 1706 on Leibniz – flirtations with the *vinculum substantiale* aside – did think" (ibid. 54). Again, regarding the comments about animals as an "affair" presumes a short-lived, episodic adventure that soon came to an end.

In light of these claims from some of the most distinguished commentators, it is clear that the textual picture needs to be examined systematically. Without this, one can be given the impression that the textual cost of ignoring animals is negligible. Sleigh lists two problematic texts; Latta and Mates (in the epigraph) make it sound as if Leibniz always takes animals to be aggregates of monads. Cover and Hawthorne – like Erdmann and Russell before them – do better on this score. They hold that, while there are many texts, they contain philosophically second-rate thoughts.

So I will present the relevant passages largely unedited, and ordered when possible by date. They must be cited because the burden of proof rests squarely on me to show that Leibniz held animals to be substances in their own right throughout the mature period. This "gallery" will move some readers, but not all. The Erdmann/Russell/Cover-Hawthorne position, for instance, will find it regrettable that Leibniz was "wayward" so often, but his being wide of the mark so much does not mean the claims should be taken seriously.

Let me hasten to add that reading these texts carefully is an option, not a requirement for understanding the analyses to follow. Indeed, regardless of one's attitude towards animals, this chapter is well worth reading through because it turns out that, arguably, his holding them to be substances is not a botch.

8.3 The Principal Mature Texts

[Kant] gives licence for seeing beyond what the philosopher actually said, to what he really meant to say.

It seems unlikely, though, that a philosopher did not mean to say what he said, when he said it over and over again.

Rae Langton (1998, 1)

If, as Langton says, one finds Leibniz "over and over again" claiming that there are animals, one can only assume that he meant to say there are animals.

This collection of texts is not exhaustive. No one can claim to have an exhaustive listing on any topic until all of Leibniz's papers have been properly edited – and that will take at least another fifty years. Even among the known works, I have left out a few passages.

As the passages move from 1686 to 1716, there is an evident change from broadly Aristotelian language to more monadological terms – though

Leibniz often will try to identify one with the other.[11] (Thus "primitive passive power" is sometimes said to be equivalent to "prime matter" – e.g., G 2 252/L 530.) That is, the terminology of "substantial forms" or "entelechies" or "souls" joining with matter to form corporeal substances is used prior to the advent of monads (around 1698). After that this terminology is often used alongside the construal according to which dominant monads supervise the subordinate monads in an "organic" or "natural" body, thereby forming an animal.

The texts are as follows:

(1) Assuming that the bodies that make up an *unum per se*, as does man, are substances, that they have substantial forms, and that animals have souls, we must admit that these souls and these substantial forms cannot entirely perish. ... For no substance perishes, although it can become completely different.
(1686, DM 34: A VI 4 B, 1583 (N. 306)/AG 65)

(2) [E]ither there are no corporeal substances and bodies are merely phenomena ... or ... in all corporeal substances there is something analogous to the soul, which old authors called a form or species.
(c. 1686, A Specimen of Discoveries, G 7, 314/PW 81)

(3) *A corporeal substance can neither arise nor perish except by creation or annihilation.*
(c. 1689, Principia Logico-Metaphysica, or "Primary Truths," A VI 4 B
1649 (N. 325): C 523/PW 92/AG 34)

(4) From the Correspondence with Arnauld

(a) The soul, however, is nevertheless the form of its body, because it is an expression of the phenomena of all other bodies in accordance with the relationship to its own. ... If the body is a substance and not a simple phenomenon like the rainbow, nor an entity united by accident or by aggregation like a heap of stones, it cannot consist of extension, and one must necessarily conceive of something there that one calls substantial form, and which corresponds in a way to the soul.
(4/14 July 1686, LA 58)

(b) Substantial unity requires a complete, indivisible, and naturally indestructible entity, since its concept embraces everything that is to happen to it, which cannot be found in shape or in motion ... but in a soul or substantial form after the example of what one calls *self*. These are the only truly complete entities. ... I cannot say with certainty whether there are genuine corporeal substances other than the animate ones, but at least souls are useful in providing us by analogy with some knowledge of the others.

I accord substantial forms to all corporeal substances that are more than mechanically united. ... if there are no corporeal substances such as I can accept, it follows that bodies will be no more than true phenomena like the rainbow.

(28 November/8 December 1686, LA 76–7)

(c) But if one considers as the matter of a corporeal substance not formless mass but a secondary matter which is the multiplicity of substances of which the mass is that of the total body, it may be said that these substances are parts of this matter, just as those which enter into our body form part of it, for as our body is the matter, and the soul is the form of our substance, it is the same with other corporeal substances. ... It is true that the whole which has a genuine unity can remain strictly the same individual, although it loses or gains parts, as we experience in ourselves; thus the parts are only temporarily immediate requisites.

(9 October 1687, LA 119–20)

(d) [A]ssuming there is a soul or entelechy in animals or other corporeal substances, one must argue from it on this point as we all argue from man who is an entity endowed with a genuine unity conferred on him by his soul, notwithstanding the fact that the mass of his body is divided into organs, vessels, humors, spirits, and that the parts are undoubtedly full of an infinite number of other corporeal substances endowed with their own entelechies.

(9 October 1687, LA 120)

(e) ... I think I have shown that every substance is indivisible and consequently every corporeal substance must have a soul or at least an entelechy which is analogous to the soul, since otherwise bodies would be no more than phenomena.

(9 October 1687, LA 121)

(f) [E]very substance contains in its present state all its states past and future, and even expresses the whole universe according to its point of view ... and in particular according to the connection with the parts of its body, of which it is a more immediate expression; and consequently nothing occurs to it except from its own depths and by virtue of its own laws. ... As for corporeal substances, I maintain that mass, when one considers only what in it is divisible, is a pure phenomenon, that every substance has a genuine unity, in metaphysical rigor, and that it cannot be divided, engendered, or corrupted, that the whole of matter must be full of substances animate or at least living.

(9 October 1687, LA 126)

(g) [T]here must be everywhere in the body indivisible substances, which cannot be engendered or corrupted, having something corresponding to souls. [A]ll these substances have always been and will always be united to organic bodies capable of being transformed in various ways. [E]ach of these substances contains in its nature the law by which the series of its operations continues, and all that has happened and will happen to it. All its actions come from its own depths, except for dependence on God. [T]he union of soul and body ... consists only of that perfect mutual harmony deliberately set up by the order of the first creation, by virtue of which every substance according to its own laws, acts in harmony with what the others require.

(23 March 1690, LA 135–6)

(5) [T]he organic bodies of substances included in any mass of matter are parts of that mass. So in a fish pond there are many fishes and the liquid in each fish is, in turn, a certain kind of fish pond which contains, as it were, other fishes or animals of their own kinds; and so on to infinity. And therefore there are substances everywhere in matter just as points are everywhere in a line. And just as there is no portion of a line in which there are not an infinite number of points, there is no portion of matter in which there are not an infinite number of substances. But just as a point is not a part of a line, but a line in which there is a point is such a part, so also a soul is not a part of matter, but a body in which there is a soul is such a part of matter. [I]f the animal is conceived of as a thing having parts, that is, as a body divisible and destructible, endowed with a soul, then it must be conceded that the animal is part of matter, since every part of matter has parts. But it cannot then be conceded that it is a substance or an indestructible thing. And it is the same for man. For if a man is the I itself, then he cannot be divided, nor can he perish, nor is he a homogeneous part of matter. But if by the name 'man' one understands that which perishes, then a man would be part of matter, whereas that which is truly indestructible would be called 'soul,' 'mind,' or 'I,' which would not be a part of matter.

(March 1690, Notes on Fardella, A VI 4 B, 1671 (N. 329): Leibniz
1857, 322–3/AG 105)

(6) [I]t is necessary that what constitutes corporeal substance is something which corresponds to what in us is called 'me,' which is indivisible and yet active: for being indivisible and without parts it will not be a being by aggregation, but being active it will be something substantial. There is reason to think that there is something similar in animals, which makes them capable of sensation and which is called their soul. In fact it seems that in every kind of organic species, there must be something which corresponds to the soul, and which philosophers have called a substantial form ... . But even if we do not want to say anything

definite about animals, plants or any other species in particular, we must still recognize in general that everything has to be full of such species, which contain in themselves a principle of true unity which is analogous to the soul, and which is joined to some kind of organized body. Otherwise we would find nothing substantial in matter, and bodies would only be phenomena or like very orderly dreams.

(c. 1694, Draft of NS, G 4, 473/WF 23)

(7) For, since every *substance* which has a genuine unity can begin or end only by a miracle, it follows that they can come into being only by creation and end only by annihilation. It is natural, then, that an animal, since it has always been living and organized ... should always remain so.

(1695, NS 4, 7, G 4, 479, 481/WF 12, 14)

(8) [M]atter without souls and forms or entelechies is purely passive, and souls without matter would be purely active. A complete corporeal substance, which is really one – what the School calls *unum per se* (as opposed to a being by aggregation) – must result from an active principle of unity, and also from a mass of the kind which makes up a multitude, and which would be solely passive if it contained only primary matter. By contrast, secondary matter, or the mass which makes up our body, contains parts throughout, all of which are themselves complete substances because they are other animals, or organic substances, which are individually animated or active. But the collection of these corporeal organized substances which makes up our body is united with our soul only by the relation which arises between the sequences of phenomena which develop from the nature of each separate substance. And all of that shows how one can say on the one hand that the soul and the body are independent of each other, and on the other hand that the one is incomplete without the other, since the one is never naturally without the other. [S]o far as plants, animals, and all kinds of living thing in general are concerned there is reason to believe that just as soon as the body is truly organic in itself the soul is united to it, and that death can naturally strip away from the soul only some of the grosser parts of its organic body.

(c. 1694, "Supplement to the Explanation of the New System," G 4 572–3/WF 138–9)

(9) All bodies are actually divided into an infinite number of parts, so that if there were nothing but extension in bodies, there would not be corporeal substance, nothing of which one could say "Here is truly one substance." For all corporeal mass is an aggregate of other masses, and those of others, and so on to infinity. Thus bodies would be reduced to pure appearances if they had in themselves only extension or a multitude, and nothing in which there was a principle of true unity.

(c. 1694, to Alberti, G 7, 444)

(10) [T]he number of simple substances which make up a mass, however small that mass may be, is infinite, since in addition to the soul which constitutes the real unity of an animal, the body of a sheep (for example) is actually subdivided: that is to say, it too is an assemblage of invisible animals or plants, which themselves are also compounded, in addition to also having that which makes up their own real unity.

(1695, Reply to Foucher, G 4, 492/WF 46/AG 147)

(11) I believe that it is not properly the matter which is sensitive, since this is nothing but an aggregate of substances rather than one substance, but that it is rather the corporeal substance, which always has something analogous to feeling and life, being provided with an organic matter as well as a soul or if you will, a form.

(December 1696, to Billettes, G 7, 453/L 473)

(12) [T]he soul ... must express what happens, and indeed what will happen, in its body, and, because of the connection or correspondence of all the parts of the world, it must also express in some way what happens in all the others.

(July 1698, Clarification for Bayle, G 4, 523/WF 84–5/L 496)

(13) (3) You ask me to divide for you a portion of mass into the substances of which it is composed. I respond, there are as many individual substances in it as there are animals or living things or things analogous to them. (4) What I call a complete monad or individual substance is not so much the soul, as it is the animal itself, or something analogous to it, endowed with a soul or form and an organic body. (5) You ask how far one must proceed in order to have something that is a substance, and not substances. I respond that such things present themselves immediately and even without subdivision, and that every animal is such a thing. For none of us is composed of the parts of our bodies. (6) You fear that matter is composed of that which is not quantitative. I respond, it is no more composed of souls than it is composed of points.

(20/30 September 1698, to Bernoulli, GM 3, 542/AG 167–8)

(14) [T]he active is incomplete without the passive, and the passive without the active ... It has long seemed ridiculous to me to suppose that the nature of things has ... provided souls only to ... human bodies ... when it could have provided them to all bodies ... I do not believe there is any minimal animal or living being, that there is any without an organic body, or any whose body is not, in turn, divided into many substances. [T]here are animals in the world as much greater than ours as ours are greater than the ani-

malcules of the microscopists, for nature knows no limits. And so it is possible . . . that there should be worlds not inferior to our own in beauty and variety, in the smallest motes of dust, in fact, in atoms. And ... nothing prevents animals from passing over into such worlds by dying. For I am of the opinion that death is nothing but the contraction of an animal, as generation is nothing but its unfolding.

> (18 November 1698, to Bernoulli, GM 3, 551-3/L 511-13/
> AG 168-9)

(15)   In bodies I distinguish corporeal substance from matter, and I distinguish primary from secondary matter. Secondary matter is an aggregate or composite of several corporeal substances, as a flock is composed of several animals. But each animal and each plant is also a corporeal substance, having in itself a principle of unity which makes it truly a substance and not an aggregate. And this principle of unity is that which one calls soul, or it is something analogous to the soul. But, besides the principle of unity, corporeal substance has its mass or its secondary matter, which is, again, an aggregate of other smaller corporeal substances – and that goes to infinity. However, primitive matter, or matter taken in itself is what we conceive in bodies when we set aside all the principles of unity, that is, it is what is passive, from which arise two qualities: resistance, and tardiness or inertia. ... Thus one can say that matter in itself, besides extension, contains a primitive, passive power. But the principle of unity contains the primitive active power, or the primitive force, which can never be destroyed and always persists in the exact order of its internal modifications, which represent those outside it. As a result, that which is essentially passive cannot receive the modification of thought without receiving, at the same time, some substantial active principle which would be joined to it; and, consequently, matter considered apart cannot think, but nothing prevents active principles or principles of unity, which are found everywhere in matter, and which already essentially contain a kind of perception, from being elevated to the degree of perception that we call thought. Thus even though matter in itself cannot think, nothing prevents corporeal substance from thinking.

> (1699, Draft to Burnett, G 3, 260–1 (also at 157–8)/
> AG 289–90)

(16)   When I say that the soul or entelechy cannot do anything to the body, then by the body I mean, not the corporeal substance whose entelechy it is, which is one substance, but the aggregate of other corporeal substances that constitute our organs; for one substance

cannot influence another, and therefore not an aggregate of others. So I mean this: whatever happens in the mass or aggregate of substances according to mechanical laws, the same thing is expressed in the soul or entelechy [or if you prefer, in the monad itself or the one simple substance constituted by both activity and passivity] by its own laws. But the force of change in any substance is from itself or its own entelechy. [Remark in brackets presumably was not sent to De Volder]

(9 January 1700, to De Volder, G 2, 205–6/Ad 283)

(17)   This substance, of course, is one *per se*, and not a mere aggregate of many substances, for there is a great difference between an animal, for example, and a flock. And further, this entelechy is either a soul or something analogous to a soul, and always naturally activated some organic body, which, taken separately, indeed, set apart or removed from the soul, is not one substance but an aggregate of many, in a word, a machine of nature.

   Moreover, a natural machine has the great advantage over an artificial machine, that ... it is made up of an infinity of entangled organs. And thus, a natural machine can never be absolutely destroyed just as it can never absolutely begin, but it only decreases or increases, enfolds or unfolds, always preserving, to a certain extent, the very substance itself and, however transformed, preserving in itself some degree of life.

(May 1702, *On Body and Force*, G 4, 395–6/AG 252–3)

(18)   I am inclined to believe that all finite immaterial substances ... are joined to organs and accompany matter and even that souls or active forms are found everywhere. And to constitute a complete substance matter cannot dispense with them, since force and action are found everywhere in it.

(1702, *On What is Independent of Sense and Matter*, G 6, 507/L 552)

(19)   [I]f someone says that force and perception are essential to matter, he is taking matter as the complete corporeal substance, which includes form and matter, or soul together with organs.

(1702, to Queen Sophie Charlotte, G 6, 506/AG 191)

(20)   I have shown that the soul with its functions is something distinct from matter but that it nevertheless is always accompanied by material organs and also that the soul's functions are always accompanied by organic functions which must correspond to them and that this relation is reciprocal and always will be.

[N]ot only particular souls but animals themselves subsist and there is no reason for believing in a complete extinction of souls or even a complete destruction of the animal.

(1702, *Reflections on a Single Universal Spirit*, G 6, 533, 535/
L 556, 558)

(21)   Matter (I mean here secondary matter, or a mass) is not a substance, but substances, like a flock of sheep, or a lake full of fish. I count as corporeal substances only nature's machines, which have souls or something analogous; otherwise there would be no true unity.

In all corporeal substances I recognize two primitive powers, namely entelechy or primitive active power, which is the soul in animals and mind in man, and which in general is the substantial form of the ancients; and also first matter, or primitive passive power, which produces resistance. So properly speaking it is the entelechy which acts, and matter which is acted on; but one without the other is not a complete substance.

(22 March 1703, to Jaquelot, G 3, 457–8/WF 200–1)

(22)   When I say that even if it is corporeal, a substance contains an infinity of machines, I think it must be added at the same time that it forms one machine composed of these machines and that it is actuated, besides, by one entelechy, without which it would contain no principle of true unity.

If you think of mass as an aggregate containing many substances, you can still conceive of a single pre-eminent substance or primary entelechy in it. For the rest, I arrange in the monad or the simple substance, complete with an entelechy, only one primitive passive force which is related to the whole mass of the organic body. The other subordinate monads placed in the organs do not make up a part of it, though they are immediately required by it, and they combine with the primary monad to make the organic corporeal substance, or the animal or plant. I therefore distinguish: (1) the primitive entelechy or soul; (2) primary matter or primitive passive power; (3) the complete monad formed by these two; (4) mass or secondary matter, or the organic machine in which innumerable subordinate monads concur; and (5) the animal or corporeal substance which the dominating monad makes into one machine.

(20 June 1703, to De Volder, G 2, 250, 252/L 530–1)

(23)   From the *New Essays* (1703–1705)

(a) Organization or configuration alone, without an enduring principle of life which I call 'monad,' would not suffice to make something remain numerically the same, i.e. the same individual. ... [O]rganic bodies as well as others remain 'the same' only in appearance, and not strictly speaking. It is rather like a river whose water is continually changing, or like Theseus's ship which the Athenians were constantly repairing. But as for substances which possess in themselves a genuine, real, substantial unity ... one can rightly say that they remain perfectly 'the same individual' in virtue of this soul or spirit which makes the *I* in substances which think. If plants and brutes have no souls, then their identity is only apparent, but if they do have souls their identity is strictly genuine, although their organic bodies do not retain such an identity. ... In fact, an organic body does not remain the same for more than a moment; it only remains equivalent. ... [A] single individual substance can retain its identity only by preservation of the same soul.

(NE 231–2)

(b) *I* and *he* are without parts, since ... he continues to exist as really the same substance, the same physical *I*; but we cannot say – with complete fidelity to the truth of things – that the same whole continues to exist if a part of it is lost. And what has bodily parts cannot avoid losing some of them at every moment. ... [S]ouls are not 'indifferent to any parcel of matter', as it seems to you that they are; on the contrary they inherently express those portions with which they are and must be united in an orderly way. ... I would not wish to maintain that my finger is part of *me*; but it is true that it belongs to me and is a part of my body.

(NE 238, 240–41)

(c) There is reason to think that there is an infinity of souls, or more generally of primary entelechies, possessing something analogous to perception and appetite, and that all of them are and forever remain substantial forms of bodies. ... [T]he soul and the machine ... agree perfectly. Though they have no immediate influence on each other, they mutually express each other, the one having concentrated into a perfect unity everything which the other has dispersed throughout its multiplicity.

(NE 318)

(d) [P]erfect unity should be reserved for animate bodies, or bodies endowed with primary entelechies; for such entelechies bear some analogy to souls, and are as indivisible and imperishable as souls are. ... [The entelechies'] organic bodies are really machines, although as much superior to the artificial ones which we design as is the Designer of those natural ones to us. For the machines of nature are as imperishable as souls themselves, and the animal together with its soul persists for ever.

(NE 328–9)

(24)   Whether these principles of action and of perception are then to be called *forms, entelechies, souls,* or *minds,* and whether these terms are to be distinguished according to whatever notions one may choose to assign to them, things will not be changed in any way. You may ask what becomes of these simple beings or souls that I put in animals and other created things in so far as they are organic wholes; my reply is that they need be no less inextinguishable than ours, and that they can be neither produced nor destroyed by the forces of nature.

But to extend the analogy with what we feel at *present* in our *own* bodies to the *future* and *past*, as well as to *other* bodies, I hold not only that these souls or entelechies all have with them some kind of organic body appropriate to their perceptions, but also that they always will have, and always have had, as long as they have existed: so not only the soul, but also the animal itself (or what is analogous to the soul and to the animal, so as not to argue about names) remains, and thus that generation and death can only be developments and envelopments of which nature, as is her custom, gives us several visible examples to help us to work out what she keeps hidden. And as a consequence neither iron nor fire, nor any other violence of nature, whatever ravages they wreak on an animal's body, can ever prevent the soul from retaining a certain organic body, in as much as *organism*, that is to say order and ingenuity, is something essential to matter produced and arranged by the sovereign wisdom, since products always retain some trace of their author. This leads me to think also that there are no minds entirely separate from matter (except the first and sovereign being), and that spirits, however marvelous they may be, are always accompanied by appropriate bodies. The same must also be said of souls, even though they may be described as separate with respect to this gross body. So you see, madam, that all this is only to suppose that *things are everywhere and always just as they are in us now* (leaving the supernatural aside).

(May 1704, to Lady Masham, G 3, 339–40/WF 205–6)

(25)   You remark that it appears that the bodily organs serve no purpose, if the soul is self-sufficient. I reply that if Caesar's soul (for example) were alone in nature, the creator of things need not have given it any bodily organs. But this same creator also wanted to make an infinity of other beings, which are contained in one another's bodily organs. Our body is a kind of world full of an infinity of creatures which also deserved to exist, and if our body were not an organic whole, our microcosm or little world would not have all the perfections it should have, and the big world itself would not be as rich as it is. This also is the reason why I have said that *being organic is essential* not in general to matter, but only *to matter as arranged by a sovereign*

wisdom. And this also is why I define *an organism*, or natural machine, as a machine of which each part is a machine, and consequently as one such that the complexity of its construction continues to infinity, no part being so small that this does not apply, whereas by contrast, the parts of our artificial machines are not themselves machines.

(30 June 1704, to Lady Masham, G 3, 356/WF 214)

(26) [V]ital principles are spread throughout all nature and are immortal, since they are indivisible substances of *unities*, while bodies are multitudes subject to destruction through the dissolution of their parts. When I am asked if they are substantial forms ... if this term is taken to mean ... that the rational soul is the substantial form of man, I agree. ... For vital principles belong only to organic bodies. It is just as reasonable that there should be substances capable of perception below us as above us, so that our soul, far from being the lowest of all, finds itself in the middle, from which one may rise or sink. Otherwise there would be a deficiency in order, or what some philosophers call a *vacuum of forms.*
I believe that not merely the soul but the whole animal subsists. [S]ince the mechanisms of nature are mechanisms down to their smallest parts, they are indestructible, since smaller machines are enfolded in greater machines into infinity.
[I]f matter is arranged by divine wisdom, it must be essentially organized throughout and there must be machines in the parts of the natural machine into infinity, so many enveloping structures and so many organic bodies enveloped, one within the other, that one can never produce any organic body entirely anew and without any preformation, nor any more destroy entirely an animal which already exists.

(1705, *Considerations on Vital Principles*, G 6, 539, 543–4/
L 586, 588–9)

(27) A corporeal substance has a soul and an organic body, that is, a mass composed of other substances. It is true that the same substance thinks and has extended mass joined to it; but it hardly consists of extended mass since any of those things could be taken away, leaving the substance intact. Furthermore, all substance perceives, but not all substance thinks. Thought really belongs to monads; indeed, all perception does, but extension belongs to composites.

(1706, J-G Wachteri de Recondita Hebraeorum Philosophia,
Leibniz Review 12:7/AG 275)

(28) [W]e mean something when we speak of the union of the soul with the body to make thereof one single person. ... I admit a true union

between the soul and the body, which makes thereof a suppositum. This union belongs to the metaphysical, whereas a union of influence would belong to the physical. But when we speak of the union of the Word of God with human nature we should be content with an analogical knowledge, such as the comparison of the union of the soul with the body is capable of giving us. It is the same with the other Mysteries, where moderate minds will ever find an explanation sufficient for belief, but never such as would be necessary for understanding. A certain *what it is* is enough for us, but the *how* is beyond us, and is not necessary for us.

(1710, *Theodicy*, Preliminary Discourse §55–6, G 6, 81/T 104)

(29)   I hold that each soul, or monad, is always accompanied by an organic body, though one which is in perpetual change – so much so that the body is never the same, even though both the soul and the animal are. These rules also hold of the human body; but obviously in a more excellent manner than with the other animals which are known to us, since man must remain not only an animal, but also a person and citizen in the city of God.

(8 July 1711, to des Maizeaux, G 7, 535/WF 239)

(30)   Now *body* is either corporeal substance, or a mass composed of corporeal substances. I call *corporeal substance* what consists in a simple substance or monad (*i.e.* a soul or something analogous to a soul) and an organic body united with it. But *mass* is an aggregate of corporeal substances, as cheese sometimes consists of a concourse of worms. ... [A]ny mass contains innumerable monads, for although any one organic body in nature has its corresponding monad, it nevertheless contains in its parts other monads endowed in the same way with organic bodies subservient to the primary one.

(12 August 1711, to Bierling, G 7, 501–2/R 226/Rutherford 1995, 172)

(31)   I consider the explanation of all phenomena solely through the perceptions of monads functioning in harmony with each other, with corporeal substances rejected, to be useful for a fundamental investigation of things.

(16 June 1712, to Des Bosses, G 2, 450/L 604)

(32)   A substance is either simple, such as a soul, which has no parts, or it is composite, such as an animal, which consists of a soul and an organic body. But an organic body, like every other body, is merely an aggregate of animals or other things which are living and therefore organic, or finally of small objects or masses; but these also are finally resolved into living things, from which it is evident that all

bodies are finally resolved into living things, and that what, in the analysis of substances, exist ultimately are simple substances – namely, souls, or, if you prefer a more general term, *monads*, which are without parts. For even though every simple substance has an organic body which corresponds to it ... yet by itself it is without parts. And because an organic body, or any other body whatsoever, can again be resolved into substances endowed with organic bodies, it is evident that in the end there are simple substances alone, and that in them are the sources of all things and of the modifications that come to things.

(c. 1712, *Metaphysical Consequences of the Principle of Reason*,
C 13–14/PW 175)

(33) A *simple substance* is that which has no parts. A *composite substance* is a collection of simple substances, or *monads*. ... Composites or bodies are multitudes; and simple substances – lives, souls, and minds – are unities.

[E]ach distinct simple substance or monad, which makes up the center of a composite substance (an animal, for example) and is the principle of its unity, is surrounded by a *mass* composed of an infinity of other monads, which constitute the *body belonging to* this central monad, through whose properties the monad represents the things outside it, similarly to the way a center does. And this body is organic when it forms a kind of automaton or natural machine, which is not only a machine as a whole, but also in its smallest distinguishable parts.

Each monad, together with a particular body, makes up a living substance. ... [A] living thing is called an *animal* as its monad is called a *soul*.

Thus, not only souls, but also animals cannot be generated and cannot perish. They are unfolded, enfolded, reclothed, unclothed, and transformed; souls never entirely leave their body, and do not pass from one body into another that is entirely new to them.

(1714, PNG §1, 3, 4, 6, G 6, 598–9, 601/AG 207–9

(34) §62: Thus, although each created monad represents the whole universe, it more distinctly represents the body which is particularly affected by it, and whose entelechy it constitutes. §63: The body belonging to a monad (which is the entelechy or soul of that body) together with an entelechy constitutes what may be called a *living being*, and together with a soul constitutes what is called an *animal*. §64: Thus each organized body of a living being is a kind of divine machine or natural automaton, which infinitely surpasses all artificial automata. For a machine constructed by man's art is not a machine in each of its parts. ... But natural machines, that is, living bodies,

are still machines in their least parts, to infinity. §70: [E]ach living body has a dominant entelechy, which in the animal is the soul; but the limbs of this living body are full of other living beings, plants, animals, each of which also has its entelechy, or its dominant soul. §72: Thus the soul changes body only little by little and by degrees, so that it is never stripped at once of all its organs. §77: [N]ot only is the soul ... indestructible, but so is the animal itself, even though its mechanism often perishes in part, and casts off or puts on its organic coverings.

(1714, Mon/AG 221–3)

(35)   (On a chart sent to Des Bosses, beneath "Substance" the following two entries are made, where the phrase "Substance or Modification" is ranked under "A unity *per se*; a full being.") Simple, a monad, like minds, souls, which are subject to no influence by other creatures [and, in a separate column] Composite (like animals or other organic beings) which always remains unchanged and adheres to a dominant monad but is subject to the influence of other composite substances.

(19 August 1715 letter to Des Bosses, G 2, 506/L 617)

(36)   And *secondary matter* (*e.g.* an organic body) is not a substance ... it is a collection of several substances, like a pond full of fish, or a flock of sheep, and consequently it is what is called *unum per accidens* – in a word, a phenomenon. A true substance (such as an animal) is composed of an immaterial soul and an organic body, and it is the compound of these two which is called *unum per se*.
[S]ouls agree with bodies, and among themselves, by virtue of the pre-established harmony, and not at all by mutual physical influence, save for the metaphysical union of the soul and its body, which makes them compose an *unum per se*, an animal, a living being.

(4 November 1715, to Remond, G 3, 657–8/R 226/
Rutherford 1995, 175)

(37)   [T]here are no created substances wholly destitute of matter. For I hold with the ancients, and according to reason, that angels or intelligences, and souls separated from a gross body, have always subtile bodies, though they themselves be incorporeal.

(18 August 1716, to Clarke, 5.61)

8.4 Idealism: Well-Founded Animals

An aggregate on the Well-Founded Phenomena account was construed as a "real phenomenon (*p*) quasi-caused by the monadic aggregate." There it was possible to regard both *p* and the "monadic aggregate" as aggregates. It is the monadic aggregate that concerns me here. When the monads in a monadic aggregate achieve a machine-like structure amongst themselves, that aggregate becomes, I will say, a *monadic machine*.

On the account of ordinary aggregates, p was well-founded by an ordinary monadic aggregate. Now, when p is a well-founded phenomenon of a machine, it is well-founded by the monads in a monadic machine. Such machines, when ganged together, form a "machine composed of machines," which Leibniz calls a "natural machine" because it is found ready-made in nature. Finally, the natural machines, taking their monads with them of course, are caught up into animals when they cooperate appropriately with a "dominant monad." Such animals – always perceived in the "guise" of their natural machines – can be termed "well-founded animals."

Now the bit about a "machine-like structure" that transforms ordinary monadic aggregates into fancy ones merits comment. The arrangement of the items in a monadic machine must be roughly analogous to the arrangement of physical parts in a physical machine. But in this account the items to be arranged in a machine-like way are of course Idealist, world-apart monads. Thus there is no way to improve on that vague characterization of their arrangement.

Recall that "quasi-causation" was introduced as a cambridge relation between the monadic aggregate and $Monad_1$ – the one aware of p. This preserved the Canonical Metaphysics. The relations between all the monads in the monadic aggregate were also cambridge. But with cambridge relations maintained everywhere, the notion of a "machine-like arrangement" between world-apart monads must be due to "quasi-constitution," for want of a better term.

For *machines are possible only in virtue of relations* – real relations, of course. In the famous mill example (Mon 17) one is forbidden from supposing that moving levers could explain perception. That sounds plausible, but it simply underscores the problem confronted here. There is no analogy whatever between a line-up of gears and pulleys and a line-up of purely mental perceiving substances.

Another way of putting the point is this. The account of machinehood offered here is completely *uninformative*. Because real relations are altogether banished, there are in principle no details about how a monadic aggregate is transformed from an ordinary one into a machine. And, looking ahead in this section, for the same reason the account of animals built on it will be uninformative. For after one adds a "dominant monad" to a "natural machine," this dominant monad will (of course) be permitted to maintain only cambridge relations with the monads in its natural machine. And such relations yield no account whatever of the way in which the dominant monad is able to make the amalgam into "one machine" (G 2, 252/L 531). The machine can only be said to be quasi-constituted by the dominant monad. One would have hoped that the appropriateness of calling it a "machine" could be assessed somewhere along the line. But it cannot in this account. Machine hood becomes a mere postulate of mechanistic explanation.

Still, even with these limitations one can state abstractly what is required for there to be well-founded animals. First I develop an account of *natural machines* based on passages found in 8.3. Artificial machines like robots are set aside because they haven't the required complexity to be "knighted" by dominant monads so as to form animals. Leibniz's claim for a natural machine that "the complexity of its construction continues to infinity" (G 3, 356/WF 214) is taken to mean that humans who explore machines will never "bottom out" on monads. In metaphysical truth, looking at machines from a God's-eye view, there is a bottoming out on monads. Conceptually one can proceed to the limit of this decomposition and say that, as in the case of all aggregates, they ultimately decompose into monads even while maintaining that perceptually they never do.

I can now pin down the differences between "monadic machines" and "natural machines" as follows:

Monadic Machine

m is a *monadic machine* at *t* iff: at *t*, the monads in the monadic aggregate that quasi-causes a phenomenon aggregate, *p*, in *Monad$_1$*:

i) have an arrangement that is analogous to the arrangement of parts in a physical machine, and
ii) jointly quasi-constitute a machine, *m*; and
iii) *Monad$_1$* (possibly unconsciously) considers *p* a unified, colored, and extended machine.

m is a *monadic machine* that persists from *t1* to *tn* iff: at each *tj* between *t1* and *tn*, *Monad$_1$* is in some *cj* ε {C1} such that: *cj*'s (possibly unconsciously held) representational content includes a phenomenon aggregate, *p*, which is quasi-caused by the monads in the monadic aggregate that:

i) have an arrangement that is analogous to the arrangement of parts in a physical machine, and
ii) jointly quasi-constitute a machine, *m*; and
iii) *Monad$_1$* (possibly unconsciously) considers *p* the same unified, colored, and extended machine from *t1* to *tn*.

Here, the *p* that appeared as a plain "well-founded aggregate" in 5.3.2 gains the additional quality of being considered a "machine" by some particular monad, or *Monad$_1$*. Given universal mirroring, every finite mind will have such *p*s in its representational content – *p*s ultimately quasi-caused by monads arranged machine-wise in the monadic machine.

From this "base step," one can proceed to build more complex natural machines that quasi-cause *p*:

Natural Machine

n is a *natural machine* at *t* iff: at *t*, the *m*s that quasi-cause a phenomenon aggregate, *p*, in $Monad_1$:

i) have an arrangement that is analogous to the arrangement of parts in a physical machine, and
ii) jointly quasi-constitute a machine, *n*; and
iii) $Monad_1$ (possibly unconsciously) considers *p* a unified, colored, and extended machine.

n is a *natural machine* that persists from *t1* to *tn* iff: at each *tj* between *t1* and *tn*, some $Monad_1$ is in some *cj* ε {C1} such that: *cj*'s (possibly unconsciously held) representational content includes a phenomenon aggregate, *p*, which is quasi-caused by some *m*s that:

i) have an arrangement that is analogous to the arrangement of parts in a physical machine, and
ii) jointly quasi-constitute a machine, *n*; and
iii) $Monad_1$ (possibly unconsciously) considers *p* the same unified, colored, and extended machine from *t1* to *tn*.

The "partly delusive experiences" (Broad 1975, 92) quasi-caused by the monads will be *p*s that are considered either machines-at-a-time, or persisting machines. Given universal mirroring and no requirement that the perceiving monad be capable of reflection, every *p* will be in every finite mind.

With these definitions in hand, I can specify the conditions for well-founded animals. In what follows, 'dominant monad' refers indifferently to what, in the early and middle mature periods was called a "soul" or "substantial form," and in the later period was sometimes referred to as a "dominant soul" or "entelechy."

Well-Founded Animals:

A is an *animal* at *t* iff: at *t* there is an *n* to which a dominant monad, *D1*, is quasi-united so that it forms a living thing, *A*.

A is an *animal* that persists from *t1* to *tn* iff: at each *tj* between *t1* and *tn*, a dominant monad, *D1*, is quasi-united with an *n* (which shares at least one monad with the *n* to which *D1* was quasi-united at the immediately preceding *ti*), so that it forms a living thing, *A*.

Cambridge constraints are obeyed here. Given universal mirroring and the analysis of *n*, it follows that every animal is represented as a *p* – an appearance of a natural machine – in every finite mind.

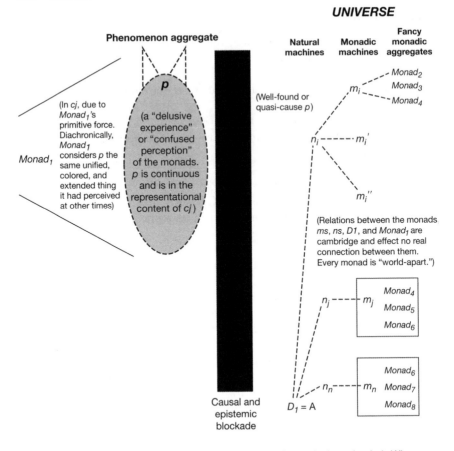

i, j, and *n* represent three adjacent times in the career of a particular animal, *A*. When an *n* "combines" with a particular dominant substance, *D1*, *A* is "formed." Everything to the right of the blockade is non-extended. Extension enters into the picture only in *p*, which is extended because of the confused "considerings" of *Monad₁* – due largely to the work of the "perceptual continuum."

Figure 8.1. Idealism: Well-Founded Animals

In relation to the persistence conditions, Leibniz explicitly allows natural machines to take on and lose parts constantly (see, e.g., C 16/PW 178). Thus in the diachronic version there is no requirement that the same *n* partly constitute a persisting animal during its entire career. Still, he insists that " ... souls never leave the whole of their body, and do not pass from one body to another which is entirely new to them" (G 6, 601/MP 199). Thus each *n* must share at least one monad with the previous *n* with which *D1* was united. A given *n* is a "temporarily immediate requisite" (LA 120; G 2, 252/AG 177) for an animal, but that particular *n* need not partly compose it at any other time. *D1*, governed as it is by its complete concept, carries identity. Here "living thing" means something which is alive only in a very general sense – it may be something as lowly as an amoeba or plant.

The claim that *D1* "quasi-unites with *n* so that it forms a living thing, *A*" signals a problem for this analysis insofar as it would speak for Leibniz. For, as we've seen, Leibniz himself is quite clear that animals have a genuine unity, as opposed to the fake unity of aggregates. And *quasi-unity is not unity.* Unity would have to involve "meddler" relations between *D1* and the monads in *n*. But cambridge strictures proscribe such relations, allowing animals to shatter into disjoint bits – to become a Humpty Dumpty that can't be "put together again" because it was never put together in the first place.

As in the case of the Well-Founded Phenomena analysis, the most striking absence here is a respectable subject of predication for what's mind-independent. One can agree to call *D1+n* an "animal," but since cambridge relations make genuine ties between its constituents impossible, the unity is only "quasi." If all that exist are monads and their perceptions, animals must, like well-founded aggregates, be phenomenal aspects of perceptions, or *p*s.

But Leibniz's animals can't be *p*s. Four reasons are offered. Each is decisive. Together they are annihilating.

First, if animals were *p*s they could not be true unities. It became clear in Chapter 3 that phenomena were declared continuous and thus unfit for true unity. Second, *p*s are mind-dependent, while Leibniz's animals must be mind-independent. There is no way one could intelligibly predicate of a mind-dependent *p* such properties as "contains monads" or "contains other animals" or "is active" or "is divided into substances." Third, Leibniz often distinguishes between aggregates and animals, as when he writes, "each animal and each plant is also a corporeal substance, having in itself a principle of unity which makes it truly a substance and not an aggregate" (G 3, 260/AG 289). If animals were *p*s, they would be aggregates. So the scope of the "Divisibility Argument" extends to aggregates but not animals.[12] Fourth, if animals were *p*s they could not be composed ultimately of simples (monads), whereas it is very important for the cohesion of the mature system (and adherence to the "Simples Rule" of Chapter 2) that the simples compose everything else. That is why, in text 32 from 8.3, he says that an animal's organic body ultimately decomposes into "living things" or "simple substances." *p*, by contrast, is composed of continuous sub-*p*s to infinity.

These objections by now need no elaboration. They bolt the door against any attempt to classify animals as phenomena and thus "work them into" Idealism.

Evaluation of Well-Founded Animals

Looking at the big picture, this analysis shows that one can spell out, in abstract terms, what it takes for Leibniz's account of nested machines dominated by a special monad to be instantiated within the constraints of Idealism. But it also shows how forced and unnatural the "fit" is.

Indeed, the diagram of this position reveals all in a single stunning glance. The entire metaphysics – what is going on in the universe – is irrelevant to our knowledge of animals because it's necessarily sundered from the knowing subject by the "Blockade." Moreover, any mind-independent animals procured by the metaphysics are scattered objects that make Leibniz's claim of perfect unity utterly laughable. At the same time, *p* is helpless to provide a home for animals.

The price of Idealism is now nearly unpayable. The number of texts that turn out, not just difficult to understand, but unintelligible burgeons out of control. Martha Bolton has claimed that a major problem in today's Idealist climate is that animals "keep popping up all over the place" in the mature corpus.[13] So many texts uphold the true unity of mind-independent animals that the task of explaining each of them away and construing them as consistent with Idealism is never-ending.[14] One is probably better advised simply to write animals off rather than trying to bend the texts to say what one needs them to say.

8.5 Realism: Animals as Variable Embodiments

> It being well beyond the concerns of this work to undertake a systematic treatment of Leibniz's views of corporeal substance, we leave it to others to offer an account of what those readers [who recognize simple and composite substances] will purport to be a second class of *per se* unities. (Perhaps we would be pleasantly surprised by the payoffs of such a project. For now, we are very skeptical indeed.)
>
> J. A. Cover and John Hawthorne (1999, 55)

Indeed, "writing off animals" is precisely the position expressed in these words. Cover and Hawthorne unapologetically choose Idealism and the Exclusivism it requires. With that choice made, their skepticism is well-founded. Within the strictures of Idealism, it would be "surprising" indeed if anything illuminating could be said about animals and their *per se* unity. I confess that if I had to decide to keep or discard animals based only on the "Well-Founded Animals" account just examined, I would toss them. These authors are convinced that "the simple perceiving monads" are the only *per se* unities. As "the mere co-existence of certain simple substances" is sufficient for the existence of a "so-called corporeal substance," animals must be rejected (Cover and O'Leary-Hawthorne 1999, 54–5).

But, while any Idealist account of this "second class of *per se* unities" seems doomed, it might succeed elsewhere in Leibniz's system. That system contains a healthy Realist theory, and the Realist account I'm about to offer is systematic and pleasantly surprising.

Chapter 6's principal Realist analysis of aggregates as "Rigid Embodiments" provides the launching point for this different account of animals. The Idealist's "Well-Founded Animals" account idled most of Leibniz's machinery and produced no mind-independent, discrete animals. By contrast, this analysis is able to embrace the reality of animals and deploy much of Leibniz's metaphysical machinery. The animals so formed are genuine substances, on a par with monads. Following Leibniz, monads here act as the constituents of "basic animals," with those animals serving as substances in higher-order animals.

Begin then by noting that an animal can be treated as a *variable embodiment* – a whole, again, developed by Kit Fine as a way of understanding changing particulars like "the water in the river." The analysis is designed to dovetail with the rigid embodiment analysis that played a key role in our comprehensive analysis of aggregates. A variable embodiment takes rigid embodiments as arguments and is determined by a function that tracks a series of rigid embodiments over time. Fine's own description is given in a footnote and the example changed from rivers to "Rick's music collection" for the sake of intuitive clarity.[15]

So Rick's music collection is a variable embodiment because the rigid embodiments – specific pieces of music, electronic files, and discs standing in appropriate relations – it tracks differ wildly over time. Despite the variation, the collection remains the same variable-embodiment-whole. One could, anticipating Leibniz a bit, add a constraint according to which the collection endures only if at least one item in a given rigid embodiment is "passed on" to the next embodiment of the collection. Indeed, that is a reasonable request, though nothing is going to prevent someone from using "same collection" to refer to an entirely new set of musical objects.

Note that such collections, like rivers, can be ephemeral. Rick can sell his entire collection before moving overseas for three years, then buy a completely different one when he returns from his stint in the Peace Corps. And what he has at the end is still, as he would say, "my music collection."

But it turns out that Leibniz will not need to accommodate variable embodiment wholes whose rigid embodiment manifestations are subject to "gaps." The controlling "principle of variable embodiment" for Leibniz's animals is the complete concept of the dominant monad. Complete concepts determine the sequence of states, without interruption, from the beginning to the end (if there is an end) of a monad's career. In terms of embodiments, they determine the sequence of rigid embodiments that monad will have – again without interruption so that it is never left disembodied.

Chapter 6's analysis of aggregates as rigid embodiments will be used to develop an account of the bodies of animals, where these become the arguments for the animal's complete concept. As one might say, these bodies provide animals' various perceivable manifestations at different times.

Call rigid embodiments whose substances – "*S*s" – maintain a machine-like structure *embodiment machines*. (These correspond to what were called, in the Well-Founded Animal account, "monadic machines.") I first develop an account of embodiment machines. These are used to construct what Leibniz called "natural machines" – roughly nested collections of lesser machines. Finally the natural machines are plugged into functions (complete concepts) that yield animals as variable embodiments. (Sometimes hereafter 'variable embodiment' will be abbreviated 'embodiment'.)

Embodiment machines would be analyzed as follows:

Real Emb-MACH: m is a *embodiment machine* at t iff: at t,

1   The Ss exist; and
2   The Ss/**M** (are so related that they
    i)   constitute an object, m, by maintaining an order analogous to that between the parts in a physical machine; and
    ii) provide a base for the supervening properties of m; and
    iii) ensure that m's derivative reality, activity, and force supervene directly on the primitive reality, activity, and force of each of the Ss); and
3   If finite minds are thinking (possibly unconsciously) of m, they are (possibly unconsciously) judging that 'F' is properly predicated of m, where
    i)   F is an accurate guide to the true nature of m when it:
       a) characterizes m as real, active, or possessing force, or[16]
       b) characterizes m as a direct supervenience rigid embodiment; and
    ii) F is not an accurate guide to the true nature of m when it characterizes it as a unity; and
    iii) the perceptual continuum explains why 'extended body' is often predicated of m; and
    iv) the presence of mechanical concepts in finite minds explains why 'machine' is often predicated of m; and
    v)   if some finite mind, $S1$, is judging (possibly unconsciously), "m is the same F as the one I perceived before," the judgment will be open to error due to factors that include an inadequate knowledge of:
       a) precisely which Ss are present at the two times; and
       b) whether the Ss constitute an m at the two times; and
       c) whether m is an F at the two times.

'Machine' designates equivalent predicates in all possible natural languages. **M** is the **R** suited to relating substances so that they constitute embodiment machines with appropriate supervenience strictures observed. m all by itself is just as much an uncharacterized object as was w on the analysis of aggregates. I change the variable from "w" to "m" only to indicate that these aggregates, unlike plain ws such as piles of stones, will often have 'machine' predicated of them. The "machinehood," unity, and extension of m are wholly in the mind doing the judging. A God's-eye view of m would show only the Ss "so related." In (2) (i) the "order analogous that to that of parts in a physical machine" is not elaborated upon because, as was evident in the last section, it can't be. Providing a "base for the supervening properties of *m*" also is left in its abstract form because there is no way to tell, e.g., how *m*'s mechanical properties are supported by the Ss' nonmechanical properties.

As in the case of every aggregate, all I know for sure about *m* is that it is real, active, and has force, and that it is properly regarded as a rigid embodiment. Mechanical concepts in finite minds in (3) (iv) – whose first nascent stirrings appeared long ago in proto-atomist metaphysicians and have been revived again and again in mechanical philosophies – explain why one is disposed to look at *m*s as machines.

Yes: *m* is not a machine until it is regarded as a machine or judged to be a machine. Apart from the predicating mind, it is just a real, active, and force-possessing rigid embodiment whole. Some may find it counterintuitive to suppose that Leibniz's machines aren't "really" machines. But the task here is to give an intelligible account of what is intuitive, and that has been done. I have gone down this road because I am intent on preserving the critique of extension, and that means keeping extension pinned in the mind. If I countenance mind-independent, extended *m*s, the game is up. So all primary and mechanical qualities show up at best as Fs that the mind predicates of *m*.

Again from this base step I proceed to *natural machines*:

Real Nat-MACH: *n* is a *natural machine* at *t* iff: at *t*,

1 An infinite number of *m*s exist; and
2 The *m*s/N (are so related that they
   i)   constitute an object, *n*, by maintaining an order analogous to that between the parts in a physical machine; and
   ii) provide a base for the supervening properties of *n*; and
   iii) ensure that *n*'s derivative reality, activity, and force supervene directly on the primitive reality, activity, and force of each of the Ss in the *m*s).
3 If finite minds are thinking (possibly unconsciously) of *n*, they are (possibly unconsciously) judging that 'F' is properly predicated of *n*, where
   i)   F is an accurate guide to the true nature of *n* when it:
        a) characterizes *n* as real, active, or possessing force, or
        b) characterizes *n* as a direct supervenience rigid embodiment; and
   ii) F is not an accurate guide to the true nature of *n* when it characterizes it as a unity; and
   iii) The perceptual continuum explains why 'extended body' is often predicated of *n*; and
   iv) The presence of mechanical concepts in finite minds explains why 'machine' is often predicated of *n*; and

v)   If some finite mind, *S1*, is judging (possibly unconsciously), "*n* is the same F as the one I perceived before," the judgment will be open to error due to factors that include an inadequate knowledge of:
a) precisely which *m*s are present at the two times; and
b) whether the *m*s constitute an *n* at the two times; and
c) whether *n* is an F at the two times.

N is the **R** in virtue of which *m*s constitute natural machines with appropriate supervenience relations intact. Since *m*s are parts of *n*, (3) (v) (a) says that the judging mind will have to keep track of which ones are present.

On (2) (i) one has a better grasp of the constitution conditions for *n* than one did in the case of *m*s. For when thinking of *m*s as machines, one conceptually bestows upon them myriad mechanical qualities and relations. And those mechanical features can be used to derive an account of how *n*s are configured – one that parallels fairly closely the arrangement of parts in a physical machine. A toy example: a complex machine *n* is constituted from *m1* and *m2* – say, respectively, a cogged wheel and a slotted one that fit together nicely. I conceive of the *m*s as extended and as having a certain shape and solidity. Then *n* would be the result of bringing them into spatial proximity and appropriate contact so that one wheel can drive the other. These details are available when *m* and *n* are taken to fall under the concept, "machine."

Animals now can be analyzed as variable embodiments. Some shorthand will help streamline the analysis. '*D1*' will denote a particular dominant substance, so an animal at a time is '*D1nt*'. That is, a particular manifestation of the cow Zoe, say, at a particular time is Zoe's dominant monad, *D1*, unified with the natural machine *n* at time *t*. Persistence for Zoe will be represented as a particular *D1* suited up with various natural machines at different times – abbreviated by '*D1nt1, D1nt2*,' etc.

I will first present the Realist analysis informally as applied to Zoe. The formal analysis in definition form will follow.

Zoe is created when God takes a monad, *D1*, destined to be the soul or dominant monad for an animal and joins it to a given natural machine, *n1*, so that *D1* and *n1* together form a perfect unity. From that time forward *D1* will never again be disembodied, though *n1* will soon be replaced by other, different *n*s. *D1*'s complete concept determines "which *n* comes next" in its possibly infinite future career, always ensuring that the new *n* shares at least one substance with the old *n*. If there weren't this "sharing" of a substance between bodies, *D1* would be disembodied – even if for a very brief time. Zoe may not look anything like a cow to finite perceivers on the first day of her creation. She may be invisible, or look like a stone or a fish or a piece of charcoal. *D1*'s body's size and perceived qualities may vary dramatically, since identity is carried wholly by *D1*. At some point *D1* takes on an *n* that is perceived by humans as a cow. At this point Zoe is attributed extension, mass, and mobility. Zoe remains from the beginning to the end unextended – $D1n1$, $D1n2$, etc. The terms predicated of Zoe bring with them concepts of extension and other primary qualities. Accurate judgments about Zoe attribute to her reality, activity, force, life, and indivisibility, or say she is an organism, substance, or a variable embodiment. Judgments such as 'Zoe is the same cow as was in this pasture yesterday' will be open to error because of an inadequate knowledge of whether "yesterday's n" and "today's n" are dominated by $D1$, whether the two ns have met the "overlapping S" requirement in the intervening time, and whether in both cases the animals are cows.

More formally:

Real Emb-ANIMAL:

A is an *animal* at t iff: $D1nt = A$, iff: at t, a natural machine, n, provides a body for a dominant substance, $D1$, which is united so completely with n that it forms a genuine unity, A.

A is an *animal* that persists from ti to tn iff: $\{D1nti, \dots, D1ntn\} = A$, iff:

1 the complete concept of some dominant substance, $D1$, specifies that at each tj between ti and tn, a specific natural machine, nj (which shares at least one S with ni), shall be its body; and
2 $D1$ is united so completely with nj that it forms a genuine unity, A; and
3 If finite minds are thinking (possibly unconsciously) of A, they are (possibly unconsciously) judging that 'F' is properly predicated of A, where:
   i)   F is an accurate guide to the true nature of A when it characterizes it as a perceiving and striving unity that is real, active, and possesses primitive force, or as a living indivisible organism, a composite or corporeal substance, or a variable embodiment; and
   ii) If some finite mind, $S1$, is judging (possibly unconsciously), "A is the same F as the one I perceived before," the judgment will be open to error due to factors that include an inadequate knowledge of:
        a) whether each A is dominated by $D1$; and
        b) whether each A has met the "overlapping S" requirement in (1) during the intervening time; and
        c) whether each A is an F.

As animals are always seen in the guise of the n that is their body (or "manifestation") at any given time, some parts of the analysis of n apply to A. In particular, the perceptual continuum explains why animals are often thought to be extended, and mechanical concepts explain why they are

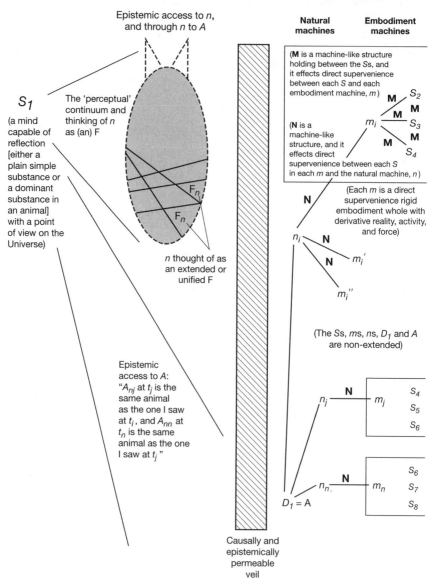

UNIVERSE

Epistemic access to *n*,
and through *n* to *A*

Natural machines   **Embodiment machines**

(**M** is a machine-like structure holding between the *S*s, and it effects direct supervenience between each *S* and each embodiment machine, *m*)

S₁

(a mind capable of reflection [either a plain simple substance or a dominant substance in an animal] with a point of view on the Universe)

The 'perceptual' continuum and thinking of *n* as (an) F

(**N** is a machine-like structure, and it effects direct supervenience between each *S* in each *m* and the natural machine, *n*)

(Each *m* is a direct supervenience rigid embodiment whole with derivative reality, activity, and force)

F_n

F_n

n thought of as an extended or unified F

(The *S*s, *m*s, *n*s, D_1 and *A* are non-extended)

Epistemic access to *A*:
"A_{nj} at t_j is the same animal as the one I saw at t_i, and A_{nn} at t_n is the same animal as the one I saw at t_j"

S_4
S_5
S_6

S_6
S_7
S_8

$D_1 = A$

Causally and epistemically permeable veil

i, j, and *n* represent three adjacent times in the career of a particular animal, *A*. D_1 is a particular dominant substance whose complete concept specifies that its career includes $\{D_{1ni}, D_{1nj}, D_{1nn},\}$. A different veil would intervene between non-reflective minds and *n*. Lucky minds could know *n* and *A* themselves without any guise – as God does.

Figure 8.2 Realism: Embodiment Analysis of Animals

considered machines. Animals are considered, from a common-sense stand-point, extended – roughly, "organized masses of cells." But their true metaphysical nature is the decidedly unextended and arcane metaphysical entity, '*D1n*'.

It is crucial to realize that Zoe is a perfect unity because she is welded together by God in a special act of creation. Why crucial? Because the commentators have made so much of the unity question for animals.[17] Leibniz has, they tell us, no account of the unity of animals. And they're right.

But that's natural given what he says in texts 28 and 36 in 8.3. Recall that in the study of aggregates (Chapter 6) I appealed to the doctrine of divine conservation to show that Leibniz countenances some non-cambridge Rs in his metaphysics. Here, however, he points out explicitly that the relation between (in our terms) *D1* and *n* is non-cambridge. In 28 he says the union of soul and body is "metaphysical" and must be understood on analogy with mysteries like the incarnation. For such mysteries, "*what it is*" must suffice since "the *how* is beyond us." And in 36 he says, most point-edly, that souls agree with bodies according to the pre-established harmony "save for the metaphysical union of the soul and its body" which makes them a "*unum per se.*" There is not even a hint that he can explain this exception to the general "cambridge relations rule." Thus there is a powerful textual basis for the genuine, mind-independent unity this analysis attributes to *A* – for there being (in Cover and Hawthorne's words) "a second class of *per se* unities."

Of course, quite independently of the analysis, given that God is the one fusing *D1* with *n*, it's unremarkable that finite stumbling minds can't penetrate the divine mystery. This is a special act of creation. As with all miracles, it harbors mysteries beyond human ken. "How is it done?" can't be answered any more than: "How does he make a soul?" or "How does he make some energy?"

In my earlier work I wrote that a corporeal substance is formed when a dominant monad *D1* "unites itself so completely with {C} [an infinite col-lection of substances] that together with {C} it forms a living thing" (Hartz 1992, 539). I attributed the uniting power of the dominant monad to "magic" there, and that is the position I just defended. But there is a subtle difference between that analysis and the one offered here. "(2)" in Real Emb-ANIMAL above reads "*D1* is united so completely with *nj* that it forms a genuine unity." The difference between the two accounts is this. In the earlier article I held to an eliminative reduction for aggregates like "*nj*," and so there was nothing for *D1* to unite with except the individual substances *nj* redu-ces to. Now, as I hold *nj* to be a freestanding mind-independent aggregate that is irreducible to its substances, *D1* can unite with *nj* itself. This is more consonant with Leibniz's text, as it is nearly always a fancy aggregate that the dominant monad is said to unite with to form an animal. (My 1992 claim that "*D1* unites itself so completely with substances" was almost as radical, for I was there claiming that animals were substances in a way that is incompatible with Idealism. Only the details have changed here.)

Within this study, one very important point connected with God's creation of animals is this. *Animals are simples.* Monads were said to be simples because they lack any parts. Animals are simples because their complexity is miraculously done away given divine fusion of a substantial form and some matter (or, equivalently, a dominant monad and its organic body). Again and again in the passages cited Leibniz sees the need to hold that not merely the substantial form but also the whole substance is, as he says to Arnauld "indestructible and ingenerable" (LA 78).[18] In that context, the substance is an animal, and this doctrine is reiterated throughout – even after the advent of monads. Thus he claims reproduction must, despite appearances, be transformation. On the first day of creation, all the non-rational animals that ever were going to exist had to be created by God as genuine unities despite their "temporarily required" (LA 120) bodies' lack of unity. A rational soul requires a special creation (AG 75) but the human animal arising from its fusion with a series of bodies enjoys, from that moment on, the same sort of genuine unity – again, despite the disunity of each body (LA 120).[19]

I can hear an objector saying: "Only monads are really simple. It must be some sort of second-rate simplicity that animals have – the only substances are the monads!" Reply: a careful look at what Leibniz says about Idealist monads reveals that they too have conceptually distinguishable constituents. In the early mature period, it was Aristotelian form/matter composites that were the exemplary substances. Even after monads appeared, two distinguishable aspects are attributed to the monad. Thus he says in the "five-part anatomy" that he distinguishes "(1) the primitive entelechy or soul" and "(2) primary matter or primitive passive power" from "(3) the complete monad formed by these two" (G 2, 252/L 530). Absolute simplicity is not on even for monads. The monad needs a passive force to offset its active force, otherwise its finitude couldn't be accounted for and it could play no role in explaining the recalcitrance of matter. Even though these two "aspects" can never actually be found in isolation from one another – any more than an Aristotelian form can be yanked free of some matter – it nevertheless remains true that monads are composites.

Animals are also composites, yet simple. Theirs is a more complicated composition, of course, since it incorporates this monadic composition but adds to it the organic machine's composition and the further composition of that machine with a special monad – in "(5) the animal or corporeal substance which the dominating monad makes into one machine" (G 2, 252/L 531).

Evaluation of Embodiment Analysis of Animals

It is hard to exaggerate the importance of this account. It achieves a breathtaking comprehensiveness and unity for the mature metaphysics never before envisioned.

Since this analysis incorporates rigid embodiments, it inherits most of the advantages enjoyed by the Comprehensive Rigid Embodiment analysis of aggregates (6.6.7). They will not be rehearsed here, though they are quite impressive in themselves.

Perhaps the best way to point out the Embodiment Analysis's strengths is to indicate how it accommodates Leibniz's doctrines expounded in other chapters above.

From Chapter 1

(a) It illustrates Leibniz's Theory-Pluralism. He remains committed both to the Idealist theory with all its restrictions *and* to the Realist theory where animals thrive and monads do all sorts of things they could not do on the other theory. The Idealist "war on animals" is not necessary because all animals – including *Homo sapiens* – are provided habitat under the aegis of a different theory.

From Chapter 2

(a) It presents a Simples metaphysic. The monads are partless, and once formed, animals function as simples because they are indivisible true unities not susceptible to divisibility.[20] Their compositeness is not a threat to their simplicity. That is huge news, really. It makes it unnecessary to retreat to Idealism in order to avoid problems with animal unity. Animals can enter into the composition of aggregates and other animals as well as can monads. Since they are non-extended, they do not bring extension with them any more than do monads.

(b) It lives up to the "Simples Rule" (2.3). That rule, recall, required every Simples Metaphysic to individuate a composite by (i) individuating its simples and (ii) constructing intelligible supervenience relations between the properties of simples and those of the composite On (i): the individuation of every composite – aggregate or animal – is guaranteed by its direct tie to the substances that make it up. Aggregates as clumps of *S*s are individuated only by reference to the already-individuated *S*s. And animals are individuated by their dominant substances. On (ii): this analysis requires direct (hence intelligible) supervenience of an organic body's derivative reality, activity and force on the primitive versions of these in its constituent substances.

From Chapter 3

(a) The perceptual continuum is used to explain why animals are known through extended bodies. The animal itself is not extended, and neither is its body – though of course the body typically appears to finite perceivers to be extended.

(b) Animals as well as monads avoid the Divisibility Argument and the problems faced by extended things – corroborating the claim (above) that they are simples. Indeed, Leibniz says precisely this (GM 3, 542/AG 168) at about the time monads were invented (1698). His unabashed reference to animals as the stopping point in decomposition shows that, especially in the early mature corpus, animals are indivisible extensionless substances – simples. That was a role soon to be shared by monads. Thus, on this inclusive analysis of animals as embodiments, non-extended substances in a non-extended natural machine can be supervised by a non-extended dominant substance so that a non-extended "basic animal" emerges. Then that non-extended basic animal can play a role in the formation of non-extended "upper level animals."

(c) The texts claiming that aggregates are "actually divided" into substances – throughout the mature corpus, animals! – make perfect sense on this picture. References to a "world of innumerable creatures" in each particle of matter are clearly borne out here.

From Chapter 6

(a) The Rigid Embodiments and direct supervenience developed there find their full fruition in this analysis, which relies crucially on them in building mind-independent animals out of substances.

(b) The principal claim of this chapter was that Realism's "aggregate thesis" is superior to Idealism's "phenomenalist" analysis of bodies. The fact that those Realist themes pay rich dividends in expounding the mature system, while Idealist themes cannot, abundantly supports that claim.

What a theory!

8.6 Compatibilist Animals

A remaining issue concerns animals as viewed by the "Compatibilists" examined in Chapter 7. I argued that their attempt to square Idealism with Realism on aggregates was unsuccessful. But one issue which was left for later discussion was the Compatibilist line on animals. I now turn to it.

As I said above, Robert M. Adams deserves credit for putting Leibniz's doctrine of animals on the map in English-language commentary in his groundbreaking 1983 article, "Phenomenalism and Corporeal Substance in Leibniz." Since Adams's later book breaks a bit with the earlier article and offers a Compatibilist interpretation of animals, his views will be closely explored here. The Compatibilist theory of Donald Rutherford will also be examined.

In his earlier article, Adams presents Leibniz as a "two-substance" theorist. Working largely from the seminal text (number 22 in 8.3 above: G 2, 252/L 530–1) to De Volder giving the 5-part anatomy of corporeal substance, Adams writes:

Leibniz clearly distinguishes the corporeal substance (5) both from its organic machine and from its dominant monad. It is something formed by the combination of those two. This appears to rule out one tempting interpretation. Cassirer identified corporeal substance with the monad itself "insofar as it is endowed with a particular organic body, according to which it represents and desires" [Cassirer 1902, 408]. Cassirer added that this corporeal endowment is "only a determination of the *content of consciousness*" of the monad. On this reading, the corporeal substance is a substance because it is a monad and corporeal because it is endowed with an organic body.

Adams (1983, 229)

Adams then rightly points out that in addition to the De Volder passage, many others block out the Cassirer suggestion – especially those that assert that a corporeal substance includes "a mass or organic body as well as a dominant monad." While the organic body is an aggregate, the corporeal substance "is not an aggregate" and "is not a mere phenomenon." It also "is not simple, as monads are," and that launches the question about the unity of creatures like this – something that is "at the center of the gravest difficulties and instabilities in Leibniz's theory of the physical world" (Adams 1983, 229–30).

For the reasons Adams gives, joined by the many reasons already given, there seems no option but to attribute to Leibniz a two-substance conception and to proscribe Cassirer's dangerous proposal.

Dangerous? Yes. Why? Because it plays fast and loose with identity. On that proposal, I can have my monads and my animals, and yet magically only count one object, depending on which way the "quas" are facing. Insofar as the monad is a monad, it is simple; insofar as that same monad is an animal, it is composite. When one says it fast, it seems possible. But notice that the subject of predication changes. The same object can't be both simple and complex any more than the same integer can be both odd and even, or the same object can be both a mind-dependent phenomenon and a mind-independent congeries of substances.

So in addition to all the Leibnizian reasons for rejecting the Cassirer proposal – reasons given in embarrassingly abundant detail by Adams himself in his article – there are sound philosophical reasons for its rejection (see, e.g., Wiggins 1980, 2001). If one "identifies" animals with monads one defies Leibniz's Law as applied to these objects. Given that the relation at issue is absolute identity, they are two, not one. And that would appear to be the end of the matter.

But Cassirer emerges the victor in Adams's book. Adams has reconsidered the matter and now favors – though with admittedly sparse textual evidence – the "qualified monad conception" of corporeal substance. The view is described thus: "The monad can be called a *corporeal* substance inasmuch as it *has* a body. A corporeal substance, on this view, is not a monad *plus* a body, but a monad *as having* a body" (Ad 269). Adams then expounds many texts, some of which seem to favor the two-substance conception while others are at least amenable to the one-substance conception, concluding that the two-substance conception is "the only one that we can be certain that Leibniz held at any time" (Ad 285).

Is the one-substance conception viable? I want to ask whether this "one-substance conception" can render intelligible Leibniz's claims about animals – indeed, whether this conception can render intelligible claims Adams himself attributes to Leibniz. By this time in the book, Adams faces two separate problems. (1) his qualified monad conception would "modalize" bodies, making them ways monads are, as a smile is a way a face is configured. The smile cannot then be yanked away from the face – as in *Alice* (Chapter 6) the Cheshire Cat's smile was supposed to have remained even after the animal had altogether disappeared. On this construal, the bodies aren't freestanding so that they can combine with anything – especially (except trivially) the monad they are a mode of. Yet Leibniz is always thinking of the body as combining with a separate monad. (2) The earlier phenomenalization of aggregates means this idiom of "combination" is now out of place.[21] For there is no intelligible sense in which a dominant monad can combine with its or any other mind's appearance. Whatever combining there is will already be done in virtue of the appearance being in the mind; "dominance" as a further step is otiose and unnecessary. Yet Leibniz is clearly thinking of dominance as a relation holding between monads – and in virtue of its holding, there is an animal.

Both of these problems confront a central passage of the book. Adams writes,

> The monad *always* has its body, and hence the organic body is an enduring, though constructed and merely phenomenal, object permanently attached to its dominant monad (G II, 251/L 530). ... The substances that are included in an organic body can be replaced with other substances as long as the body retains the necessary organs and the same dominant monad (Mon 71–2).
>
> (Ad 266–7)

(1) The reference to an "object" with substances "included in" it is inconsistent with the qualified monad conception of bodies. (2) Even granting the existence of such an object, there is the further problem that the organic body is said to be "constructed and merely phenomenal." Its "merely phenomenal" status makes it impossible for it to do what Leibniz is here cited as saying it does – namely, that it includes mind-independent substances in it and that it is an organic body "permanently attached to" a dominant monad. It seems incoherent to assign some mind-independent dominant monad the task of attaching itself to any mind-dependent appearance – even its own.

A look at the historical context may help. The De Volder exchange in particular (from which Adams is working here) grants animals a central role in the five-part anatomy of corporeal substance (G 2, 251/L 530–1). Particularly instructive are Leibniz's own reactions to De Volder's *recounting* of Leibniz's position – a recounting that prompted the five-part anatomy as a clarification. De Volder wrote:

> I shall try to explain how I understand your hypothesis ... As long as a mass of matter is infinitely divisible, and all emptiness is removed, it has no unity. As long as the same mass is merely passive, impenetrable, and resists motion, it can do nothing unless a motive force is added, an entelechy. Since you hold the entelechy to be indivisible, together with the mass it will make a corporeal substance, a unity, a monad. However every single corporeal substance contains an infinity of machines within it, each equipped with its own forces, and each of these again contains an infinity of others, and so on in this way to infinity.
>
> (G 2, 244–5)

Were Leibniz an Idealist intent on disembodying corporeal substances, one would expect him to come back and deny all this talk of machines and corporeal substances and mass. Instead, he agrees that De Volder has got it about right, with the provision that one entelechy actuates and forms into "one machine" the infinity of lesser machines (G 2, 250/AG 175/L 529).

This point is damaging to Compatibilist arguments because some of Leibniz's baldest phenomenalist claims (G 2, 264/L 535; G 270/L 537) were made to De Volder a year later. And on this interpretation, those sort very ill with his dramatic commitments, to the same correspondent in the same time period, to masses and machines and truly unified animals. In fact, it's hard to understand why the one 1704 De Volder text – "there is nothing in things except simple substances, and in them perception and appetite" (G 2, 270/L 537) – has such a grip on commentators.[22] Why should this, rather than the aggregate thesis, be anointed "the most fundamental principle of Leibniz's metaphysics" (Ad 217)? Its being taken as *exclusively* Idealist is especially problematic, as I argued earlier. A look at the De Volder Doctrine Table shows Realist aggregate thesis doctrines routinely endorsed, with enough references to animals to show that they remained among his commitments.

Rutherford's Compatibilism, while not endorsing the "qualified monad conception," is quite similar to Adams's in that it includes a healthy commitment to Idealism. Because of that, he faces some of the same problems.

Rutherford follows Leibniz's texts, admitting that phenomenalism about bodies cannot account for soul-body harmony:

> It is clearly his view that this doctrine is designed to explain an agreement between the orderly progression of a soul's perceptions and the changes that occur in something external to it: its organic

body. No other construal can be placed on a passage such as [PNG 3].

(Rd 216)

Even so, Idealism asserts itself soon after when the "external body" is said to be "a mass the soul perceives as an extended thing." Rutherford continues, "To talk of 'bodies' at all in his scheme must be regarded as a type of shorthand. What exist ultimately for Leibniz are soullike monads and their intrinsic accidents" (Rd 217).

And that sets up a dilemma. Rutherford says that, given these phenomenalist strictures on organic bodies,

> we might wonder whether the organism or soul-body composite is even a coherent ontological type or whether it is, instead, a sort of category mistake: an entity formed by illicitly combining what is mere appearance (the body) with what is truly real (the soul). To answer this doubt, we must modify somewhat our account of the relationship between bodies and souls. Although the soul-body distinction is properly characterized as a distinction between two epistemological perspectives, it is not only that. Along with this distinction comes a crucial ontological claim: that bodies are themselves pluralities of monads. For Leibniz, the term "body" does not refer merely to an appearance or phenomenal object. Instead, a body *is* a plurality of monads, which happens to give the appearance of being an extended object when apprehended by other finite monads.

(Rd 218)

In essence, the solution to the problem of animals is to fall back on Leibniz's equivocation on 'body'. A body, one is being told, can be *either* an appearance *or* a plurality of monads, depending on which is needed. That is, the same thing can be either of those, though the one is mind-dependent and the other isn't. On this account, since a "plurality of monads" is needed for organisms to be "coherent ontological types," bodies are pluralities of monads for that purpose. But those same bodies (as I suppose on this view) could also magically be mere appearances. Without elaboration one is assured that this addition to the account "raises no new problems" and that the two pictures "converge on one reality" (Rd 218).

I conclude that Compatibilists will always confront impassible barriers to a proper understanding of Leibnizian animals.

9   A Final Look

The journey from beginning to end has been difficult but has had its rewards. Chief among them is a new appreciation of the coherence, breadth, and depth of Leibniz's thought. It offers an unusual degree of freedom to those studying philosophy, and contains a consummate richness almost unimaginable in other more straight-laced schemes. Storms erupting over inconsistencies are replaced by a glassy sea once the relevant claims are seen as alternative theories rather than as Truths.

If they are Truths, the picture is quite bleak. For two theses have now been established beyond doubt: (1) Idealism and Realism are inconsistent and (2) Idealism and Realism are endorsed together in all of Leibniz's major mature works. Attributing incoherent Truth-Pluralism to Leibniz would be inevitable if Theory-Pluralism hadn't come along to save the day.

One is left wondering what Leibniz himself was thinking when he so regularly and inextricably interfused Idealism with Realism. I have tried to figure out how he could operate with such a major "psychic division" going all the time. I can't fathom doing it myself – I would definitely be a "one view" theorist! But in many ways it's just like Leibniz to push his way through obstacles in the headlong pursuit of a Renaissance and rationalist ideal.

The example that keeps coming to mind is the Florence dome. To make this dome so large, Filippo Brunelleschi was forced to use ideas and plans scavenged from disparate sources: geared hoists, Islamic mosques, buttressing techniques, classical buildings, and the ancient Roman "herringbone" pattern of bricklaying. All these had to submit to a final synthesis – realized jointly in one magnificent cupola. They could not remain individual and scattered. Through sheer force of the Renaissance will, they were combined.

And so I think it was with the Idealist and Realist elements Leibniz found in sources far and wide and close at hand. They *had* to yield to a final synthesis. If they tried to cling to their isolating individuality, they would be forced into a synthesis befitting the Renaissance ideal of unity. Anything less was unthinkable.

The reader is of course entitled to her own opinion about interpretive schemes. Taking a long view of the matter, it is enough if through this study she comes to an appreciation of the full riches of Leibniz's system.

9.1 The Tables Turned

> But we have all been taught to think of Leibniz's Idealism as the guiding principle of his metaphysical thinking, and so it hardly occurs to us to inquire with an open mind into what position Leibniz is in fact advocating in the various places of his prolific writings.
>
> David S. Scarrow (1973, 92)

It is not an exaggeration, I think, to say the tables have now turned against Idealism. Serious questions have been raised about its ascendancy – about whether it is, as Scarrow says, "the guiding principle of his metaphysical thinking."

Again, the loss of Idealist Compatibilism is crucial in this regard. For with it gone, theorists who want to maintain unadulterated Idealism yet avoid attributing incoherence to Leibniz seem forced into Exclusive Idealism. And that view now faces two challenges it didn't have to face fully before (1) How will it justify being so selective in its approach to a corpus which contains as much evidence against its view as for it? and (2) How will it justify neglecting or construing as metaphorical such a vibrant philosophical alternative as Leibniz's Realism?

Idealism has indeed traditionally regarded Realism as a threat. It worried that (1) the Realist aggregate thesis would introduce inconsistency into Leibniz's thought and hence make him an advocate of Truth-Pluralism; that (2) the aggregate thesis would mire monads with spatiality; and that (3) if one says monads are embodied in animals, one would be committed to monads' having a "corporeal nature" (Erdmann 1891, 2: 189). In each case the fears, seemingly well-founded, did not bear up under scrutiny. Theory-Pluralism answers (1), and the Realist analyses offered here avoid (2) and (3).

The sort of coherence Leibniz's system has is not the kind the commentators insisted upon – where every claim squares with every other. Instead, to maintain a formidable arsenal of metaphysical machinery with plenty of redundancy and explanatory reserves, he floats two main theories. Each one, while not cohering the other, is internally consistent. Of course the internal consistency of his Idealism was never in doubt. But the Realist theory had never been put to the test. Now it has. And it passed with flying colors.

As the tables have turned against Idealism, some readers have suggested simply tossing it out. "If it does so little explanatory work, why keep it around?" My response appeals to Theory-Pluralism, now in defense of Idealism. For it would be quite against the spirit of Theory-Pluralism to scuttle a theory if it has distinctive explanatory strengths. On a very dark day, when the chill winds of skepticism threaten to shut down all the machinations of Realism, Leibniz might need to take refuge in the warm bosom of Idealist solipsism. Those who allow Realism's frequent brilliance to blind them to the need for maintaining austere fall-back positions will pay the price on such a day.

There is in all of us, I think, a tendency to go for one view with gusto, to declare just this one True. It is a tendency which, as I've said, Leibniz himself sometimes succumbs to. But other times he points to a better way – helping us gain freedom from the intellectual bondage of sectarianism.

9.2 Is it True?

Very little has been done to assess the truth of Leibniz's positive claims about the denizens of this universe. Are there any of these things?

No metaphysics can be confirmed or disconfirmed. Its task is complete when it presents a general framework for understanding the world and our place in it. The positivist preoccupation with "verifiability" made it seem that there was something wrong with metaphysics because it didn't admit of crucial experiments that proved it right or wrong. But of course positivism was replete with metaphysical assumptions that admitted of no such test. In the end, it too was on its own. And this was quite predictable from within Theory-Pluralism, where one maintains an open mind about the nature of the world because it can't be proven that it is made up of numbers or atoms or forms or primary matter, sense-data, logical atoms, or what have you.

Still, as metaphysics go, this one is quite confirmable. Each of us is a monad, so there is no problem confirming that there are minds that perceive and strive. Each of us is also an animal, so there is no problem confirming that there are embodied substances that perceive and strive by means of their bodies. That is, things like hunger and pain and sexual experience seem possible only if the minds are hooked up pretty intimately with a body that needs food and protection and satisfaction. Add to that the plausible story Leibniz tells about the place of space, time, and God in the larger scheme and you have the metaphysics – though of course these further claims are controversial and not as open to confirmation as the two central ones having to do with monads and animals. In general, the larger story remains closer to confirmation than many of its competitors – say, the claim that one should start with not-obviously-confirmable numbers or atoms and try to build everything out of them. And the fact that this vision is tied to the earth, to common experience, makes it unnecessary to follow Paul Schrecker in regarding the *Monadology* as a fairy tale wrapped in traditional "mythological trimmings" (Leibniz, 1965, xv-xvi) that are best stripped away.

The Idealist and Realist theories themselves can legitimately avoid the Truth-question. But, as in the case of scientific theories, they admit of a more informal appraisal and can be ranked better or worse in terms of such marks as simplicity, elegance, explanatory power, and so on. I will summarize these as *aesthetic* and *explanatory*.

Aesthetic. I think both of Leibniz's theories are beautiful. Furth is right to note that it was a mighty feat to come up with his stark, pristine, all-encompassing Idealist vision – with its reduction of all else to monads and their perceptions. If that was not enough, Leibniz offers us a Realist vision of equal beauty. The Realist theory possesses a resplendent unity and comprehensiveness unimaginable on the other scheme. It is complete in the way a masterpiece is complete: nothing can be added or taken away without destroying the work. And so far the accounts seem pretty well tied.

Explanatory. It seems Idealism's explanatory power dwindles when it upholds cambridge relations. Everything thus ends up "on its own." "Explainings" become "explainings-away." Causal and all other explanatory connections are severed. Reality is replaced by Appearance. *What is* by *as if.*

By contrast, Realism has the explanatory power needed to unite otherwise scattered elements into a system. It uses real relations to ensure aggregate w exists mind-independently and in such a way as to be utterly dependent on its Ss. Then, moving on to animals, it can say how Ss unite to form an m (a special sort of w) and ms unite to form an n, and n combines with a dominant substance to arrive at last at a mind-independent animal. On the bedrock of substance Leibniz can build aggregates, and from aggregates basic animals, and then animals re-entered the picture as substances in upper-level animals.

In the end, Leibniz simply took the best science of his day and the best theology and the best philosophy and the best physics and constructed a general vision of the universe. Noting what had been discovered beneath the microscope, he thought it likely that all things usually thought dead are brimming with life, if only one had the ability to see the objects. It would be implausible to think that God singled out our little human "world" with its medium-sized dry goods as the only place where drops of water are teeming with life. The paramecium would find further organisms in *its* drops if it developed a microscope of its own, and so on and so on.

A good test of any metaphysic is to ask, "What has been left out?" I have found no answer to that question on the Realist theory developed here. At this point Leibniz reaps the rewards of having handled all aggregates with a single analysis, and all animals with a single analysis. That captures nearly everything – ships and sealing wax and planets among aggregates; cabbages and snails and humans among animals. Add in his accounts of language, space, time, and God, and there is nothing left unexplained. (Idealism also, it might be said, leaves nothing out. But so many of its explanations are "explainings-away" that often the accounts offered don't seem, to my mind, to amount to explanations at all.)

The fact that Leibniz was able to present the ingredients of that rich theory alongside the other, more familiar Idealist one is proof that he belongs among the great philosophers.

9.3 The Worth of this Study

There remains always a purely philosophical attitude towards previous philosophers – an attitude in which, without regard to dates or influences, we seek simply to discover what are the great types of possible philosophies. ... There is still, in this inquiry ... the problem as to the actual views of the philosopher who is to be investigated. But these views are now examined in a different spirit. Where we are inquiring into the opinions of a truly eminent philosopher, it is probable that these opinions will form, in the main, a closely connected system, and that, by learning to understand them, we shall ourselves acquire knowledge of important philosophic truths.

Bertrand Russell (R xi-xii; 1992: xv-xvi)

I began with Russell's claim that he had glimpsed the foundations of Leibniz's "philosophical edifice." Though my disagreements with Russell have gone deep, I end with one of his astute observations – that one worthy goal in the study of Leibniz is *understanding*. While not ignoring the historical context, "dates or influences" were of secondary value as compared with the issues of truth and argument. Indeed, I have learned from Leibniz on this journey – learned well what several "possible philosophies" look like. I have sought to give Leibniz the highest compliment. I have subjected his ideas – and interpretations of them – to the kind of punishing, unrelenting scrutiny that he subjected rival philosophies to.

There has been much in Leibniz's thought that has been left behind in this inquiry. Almost nothing is said about his early views, which often illuminatingly foreshadow mature doctrines. Many connections have already been drawn in the literature, and the task of pointing out others is a project for another day. Moreover, little has been said about the *vis viva* controversy, the details of his views of physics or theology, and other topics. Those issues seemed not in the end to play an important role in the metaphysics, though they remain important topics in the history of Leibniz's thought.

Still, for many of these topics, the way has been paved. For instance, the ultimate metaphysical foundations of *vis viva* can be found (on the Realist Rigid Embodiment account) in the derivative force that w extracts from the primitive forces in its constituent substances. And Realism answers a couple of Garber's questions about the relationship between Leibniz's physics and his metaphysics. Garber writes that (1) Leibniz appears to be a "paradox." For, if he was committed to Idealism – where "the bodies of physics ... enter *only* as phenomena" – how could he have been concerned with such issues as determining the basic laws of physics for "bodies of everyday experience" (Garber 1985, 27–8)? And (2) the "perplexity" is heightened because in some of the "standard" metaphysical works, Garber writes, Leibniz says "his metaphysics is intended to ground the true physics! What possible connection could there be between Leibniz's metaphysical conception of what there really is in the world, and his physics?" (27–8).

Paradox and perplexity have now vanished. For in the Realist theory, "bodies of everyday experience" are real and not phenomena; and the "grounding" of Leibniz's physics in his metaphysics is assured. Garber was right to claim that a Realist theory holds the answer to these questions, and a great deal of credit is owed him for bringing Realist themes to the fore in recent discussion. But Garber applied Leibniz's commitment to Realism only to animals and he restricted that commitment to the "middle years" (roughly 1676–95). Thus he was making a fairly limited claim about the extent – ontological and temporal – of Leibnizian Realism. He conceded that after this time Idealism largely prevailed (28).

I think it's clear Realism cannot be delimited and circumscribed in this way. It is everywhere in the mature thought – showing up well beyond the middle years and in the philosophical account of aggregates as well as that of animals.

Even for the topics covered here, the way is now open for further studies – say, of the details of Leibniz's Realist and Idealist theories held during various time periods and in various works and their impact on other doctrines in his system.

Looking at the Realist theory: working out its precise details is something he probably couldn't have done himself. For he was so clearly committed to an Idealist "slant" on things that he could only keep it on the "back burner" most of the time. He did his best to find points of commonality between the two perspectives. But he was never given the freedom Theory-Pluralism has granted me here.

There is much to learn from Leibniz once the demands for consistency have been set aside and the Renaissance mind, dabbling treacherously at the precipice of incoherence, bids those hiding safely in single-minded positions come out and explore with abandon the full range of options. For "pleasure disappoints, possibility never. And what wine is so sparkling, so fragrant, so intoxicating, as possibility!" (Kierkegaard 1944, I: 40)

Appendix

Guide to Doctrine Tables

These Doctrine Tables are designed to show where various important doctrines are endorsed in five major works in the mature corpus. They are arrange chronologically, and in each case I have tried to put down the number of times a doctrine is endorsed on a given page or in a given section, though no doubt some of the cases could be disputed. In parentheses I sometimes include references to translations.

These abbreviations are used only in the Doctrine Tables. First the Realist "Aggregate Thesis" doctrines (1.8) are here repeated with their abbreviations, and added to them are endorsements of animals (which I take to indicate a commitment to Realism, as argued in Chapter 8):

Cmp	*Composition*: Every body is composed of substances.
Cn	*Containment*: Every body contains substances.
D	*Divided*: Every body is actually divided into substances.
F	*Force*: Every body has derivative active force that supervenes on the primitive active force of the substances it contains.
M	*Mass*: Every body is a "mass" or aggregate of substances.
Plu	*Plurality:* Every body is a plurality.
Pr	*Presupposition*: Every plurality presupposes genuine unities.
R	*Reality*: Every body has some residual derivative reality because of the presence in it of primitively real substances.
Ss	*The Ss*: Every body *is* substances.
Sv	*Supervenience*: Every derivative quality of bodies must arise from the primitive qualities of the things it contains.
An	Endorsements of animals.

The remaining two categories fall under *Idealism* (italicized to help set them apart from Realist themes):

CM	*Canonical Metaphysics* as described in 1.7 and Chapter 5 – briefly, that the monads are the only substances, relations are ideal or reducible to intrinsic states, the "predicate in sub-

ject" doctrine holds, bodies are eliminatively reduced to phenomena, universal harmony and mirroring apply to perceptions of monads – and the following are denied: mind-body parallelism, the "aggregate thesis," and the true unity of animals.

Ph   *Phenomenalism* – the places where Leibniz says aggregates are appearances (or "phenomena") in minds. (While such claims are very much in the spirit of the Canonical Metaphysics program, when they are found explicitly in a work, they are reported here.)

So, for example, in the Arnauld Correspondence Table, LA 97: Cmp 2, Cn 1, Plu 2, Pr 2, R2, Ph. 1 means that there are, on p. 97 of LA, two occurrences of Composition, one of Containment, two of Plurality, Presupposition, and Reality, and one of *Phenomenalism*. And in the *New System* Table, NS 14: Cn 1, An 1, *CM 5, Ph 2* means that in section 14 of the *New System*, Containment and Animal are endorsed once, the *Canonical Metaphysics* five times, and *Phenomenalism* twice.

The Tables show where the principal doctrines are found, but they are not intended to be infallible guides. If the reader wishes to look further into the textual details, they will help her find relevant passages – the explicit quotation of which is too lengthy to include here.

Table 1   Discourse on Metaphysics (1686) Doctrine Table (by Section of DM)

DM §	Realism	Idealism
8 (AG 40-1)		CM 3
9 (AG 41-2)		CM 3
12 (AG 44)	An 1	
13 (AG 44-6)		CM 1
14 (AG 46-7)		CM 4, Ph 4
15 (AG 48)		CM 1, Ph 1
16 (AG 48-9)		CM 1
18 (AG 51-2)	F 1	
21 (AG 53-4)	F 1	
22 (AG 54-5)	An 1	
26 (AG 58)		CM 2
27 (AG 59)		CM 2
28 (AG 59-60)		CM 2, Ph 3
29 (AG 60)		CM 1
30 (AG 60-2)		CM 1
32 (AG 63-4)	An 1	CM 5, Ph 2
33 (AG 64-5)	An 2	CM 1, Ph 1
34 (AG 65-6)	An 2	CM 1
35 (AG 66-7)		CM 2
36 (AG 67-8)		CM 2

Table 2 Totals for Discourse on Metaphysics

Realism		Idealism	
F 2, An 7		CM 32, Ph 11	
Aggregate Thesis	2	Canonical Metaphysics	32
Animals	7	Phenomenalism	11
Total	9	Total	43

Table 3 Arnauld Correspondence (1686–90) Doctrine Table (by page number in LA – i.e., G 2)

LA (= G 2)	Realism	Idealism
39 (AG 70)		CM 1
41 (AG 71-2)		CM 2
42 (AG 72-3)		CM 2
43 (AG 73-4)		CM 3
44 (AG 74-5)		CM 2
45 (AG 75)		CM 2
46 (AG 75-6)		CM 2
47 (AG 76-7)		CM 4
49		CM 1
50		CM 1
51		CM 1
52		CM 3
53		CM 2, Ph 1
54		CM 1
55		CM 1
56		CM 2
57		CM 4, Ph 1
58	An 1	CM 3, Ph 1
74 (AG 77)	An 1	CM 1
75 (AG 78-9)	An 3	CM 1, Ph 1
76 (AG 79)	An 1	CM 1, Ph 1
77 (AG 79-80)	D 1, Pr 1, An 3	
90 (AG 81)	An 1	
91 (AG 81-2)	An 1	
92 (AG 82-3)	An 1	
93 (AG 83)	F 1, An 1	
94 (AG 83-4)	An 1	
95 (AG 84-5)		CM 2
96 (AG 85-6)	Pr 1, R 1, Sv 2	Ph 1
97 (AG 86)	Cmp 2, Cn 1, Plu 2, Pr 2, R 2	Ph 1
98 (AG 86-7)	F1, An 1	CM 1
99 (AG 87-8)	An 1	Ph 1
100 (AG 88-9)	Cmp 2, Cn 1, R 1, Sv 1, An 2	Ph 1
101 (AG 89)		Ph 5
102 (AG 89-90)		Ph 1
111	An 1	
112		CM 2, Ph 1

113	An 2	*CM 1*
114	An 3	*Ph 1*
115	F 1, An 1	*CM 1, Ph 3*
116	An 2	*CM 1*
117	An 1	*CM 1*
118	Cn 1, Plu 1, Pr 1, Ss 1, An 3	*Ph 1*
119	Cn 1, Plu 1, An 1	*CM 1, Ph 3*
120	Cn 1, D 1, Ss 1, An 2	
121	An 1	
122	Cn 1, An 2	
123	An 1	
124	An 2	*CM 1*
125	An 1	*CM 1*
126	Cn 1, An 2	*CM 3, Ph 1*
133	F 1	*CM 2*
135	Cn 1, Ss 1	
136	An 1	*CM 3*
137	F 1	

Table 4 Totals for Arnauld Correspondence

Realism		Idealism	
Cmp 4, Cn 8, D 2, F 5, Plu 4, Pr 5, R 4, Ss 3, Sv 3, An 44		CM 62, Ph 27	
Aggregate Thesis	38	Canonical Metaphysics	62
Animals	44	Phenomenalism	27
Total	82	Total	89

Table 5 *New System* (1695) Doctrine Table (by paragraph number in NS)

NS §	Realism	Idealism
2 (AG 138-9)	F 1	
3 (AG 139)	F 2, Plu 1, R 1, Sv 1, An 1	*CM 2*
4 (AG 139-40)	An 1	*CM 1*
5 (AG 140)	An 1	*CM 1*
6 (AG 140)	An 1	
7 (AG 140-1)	An 3	
9 (AG 141)	An 1	
10 (AG 141-2)	An 1	
11 (AG 142)	Cmp 1, Cn 1, M 1, Plu 2, Pr 2, R 2, Sv 1, An 1	*CM 1*
12 (AG 142-3)	An 1	
13 (AG 143)		*CM 1*
14 (AG 143-4)	Cn 1, An 1	*CM 5, Ph 2*
15 (AG 144)	An 1	*CM 2*
16 (AG 144-5)		*CM 3*
17 (AG 145)		*CM 2*

Table 6 Totals for *New System*

Realism		Idealism	
Cmp 1, Cn 2 , F 3, M 1, Plu 3, R 3, Sv 2, An 13		CM 18, Ph 2	
Aggregate Thesis	15	Canonical Metaphysics	18
Animals	13	Phenomenalism	2
Total	28	Total	20

Table 7 De Volder Correspondence (1699–1706) Doctrine Table (Selections, by page number in G 2)

G 2	Realism	Idealism
183 (L 519)	Ss 1	
184-5 (L 520)	Cn 2, Sv 1, An 1	CM 2
193 (L 521)	Cn 3, An 1	CM 1
194 (L 522)	Cn 1, An 1	
195 (L 523)	Cn 2, F 1, Plu 1, Ss 1, An 1	
205-6 (Ad 283-4)	Cmp 1, Cn 2, M 2, An 1	CM 3
239 (L 526)		CM 1
250 (L 529)	Cmp 1, Cn 4, F1, M 1, Sv 1, An 2	CM 4, Ph 1
251 (L 529-30)	F 2, Pr 2, Sv 1, An 2	CM 3, Ph 1
252 (L 530-1)	Cn 2, Sv 1, An 4	CM 2, Ph 1
253 (L 531)	Cn 1, Plu 1, An 1	
256 (Rd 234)	Sv 1	
261-2	Cmp 1, Cn 2, D 1, Plu 1, R 3, Ss 1, Sv 3	CM 1, Ph 1
263-4 (L 534-5)	Cn 1, F 1, Pr 1	Ph 2
267 (R 242)	Cn 2, D 1, M1, Plu 1, Pr 1, R 3, Sv 1	
268 (L 536)	Cmp 1, Cn 1,D 1, Sv 1	CM 1, Ph 1
270 (L 537)	F 1, Sv 1	CM 2, Ph 2
275 (AG 181)	Cn 1, M1, Sv 1	CM 4
276 (AG 182)	Cn 1, D1, M1, Plu 1, Pr 1, Ss 1	CM 2, Ph 2
277 (AG 182-3)		CM 1
278 (AG 184)		CM 2, Ph 1
278-9 (R 245)	Cmp 1, D 1, Plu 1, Pr 1	
282 (AG 185)	Cmp 1, Cn 2, D 1, Plu 1, Sv 1	CM 2, Ph 2

Table 8 Totals for De Volder Correspondence

Realism		Idealism	
Cmp 6, Cn 27, D 6, F 6, M 6, Plu 7, Pr 6, R 6, Ss 4, Sv 13, An 14		CM 31, Ph 15	
Aggregate Thesis	87	Canonical Metaphysics	31
Animals	14	Phenomenalism	15
Total	101	Total	46

Table 9   *Monadology* (1714) Doctrine Table (by Section of Mon)

Mon §	Realism	Idealism
1 (AG 213)	Cn 1	*CM 1*
2 (AG 213)	Ss 1	
3 (AG 213)		*CM 1*
4 (AG 213)		*CM 1*
5 (AG 213)		*CM 1*
6 (AG 213)		*CM 1*
7 (AG 213-14)		*CM 3*
8 (AG 214)	Sv 1	
9 (AG 214)		*CM 1*
10 (AG 214)		*CM 1*
11 (AG 214)		*CM 1*
12 (AG 214)		*CM 1*
13 (AG 214)		*CM 1*
14 (AG 214-15)	An 1	*CM 1*
15 (AG 215)		*CM 1*
16 (AG 215)		*CM 1*
17 (AG 215)		*CM 2*
18 (AG 215)		*CM 1*
19 (AG 215)		*CM 1*
20 (AG 215)		*CM 1*
21 (AG 216)		*CM 1*
22 (AG 216)		*CM 1*
23 (AG 216)		*CM 1*
24 (AG 216)		*CM 1*
25 (AG 216)	An 1	
26 (AG 216)	An 1	
27 (AG 216)		*CM 1*
28 (AG 216-17)	An 1	
29 (AG 217)		*CM 1*
30 (AG 217)		*CM 2*
36 (AG 217)	An 1	*CM 1*
47 (AG 219)		*CM 1*
48 (AG 219)		*CM 1*
49 (AG 219)		*CM 1*
50 (AG 219)		*CM 1*
51 (AG 219)		*CM 2*
52 (AG 219-20)		*CM 2*
56 (AG 220)		*CM 1*
57 (AG 220)		*CM 1*
59 (AG 220)		*CM 1*
60 (AG 220-1)		*CM 3*
61 (AG 221)		*CM 1*
62 (AG 221)	An 2	
63 (AG 221)	An 2	
64 (AG 221)	An 2	
65 (AG 221)	D 1	
66 (AG 222)	Cn 1	
67 (AG 222)	Cn 1	
68 (AG 222)	Cn 1	

69 (AG 222)	Cn 1	
70 (AG 222)	Cn 1, An 1	
71 (AG 222)	An 1	
72 (AG 222)	An 1	
73 (AG 222)	An 1	
74 (AG 222)	An 1	
75 (AG 222-3)	An 1	
76 (AG 223)	An 1	
77 (AG 223)	An 1	
78 (AG 223)	An 1	*CM 1*
79 (AG 223)	An 1	
81 (AG 223)	An 1	
82 (AG 223)	An 1	
83 (AG 223)		*CM 1*

Table 10 Totals for *Monadology*

Realism		Idealism	
Cn 6, D 1, Ss 1, Sv 1, An 23		CM 47	
Aggregate Thesis	9	Canonical Metaphysics	47
Animals	23	Phenomenalism	0
Total	32	Total	47

Table 11 Summary of Doctrine Tables

	DM	LA	NS	DeV	Mon	Total
Composition		4	1	6		11
Containment		8	2	27	6	43
Divided		2		6	1	9
Force	2	5	3	6		16
Mass			1	6		7
Plurality		4	3	7		14
Presupposition		5		6		11
Reality		4	3	6		13
Ss		3		4	1	8
Supervenience		2	2	13	1	18
Animals	7	44	13	14	23	101
Canon. Metaph.	*32*	*62*	*18*	*31*	*47*	*190*
Phenomenalism	*11*	*27*	*2*	*15*		*55*

Table 12   Totals for Doctrine Tables

Realism		Idealism	
Aggregate Thesis	150	Canonical Metaphysics	190
Animals	101	Phenomenalism	55
Total	251	Total	245

Notes

1 Introduction

1 Note that the *New System* is not always given section numbers in its transcriptions and translations. But they can easily be filled in by writing section numbers next to each paragraph in the work: in this case, 1–18.

2 Michalko 1998, 10–11.

3 See his own account of the wide scope – art, "astronomical, mechanical, and chemical observations," history, and a dictionary of technical terms familiar to craftsmen – envisioned for the Brandenburg Academy in Berlin: 6 September 1700, G 2, 210.

4 See Russell 1945, 583, 590.

5 GM 6, 236/L 436. Peter Loptson (1999, 372) has called attention to Leibniz's tendency towards "Hegelian historicism and contextualism": where "every point of view has its 'truth'" and Leibniz's thought accordingly takes on a "chameleon-like quality."

6 "That [the fish-pond] was apparently irreconcilable with his immaterial atomism troubles his modern commentators; Leibniz himself seemed to combine a confidence that his two systems really did converge with an anxiety about the details required to work this convergence out" (Wilson 1997, 175).

7 See Reston 1995, 25 ff.

8 "[T]he actual phenomena of nature are ordered, and must be so, in such a way that nothing ever happens in which the law of continuity ... or any of the other most exact mathematical rules, is ever broken. Far from it: for things could only be made intelligible by these rules, which alone are capable ... of giving us insight into the reasons and intentions of the author of things" (1702, Reply to Bayle, G 4, 568–69/WF 123).

9 See DM 14 and G 2 516/AG 202.

10 E.g. NS 13–15 and *Theodicy* I, 7: G 6, 106/T 127.

11 I will examine the doubts about animals intensively in Chapter 8. On this point of animals being a source of doubt, see Ad 240, where it is pointed out that the "vast expansion of his ontology" to include animals "brought with it an increased vulnerability to skeptical doubts." Thus the "more austere phenomenalism is sometimes visible behind the complex theory of his later years, as a rejected but respected alternative, or even as a fall-back position kept in reserve."

12 I shall henceforth omit separate reference to plants as they are on a par with animals.

13 See R, 4, 132–5; Furth (1976), 120–21.

14 Theodicy I, 30: G 6 119/T 140.

15 Garber 1985, 62 writes, "the world of the *Monadology* is as full of organisms" as the world envisaged in the correspondence with Arnauld.

16 See John Bernoulli's comment to Leibniz about the trajectory: GM 3, 714. The more general point is at G 2, 205–6/Ad 283–4.

17 G 2, 205–6/Ad 283. See also the discussion at Rd 253–8.

18 For details, see Ad, Chapter 13.

19 It is so called because in a few spots Hegel claimed, or appeared to have claimed, that contradictions can be true. He writes "there is a host of contradictory things" – for example, motion, where "Something moves, not because at one moment it is here and at another there, but because at one and the same moment it is here and not here, because in this 'here', it at once is and is not" (Hegel 1969, 440). For a full discussion, see Priest 1987.

20 Kabitz 1932, 636. The entire brief passage, written in Leibniz's hand in his copy of Berkeley's *Principles of Human Knowledge*, is translated at AG 307.

21 See, e.g., Mugnai 1992, Mates 1986, Cover and O'Leary Hawthorne 1999, and Plaisted 2002.

22 "Monads are not in bodies" (Mates 1986, 204, fn. 63).

23 Kim 1978, quotation from p. 154.

24 Kim 1984.

25 This is an abbreviation for the " if and only if" relation, or "material equivalence" as it's called in logic. The main idea is that the two items entail each other. Thus "A iff B" is equivalent to "If A then B *and* If B then A." The logical conditions on A and B must match, though strict identity of A and B is not required. In the case at hand, when two properties supervene on one another, the conditions after the "iff" must obtain, and vice versa.

26 This construal of strong supervenience is a simplified version of the one given in Kim 1991. If one is worried that simple necessarily covariant properties like "equilateral" and "equiangular" are supervenient according to this analysis, I am not much bothered by that. Let those cases be degenerate but genuine cases of supervenience. I am interested only in *contingent* relations between properties. Relations between properties in all worlds are not to the point.

2 Substance

1 "But the intelligent soul, knowing what it is and being able to say this little word 'I' which means so much, ... remains and subsists metaphysically ... " (DM 34: A VI 4 B, 1584 (N. 306)/L 325). "[B]y means of the soul or form, there is in us a true unity corresponding to what we call 'I'" (NS 11). Also G 4, 559–60/WF 113; LA 45.

2 This distinction is owed to Wallace Matson 1968, 287–8. For a development of similar ideas, see Nagel 1986.

3 Lodge 1998, 167: "This control or domination [of the soul over the body], is something we find in ourselves. It consists, in part, of our sense that we cause our bodies to move in certain ways, and perhaps more importantly that we have the ability to cause our bodies to behave in certain ways *on demand*."

4 "But to extend the analogy with what we feel at *present* in our *own* bodies to the *future* and *past*, as well as to *other* bodies, I hold not only that these souls or entelechies all have with them some kind of organic body appropriate to their perceptions, but also that they always will have, and always have had, as long as they have existed ... *Things are everywhere and always just as they are in us now* (leaving the supernatural aside) except for varying degrees of perfection" (G 3, 340/WF 205–6). It should be noted that we can attribute causation to external things because we have the innate notion of cause and effect.

5 See Jackson 1998, 19 on the physicalist's "perspective-free" account of the world.

6 See Ad 333, 340 and Hartz (1984) for discussion of this issue in connection with Leibniz.

7 See Robinson 1982, 113–23 and Armstrong 1961, 187–90. Also, less skeptically, Mackie 1973, 148–53.

8 Armstrong 1961, 187–90 and Smart 1963, 72–3.

9 Schopenhauer 1896, I: 3. This version is given a powerful voice in Foster 1982, 63–72.

10 Leibniz's complaints about the obscurity or relationality of the primary qualities pretty much entail this – see Hartz 1984.

11 "Everything happens in the body ... as if man himself were only body, or an automaton" (G 4, 559/WF 112/L 577).

12 Blackburn 1997, 16: "The trouble with physicalism is that a real world of independent, spatio-temporally located objects ... needs the categorical events of the subjective point of view to be actualized or made concrete."

13 He tells Arnauld that in explanations of composites we need to find "something at which we can stop" (LA 102 – translation from AG 90) and later writes that substances are the "absolute first principles of the composition of things" (NS 11).

14 According to which every part is necessary for a certain whole to be that whole.

15 Below this will be examined in more detail and will be called the "Divisibility Argument."

16 Prior to about 1700 – and often after that – the simples were animals, or quasi-Aristotelian form/matter composites that are *per se* unified. With the advent of monadology, however, the "substantial form" tended to be replaced by a "dominant monad" or "entelechy" – which unified an aggregate of lesser monads into a *unum per se*. Aggregates became, instead of heaps of animals, heaps of monads. A full treatment of animals must wait until Chapter 8.

17 "[F]orce must exist even in a subject which is a single substance only" (1694, in Bossuet 1909, 6: 528/WF 34)

18 "[N]o reason can be given why bodies of a certain degree of smallness are not divisible further" (c. 1689, Principia Logico-Metaphysica, or "Primary Truths," A VI 4 B 1648 (N. 325): C 522/PW 91/AG 34).

19 A theological argument is given at G 4, 495/WF 49.

20 Nevertheless, it is well to remember that in Leibniz's mind there was no sharp demarcation between the theological and non-theological. What is assumed about the natural world is nearly always tied somehow to assumptions about the Being who made it.

3 Mereology

1 The general idea is that for Leibniz space and time are orders which merely mark the relations between objects in an actual or possible system. Here there is no guarantee that objects occupy a unique "place" in the cosmos in the way that, in Newton's system, a region of Space at a Time is a unique place in the universe.

2 *On Generation and Corruption* I, 2: Aristotle 1984, 516. I will not be able to consider the use Aristotle makes of the argument.

3 As Lucretius argues (in *On the Nature of Things* I, 421–74/Oates 1940, 77), "[T]here is nothing which you can affirm to be at once separate from all body and quite distinct from void, which would so to say count as the discovery of a third nature."

4 Thus: "God in the beginning form'd matter in solid, massy, hard, impenetrable, movable particles. [T]hese primitive particles being solids, are incomparably harder than any porous bodies compounded of them; even so very hard, as never to wear or break in pieces; no ordinary power being able to divide what God himself made one in the first creation" (Newton 1952, 400, Query 31).

5 For details about Leibniz's use of this term, see, e.g., Hartz and Cover 1988.

6 GM 3, 964; Clarke L 5.106. See Antognazza 2001, 10.

7 Note that by being in the divine intellect they retain a foothold in ontology that is not available to thoroughgoing eliminative reductions of space and time.

8 "We have to accept substance without extension, for God at least could never be extended. But I believe that all created substance is accompanied by extension ... " (September 1704, to Masham, G 3, 362/WF 219).

9 As Epicurus writes, "the void can neither act nor be acted upon." Letter to Herodotus, in Oates 1940, 11.

10 See Balz 1951.

11 See, e.g., G 2, 268/L 536; G 7, 564 – both quoted in 3.6 below.

12 As I argued in 2.5 and will again in 5.1.

13 Toland is the presumed author of *"Remarques Critiques sur le Système de Monsr. Leibnitz de l'Harmonie Préetablie"* published in 1716 in the *Histoire critique de la République des lettres*. A translation and facsimile reproduction of the article appear in Francks and Woolhouse 2000. The quoted bit is on p. 106 of their translation (p. 124 of the original journal article).

14 Thus Samuel Levey: "the basic idea that matter is *actually divided* ... and not just *divisible* into parts is a resounding and pervasive theme in the theory of matter" (1999, 107).

15 c. 1714, GM 7, 17–29/L 666–73.

16 For a discussion of the formal logical relationships, as well as a textually exhaustive account of the works in which there are definitions of 'similia', 'aequalia', 'homogenea', 'congrua', and 'coincidentia', see Schneider 1988. For additional discussion, see Mugnai 1992 and Schmidt 1971.

17 GM 7, 19/L 667; "in" is irreflexive, asymmetric, and transitive. In many texts 'in' is taken to be reflexive: e.g., at G 7, 238, "A is in A" is upheld.

18 GM 7, 18–19/L 667; GM 7, 25/L 671; GM 5, 153–4; Mugnai 1992, 88–9; Schneider 1988, 176; "qualitatively identical" is reflexive, symmetric, and transitive.

19 GM 7, 19/L 667; Mugnai 1992, 89; Schneider 1988, 178; "homogeneous" is reflexive, symmetric, and transitive.

20 GM 7, 19/L 668; "part of" is irreflexive, asymmetric, and transitive (transitivity is proven at G 7, 240).

21 NE 238 (II, 27, 11).

4   Introduction to Aggregates

1 The last sentence was not in the copy sent to Arnauld, but similar material at LA 101 (quoted next) was sent. See Ad 246 for further references.

5   Idealist Analyses of Aggregates

1 See Rd 225. Also, Loeb (1981, 306) writes, "all material objects (including living bodies or organisms) are susceptible to a phenomenalistic reduction to sets of perceptions. ... "

2 G 2, 275; G 6, 590/L 625; G 3, 430/L 633.

3 20 September 1712, to Des Bosses, G 2, 460–1/L 607, cited by Furth 1976, 118.

4 'F' can be either a mass noun ('water') or a count noun ('pencil').

5 Elsewhere societies are said to be more unified than piles of stones and other aggregates because they possess a certain "intention" (to live together) and size. See Dascal 1993, 399–400.

6 This issue, raised by Adams at Ad 249, is discussed at more length in 6.7.1.

7 These relations will be more fully characterized in 6.6.1 below.

8 Broad 1975, 92. See also Jolley (1986).

9 See Jolley 1986, 49.

10 G 7, 319–22/L 363–5; less explicitly at G 2 270, 276/AG 181–82.

11 The text under consideration was written before monads appeared in Leibniz's philosophy, but I make the relevant perceivers monads because the Well-Founded Phenomena view I am working towards is nearly always put in terms of monads and their perceptions.

12 G 2, 262/L 533; G 4, 512/L 504.

13 See Sleigh 1990, 128–30 on the notion of "real causation" in a substance.

14 The formal content would express the representational content and contain non-representational appetitive and perceptual features as well.

15 Lewis 1991, 81–87. The idea is that a "mereological fusion" is "nothing over and above" the items fused (81).

16 *Notationes Generales*, Leibniz 1948, 322 = A VI 4 A, 555 (N. 131)/Ad 247. For a detailed discussion of Leibniz's view of secondary qualities, see Ad, esp. pp. 247–8.

17 "[I]n nature there is none [i.e., determined extension]; everything is strictly indefinite where extension is concerned, and what extension we ascribe to bodies is merely phenomena and abstractions" (LA 99).

18 According to which our veridical perceptions of objects are caused by some external reality – typically physical objects but in Leibniz's case, quasi-caused by external substances.

6 Realist Analyses of Aggregates

1 In a text written at about the same time, he makes the conditions mind-dependent and puts what he says about aggregates in the idiom of Idealism – in particular, Mental Constructions: "If when several things are posited, by that very fact some unity is immediately understood to be posited, then the former are called *parts*, the latter a *whole*. Nor is it even necessary that they exist at the same time, or at the same place; it suffices that they be considered at the same time. Thus from all the Roman emperors together, we construct one aggregate. But actually no entity that is really one is composed of a plurality of parts, and every substance is indivisible, and those things that have parts are not entities, but merely phenomena" (A VI 4 A, 627 (N. 147)/Leibniz 2001, 271). This is yet more evidence that Leibniz launches two quite different theories of aggregates at the same time rather than seeing a need to give one up in favor of the other.

2 This point is owed to Peter van Inwagen 1990, 22.

3 van Inwagen 1990, Chapter 2.

4 As argued in Beeley (1996), Bolton (1996), Antognazza (2001), and Mugnai (forthcoming).

5 The context for all the passages has been stripped away here. Nuances gathered from surrounding material or the historical background might color the interpretation of a given passage, but for my purposes these can be ignored.

6 This and some of the following sections are based broadly on recent work by Kit Fine (1999).

7 Indeed, this is counterintuitive, as Fine (1999, 64) notes: "it is hard to believe that [the trope is a part of the sandwich] in the same way as the standard ingredients." Thus "standard mereology" fails to analyze the sandwich correctly because no relation is specified by a plain sum, and the relation specified by a trope sum is not considered to be a part of the sandwich.

8 Fine 1999. I will expand these to include harmony and supervenience embodiments – an application not found in, or sanctioned by, Fine.

9 'Contact' is not included in Fine's analysis; it is added here to capture more of the common-sense notion of a sandwich – which puts some contraint on spatial togetherness as well as "betweenness."

10 For example, a variable embodiment would be a river or music collection, whose components are constantly changing.

11 A tiny bit of compression must be allowed, of course, to conform to the laws of physics. This will be regarded as negligible deformation.

12 I note that strictly speaking for Leibniz there would be nothing (except God's power) that could annihilate the components when these are substances.

13 This is a problem only if one sees supervenience as in some sense serving an explanatory purpose, and not just representing a "brute factual" relation between families of properties.

I have already explained (1.9) the explanatory expections Leibniz brings to bear on supervenience, and I am operating with those in mind here.

14 Weight was accounted a "character" of rigid embodiments by Fine (1999, 67). Here I make it simply one of many properties that might supervene on an arrangement of components.

15 See the discussion of "nominal definitions" in Dascal 1998, 10, and G 4, 423/AG 24.

16 As will become clear below, when supervenience relations are supplemented by others, one can construct a more satisfying account.

17 See Berra *et al.*, 1982, 78–82. See Leibniz's claim about the connection between states of bodies and secondary qualities: "[W]e cannot even understand why this rotation, these vortices, and these circles, if they are real, should bring about exactly the perceptions we have of red, heat, and noise" (G 6, 499/AG 186).

18 See G 4, 575–6/WF 141–2.

19 Of the conflict between phenomenalism and the aggregate thesis, Rutherford writes that if one says Leibniz is equivocating on 'reality' and other key terms, one ends up "ascribing a deep, and rather obvious, incoherence to his late writings" (Rutherford 1995, 147).

20 It is well to remember that Leibniz faced the question of why all relations had to be of the cambridge sort in his correspondence with De Volder – G 2, 246.

21 Leibniz 1768, VI-2, 185 – quoted in Dascal 1998, 12.

22 Of course, if God's mind is brought into the picture, objective **R**s become more plausible. A few texts lean this way: see Rd 222–6 and Lodge 2001.

23 See Dascal 1993, 399–400, where different conditions are used to distinguish various degrees of unity – e.g., between "natural" and "artificial" societies.

24 NE 238 (II, 27, 11), as noted in Simons 1987, 319.

25 We often think of ourselves as having *discovered* some of the **R**s – the "real essences" as it were. But these are nearly always theory-laden and depend on scientific theory, which could change. Thus, that water is hydrogen and oxygen "so related" might seem a timeless truth, but it remains quite defeasible given unforeseen shifts in scientific theory.

26 Dascal 1998, 10 notes that animals have confused knowledge, comprising sensation and "consecutive memory," but no language. Still, the principle of continuity is not trampled – Dascal 1998, 11.

27 I cannot restrict this to extant languages, especially in light of the claim, noted in 6.6.5, that there are "roots" for terms in most natural languages. Also see Dascal 1998, 4–12.

28 "[T]he concept of forces or powers, which the Germans call *Kraft* and the French *la force*, . . . brings the strongest light to bear upon our understanding of the true concept of substance" (1694, "On the Correction of Metaphysics," G 4, 469/L 433).

29 This is the inclusive 'or'.

30 Leibniz used this as his own example at G 2, 276/AG 182 – as cited in Chapter 3.

31 Melville 1950, 478 (Chapter 111).

32 How Locke's atom-clusters cause "ideas" in the mind is equally obscure. In addition to the traditional "causal link problem" between the physical and the mental, there is a problem with the mechanism of causation – how primary-quality-bearing atoms cause primary-quality-bearing ideas in knowers. Even more pressing is the matter of skepticism, championed by Berkeley: how do we know there is anything external in any given case? Locke himself admits problems surround the causal connection. He writes that we can retain the "certainty of our senses" given "The actual receiving of *ideas* from without, that gives us notice of the *existence* of other things, and makes us know, that something doth exist at that time without us, which causes that *idea* in us." But he adds, "perhaps we neither know nor consider how it does it. . . . " (*Essay* IV, 11, 2) and that the existence of external things may not be "altogether so certain as our intuitive knowledge" (IV, 11, 3).

33 More details about the blockade are provided in the Well-Founded Phenomena account below.

34 See Stace 1955, 43–5 for an interesting comment on Kant's veil and its historical consequences.

35 See Jackson 1998, 91–5.

36 See Nason 1945, for some details.

37 This is similar to what is called "Kantian Physicalism" by Jackson 1998, 24.

38 Kabitz 1932, 636/AG 307/Ad 224.

39 Again, at Rd 191 it is said: "For a plurality of substances to be united in a world it is in the first place necessary that they each express within their perceptual states their relation to the universe as a whole."

7 Is Realism Compatible with Idealism?

1 On the issue of convertibility for being and one that arises here: in the larger corpus Leibniz seems to observe a restriction on its scope. On that restriction, it applies only to substances, not to aggregates. Aggregates retain reality (being) even though their unity is wholly in the mind. This is confirmed twice in the De Volder exchange (G 2, 261, 267), where the "borrowed" reality of aggregates is upheld while their unity is dismissed as mind-dependent. I acknowledge the Des Bosses text: "Being and unity are convertible, and when a being is brought about through aggregation it is also one in this way, even if this being and unity is semi-mental" (G 2, 304). One can't save all the texts, and this is a very unusual one emanating from an unreliable set of letters.

2 Rutherford also writes that some "collective entities" are similar to aggregates of monads in that they are "not spatial aggregates of parts (e.g., sets of numbers)" (Rd 219).

3 See Zimmerman (1995), esp. p. 59, where a set can inherit "quasi-physical, derivative properties" from its truly physical and fundamental members. In particular, he writes, " ... a set of bits of bronze is, in a way, located where its members are; and it makes perfect sense to ascribe to it the weight the sum [i.e., aggregate] of its members would have if there were such a sum." See also p. 93 and on p. 99 there is a plausible "empirical property inheritance principle" for sets. Also Fine (1999), 66 advances a "location postulate" for physical objects considered as sets or "rigid embodiments" – roughly, objects joined by a relation (like "bunched" or "scattered"). The postulate says such embodiments are "located at the point p at t" just in case at least one of the objects is located at p at t.

4 Adams is clearly always taking the Fs to be substances, not represented substances, in this context – Ad 244–5.

5 This follows the lines of what Zimmerman calls a "sum theory of masses," according to which one says, roughly, that a mass made up of smaller masses is a unique fusion of the smaller ones (Zimmerman 1995, 65–6). On such strictures, the pirate ship's ontological status couldn't be very different from that of its constituent chips. Sure, the ship is larger than the individual chips, weighs more, and so on. But the ship can't be made of steel while the chips are plastic. Nor, if it is an aggregate of this sort, could the ship be a sense-datum or mental construction while the chips are plastic.

6 There is some backsliding from this, as when he goes on to say that "a monad characteristically represents an organic body as *its* body to the extent that it represents that body as where it is and as the instrument through which it acts" (Rd 224). One is not told how a non-spatial monad can represent its body as "where it is."

7 Quoting Rutherford more fully: "[A]ssuming the existence of certain monads, and assuming the presence of a mind capable of apprehending those monads in relation to each other, there will be determined, as a result, some aggregative being. [W]e may see Leibniz as conceiving of [the organic body that is the property of any soullike monad] in two complementary ways: on the one hand, as a mere appearance or what a monad represents as its body; on the other hand, as what that body is in itself, some aggregate of monads" (Rd 223–4). "The reduction Leibniz propounds contains elements of phenomenalism. Because the relations that determine the aggregation of monads are limited to correlations among those monads' phenomenal representations of the world, aggregates can only come to be as a result of the agreement apprehended by God among their

perceptions. There is thus a sense in which Leibniz can legitimately claim that the reality of material things is 'located in' the harmony that exists among the perceptions of monads. Granting this, however, does not entail that this theory amounts to a type of phenomenalism. Although an agreement among the perceptions of monads is presupposed in defining the relations on which aggregates depend, matter is reduced in his theory to a plurality of *substances*, not simply a plurality of their perceptions. ... In attempting to specify the ground in reality for a particular body, even God has no alternative but to identify the grounding monads in terms of the phenomena they would perceive under the condition of universal harmony" (Rd 225–6). See Wilson (1999, 375–7) for important arguments against the compatibility of "strong phenomenalism" and a metaphysic that has animals and monads composing "inanimate masses."

8 Wilson notes that Leibniz does not have a single theory of perception, and cites G 3, 622 as evidence of this (Wilson 1989, 195).

9 It is not clear this is successful. I discuss it next.

10 Note that Adams writes in this same context, "Leibniz says that bodies *are* aggregates of substances" so "it is hard to see how he could fail to think that their reality consists at least partly in the reality of the substances that are aggregated in them" (Ad 260).

11 See Hoffman (1996, esp. 113–17) for an explicit argument to this effect. Hoffman notes that the move to identify bodies with the representational content of ideas seems to erase an appearance/reality distinction for those bodies. He writes, "if bodies appear to be continuous, then they are continuous" (116). His claim seems decisive. My interest in this matter, however, is the larger point that it undercuts the Idealism behind the identification of bodies with ideas' representational contents. On another front, Berkeley's attempt to draw this distinction on the basis of "vividness" and "coherence" is a famous failure (defeated easily by vivid dreams), and rescued only by a question-begging God-caused (for real idea-collections)/us-caused (for imaginary ones) distinction.

12 Still, on this score existing Compatibilisms are internally consistent because they offer accounts of corporeal substances that are amenable to phenomenalism. Adams has the "modified one substance" theory (Ad 269–74) and Rutherford says animals are aggregates and not really substances (Rd, chapter 10).

8 Animals

1 Some are discussed in Hartz 1998.

2 Thus Catherine Wilson: "If there is anything which is truly imperishable and immortal, it must be indivisible and indestructible – and the only thing we can imagine that fits this category is the soul. ... " (1993, 671).

3 Still, Sleigh admits that "The details of the *Monadology* are not to be found here. It is not part of my claim that Leibniz really had the view of the *Monadology* in mind at this time" (1990, 115). See Wilson 1993, 669–74 for a critique of this claim – most tellingly, she asks, "[I]f the general direction of Leibniz's thought is towards immaterialism, why does the *Monadology* still contain animalculist theses ... ?" (1993, 670)

4 At that time I used 'phenomenalism' – in "mereological phenomenalism" and "supervenience phenomenalism" – to refer to bodies construed as mind-independent but still assigned to Leibniz's "middle" phenomenal level between the "ideal" and "fundamental" levels. At the phenomenal level, aggregates "are pulling their reality fom their parts" (Hartz 1992, 527). I have here dropped that use of 'phenomenalism' since this term is inevitably associated with mind-dependent appearances, and I now consider it misleading.

5 In his book, Adams favors the "qualified monad conception" of animals (Ad 269) – which is a "one-substance" theory. There, an animal is "a monad as having a body." This is discussed in 8.6.

6 Daniel Garber famously argued that animals predominate in the "middle years" – roughly from the mid-1680s to 1704 (Garber 1985; see Ad Chapter 11).

7 The text appears as number 31 in 8.3.

8 Mon and G 2, 506/L 617. The latter ironically was written to Des Bosses in 1715 – three years after the passage, to the same correspondent, that Wilson and Sleigh are relying on for the rejection of animals.

9 In observance of current practice, I drop 'O'Leary-' from John Hawthorne's name in the non-bibliographic parts of this work.

10 This ploy goes all the way back to Erdmann (1891, 2; 188). It represents what I call the "Reductio ad Vinculum" argument against animals. I cast doubt on it at Hartz 1998, 196–8.

11 For Aristotle, see e.g., *On the soul* 2, 1 (412a20).

12 Broad mistakenly says the Divisibility Argument applies to animals as well as extended aggregates (1975, 91–2).

13 Remark in conversation with the author.

14 See Hartz 1998, for a discussion of some Idealist attempts at damage control.

15 Fine (1999, 68–9): " [G]iven any suitable function or principle F (taking times to things), that there is a corresponding object standing in the same relationship to F as the variable water in the river stands to *its* principle. We call this object the *variable embodiment of F.*"

16 This is the inclusive 'or'.

17 This is the "No Principle of Unity Argument" – see Rd 273 and discussion in Hartz 1998, 202–5.

18 See text (3) in 8.3

19 Sleigh (1990, 107) is right that Leibniz does not here offer any account of the unity, though this is his golden opportunity. The silence on that point is deafening, and again shows that Leibniz held the nature of this fusion to be beyond the limits of human explanation, as I've just argued.

20 Broad writes that what I have called the "Divisibility Argument" applies to animals as well as extended aggregates: "Let them be as animated and as organic as they will, if their organisms are held to be extended, they are open to this objection" (1975, 92). The Realist analysis offered here takes away the assumption, "if their organisms are held to be extended," and so animals' susceptibility to the Divisibility Argument vanishes just as the Realist analysis of aggregates (with the non-extended whole, w, as the aggregate) made aggregates no longer susceptible.

21 For similar reasons, the attempt to phenomenalize "organism" by making it "simple substances perceiving one another in the right way" does not work – see Cover and O'Leary-Hawthorne 1999, 54.

22 E.g., Loeb 1981, 292 says this passage appears in the "philosophically serious correspondence with De Volder"; and at 309 he refers to this letter and its phenomenalist claims as a "breakthrough."

Bibliography

Adams, H. B. (1974) *The Education of Henry Adams*, E. Samuels (ed.), Boston: Houghton Mifflin.

Adams, R. M. (1983) "Phenomenalism and Corporeal Substance in Leibniz," *Midwest Studies in Philosophy*, Vol. VIII, *Contemporary Perspectives on the History of Philosophy*, P. A. French, T. E. Uehling, Jr., and H. K. Wettstein (eds), Minneapolis: University of Minnesota Press, 217–57.

Aiton, E. J. (1985) *Leibniz: A Biography*, Bristol: A. Hilger.

Anapolitanos, D. A. (1999) *Leibniz: Representation, Continuity and the Spatiotemporal*, Dordrecht: Kluwer.

Antognazza, M. R. (2001) "*Debilissimae Entitates?* Bisterfeld and Leibniz's ontology of relations," *Leibniz Review* 11: 1–22.

Aristotle (1984) *The Complete Works of Aristotle*, J. Barnes (ed.), 2 vols, Princeton: Princeton University Press.

Armstrong, D. M. (1961) *Perception and the Physical World*, London: Routledge & Kegan Paul.

Balz, A. G. A. (1951) *Cartesian Studies*, New York: Columbia University Press.

Beck, L. W. (1969) *Early German Philosophy: Kant and his predecessors*, Cambridge: Harvard University Press.

Beeley, P. (1996) *Kontinuität und Mechanismus: zur Philosophie des jungen Leibniz in ihrem ideengeschichtlichen Kontext*, Stuttgart: Steiner.

Berra, T. M., Smith, J. F., and Morrison, J. D. (1982) "Probable Identification of the Cucumber Odor of the Australian Grayling *Prototroctes maraena*," *Transactions of the American Fisheries Society* 111: 78–82.

Blackburn, S. (1990) "Filling in Space," *Analysis* 50: 62–5.

——(1997) "Spreading the World," unpublished.

Bolton, M. B. (1996) "The Nominalist Argument of the *New Essays*," *Leibniz Society Review* 6: 1–24.

Bossuet, J. B. (1909) *Correspondance de Bossuet*, C. Urbain and E. Levesque (eds), 15 vols, Paris: Hachette.

Broad, C. D. (1975) *Leibniz: an introduction*, C. Lewy (ed.), Cambridge: Cambridge University Press.

Brown, S. (1984) *Leibniz*, Minneapolis: University of Minnesota Press.

Burkhardt, H. and Smith, B. (eds) (1991) *Handbook of Metaphysics and Ontology*, Munich: Philosophia.

Carlin, L. (1997) "Infinite Accumulations and Pantheistic Implications: Leibniz and the 'Anima Mundi'," *Leibniz Society Review* 7: 1–24.

Cassirer, E. (1902) *Leibniz's System in seinen wissenschaftlichen Grundlagen*, Marburg: N. G. Elwert'sche Verlagsbuchhandlung.

Chalmers, D. J. (1996) *The Conscious Mind: In search of a fundamental theory*, New York: Oxford University Press.

Clatterbaugh, K. C. (1973) *Leibniz's Doctrine of Individual Accidents, Studia Leibnitiana*, Sonderheft 4, Wiesbaden: Steiner.

Costabel, P. (1973) *Leibniz and Dynamics: the texts of 1692*, trans. R. E. W. Maddison. Ithaca: Cornell University Press.

Cover, J. A. and O'Leary-Hawthorne, J. (1999) *Substance and Individuation in Leibniz*, Cambridge: Cambridge University Press.

Cover, J. A. and Hawthorne, J. (2000) "Leibnizian Modality Again: reply to Murray," *Leibniz Review* 10: 87–101.

Crockett, T. (1999) "Continuity in Leibniz's Mature Metaphysics," *Philosophical Studies* 94: 119–38.

Cummins, P. (1990) "Bayle, Leibniz, Hume and Reid on Extension, Composites and Simples," *History of Philosophy Quarterly* 7: 299–314.

Dascal, M. (1993) "One Adam and Many Cultures: the role of political pluralism in the best of possible worlds," in Dascal and Yakira (eds), 1993.

——(1998) "Language in the Mind's House," *Leibniz Society Review* 8: 1–24.

——(2003) "*Ex pluribus unum*? patterns in 522+ texts of Leibniz's *Sämtliche Schriften und Briefe* VI, 4," *Leibniz Review* 13: 105–54.

Dascal, M. and Yakira, E. (eds) (1993) *Leibniz and Adam*, Tel Aviv: University Publishing Projects.

Di Bella, S. (2005) *The Science of the Individual: Leibniz's ontology of individual substance*, Dordrecht: Springer.

Duchesneau, F. (1998) *Les Modèles du Vivant de Descartes à Leibniz*, Paris: Vrin.

Erdmann, J. E. (1891) *History of Philosophy*, trans. W. S. Hough, 2nd edn, 3 vols, London: Sonnenschein.

Fischer, K. (1902) *Geschichte der neurern Philosophie*, Dritter Band: *Gottfried Wilhelm Leibniz: Leben, Werke und Lehre*, Vierte Auflage, Heidelberg: Carl Winter's Universitätsbuchhandlung.

Fine, K. (1999) "Things and Their Parts," in French and Wettstein (eds) 1999, 61–74.

Foster, J. (1982) *The Case for Idealism*, London: Routledge & Kegan Paul.

Francks, R. and Woolhouse, R. S. (2000) "John Toland's 'Remarques Critiques sur le Système de Monsr Leibnitz de l'Harmonie préetablie'," *Leibniz Review* 10: 103–33.

Frankfurt, H. G. (ed.) (1976) *Leibniz: a collection of critical essays*, Notre Dame: University of Notre Dame Press.

French, P. A. and Wettstein, H. K. (eds) (1999) *Midwest Studies in Philosophy*, Vol. XXIII, *New Directions in Philosophy, Journal of Social Philosophy*, Supplement.

Freudenthal, G. (1996) "Pluralism or Relativism?" *Science in Context* 9: 151–63.

Furley, D. J. (1967) *Two Studies in the Greek Atomists*, Princeton: Princeton University Press.

Furth, M. (1976) "Monadology," *Philosophical Review* 76 (1967): 169–200; reprinted in Frankfurt (ed.) 1976, 99–135. Pagination cited follows the reprint.

Garber, D. (1985) "Leibniz and the Foundations of Physics: the middle years," in Okruhlik and Brown (eds) 1985, 27–130.

——(2004) "Leibniz and Fardella: body, substance, and idealism," in Lodge (ed.) 2004, 123–40.

——(2005) "Leibniz and Idealism," in Rutherford and Cover (eds) 2005, 95–107.

Gassendi, P. (1972) *The Selected Works of Pierre Gassendi*, ed. and trans. C. B. Brush, New York: Johnson Reprint.

Gennaro, R. J. and Huenemann, C. (eds) (1999) *New Essays on the Rationalists*, New York: Oxford University Press.

Grant, E. (1981) *Much Ado About Nothing*, Cambridge: Cambridge University Press.

Harman, P. M. (1982) *Metaphysics and Natural Philosophy*, Sussex: Harvester.

Hartz, G. A. (1984) "Launching a Materialist Ontology: the Leibnizian way," *History of Philosophy Quarterly* 1: 315–32.

——(1989) "Leibniz on Why Descartes' Metaphysic of Body is Necessarily False," in Rescher (ed.) 1989, 23–36.

——(1992) "Leibniz's Phenomenalisms," *Philosophical Review* 101: 511–49.

——(1996) "Exactly How are Leibnizian Substances Related to Extension?" in Woolhouse 1996, 63–81.

——(1998) "Why Corporeal Substances Keep Popping Up in Leibniz's Later Philosophy," *British Journal for the History of Philosophy* 6: 193–207.

Hartz, G. A. and Cover, J. A. (1988) "Space and Time in the Leibnizian Metaphysic," *Noûs* 22: 493–519; reprinted in Woolhouse 1994, vol. 3, 76–103.

——(1994) "Are Leibnizian Monads Spatial?" *History of Philosophy Quarterly* 11: 295–316.

Hartz, G. A. and Wilson, C. (forthcoming) "Ideas and Animals: The Hard Problem of Leibnizian Metaphysics," *Studia Leibnitiana*.

Hegel, G. W. F. (1969) *Hegel's Science of Logic*, trans. A. V. Miller, London: Allen & Unwin.

Heinekamp, A. (ed.) (1988) *Leibniz: questions de logique*, Stuttgart: Steiner.

Hempel, C. G. (1966) *Philosophy of Natural Science*, Englewood Cliffs: Prentice-Hall.

Hoffman, P. (1996) "The Being of Leibnizian Phenomena," *Studia Leibnitiana*, 28: 108–18.

Jackson, F. (1998) *From Metaphysics to Ethics: A defence of conceptual analysis*, Oxford: Clarendon Press.

Jammer, M. (1954) *Concepts of Space: The history of theories of space in physics*, Cambridge: Harvard University Press.

Jolley, N. (1986) "Leibniz and Phenomenalism," *Studia Leibnitiana* 18: 38–51.

——(1995a) "Review of Donald Rutherford, *Leibniz and the Rational Order of Nature*," *Leibniz Society Review* 5: 18–21.

——(ed.) (1995b) *The Cambridge Companion to Leibniz*, Cambridge: Cambridge University Press.

——(2005) *Leibniz*, London and New York: Routledge.

Kabitz, W. (1932) "Leibniz und Berkeley," *Sitzungsberichte der preussischen Academie der Wissenschaften*, Philosophische-historische Klasse, N. xxiv Jahrgang: 623–36.

Kant, I. (1787) *Critique of Pure Reason*, cited by edition and page (e.g., B 17)

Kierkegaard, S. (1944) *Either/Or*, trans. D. F. Swenson and L. M. Swenson, with revisions by H. A. Johnson, 2 vols, Princeton: Princeton University Press.

Kim, J. (1978) "Supervenience and Nomological Incommensurables," *American Philosophical Quarterly* 15: 149–56.

——(1984) "Concepts of Supervenience," *Philosophy and Phenomenological Research* 45: 153–76.

——(1991) "Supervenience," in Burkhardt and Smith (eds) 1991, 877–9.

Lange, F. A. (1925) *The History of Materialism*, trans. E. C. Thomas, London: Kegan Paul, Trench, Trubner; New York: Harcourt Brace.

Langton, R. (1998) *Kantian Humility: our ignorance of things in themselves*, Oxford: Clarendon Press.

Latta, R. (trans.) (1898) *Leibniz: The Monadology and Other Philosophical Writings*, London: Oxford University Press; reprint New York: Garland, 1985.

Leibniz, G. W. (1768) *Opera Omnia. Nunc primum collecta. ...* , L. Dutens (ed.), 6 vols, Geneva: De Tournes; reprint Hildesheim: Georg Olms, 1989.

——(1857) *Nouvelles lettres et opuscules inédits de Leibniz*, A. F. de Careil. Paris: Auguste Durand, 1857; reprint Hildesheim: Georg Olms, 1971.

——(1860) *Briefwechsel zwischen Leibniz und Christian Wolff*, C. I. Gerhardt (ed.), Halle: H. W. Schmidt; reprint Hildesheim: Georg Olms, 1963.

——(1889) *Die Leibniz-Handschriften der königlichen öffentlichen Bibliothek zu Hannover*, E. Bodemann (ed.), Hannover: Hahn, 1889; reprint Hildesheim: Georg Olms, 1966.

——(1948) *G. W. Leibniz: Textes inédits d'après les manuscrits de la bibliothéque provinciale de Hanovre*, G. Grua (ed.), Paris: Presses Universitaires de France, 1948; reprint New York: Garland, 1985.

——(1953) *Leibniz: Discourse on Metaphysics*, trans. P. G. Lucas and L. Grint, Manchester: Manchester University Press.

——(1965) *Monadology and Other Philosophical Essays*, trans. P. Schrecker and A. M. Schrecker, Indianapolis: Bobbs-Merrill.

——(1966) *Leibniz: Logical Papers*, trans. and ed. with an introduction by G. H. R. Parkinson, Oxford: Clarendon Press.

——(1998) *Philosophical Texts*, trans. R. Francks and R. S. Woolhouse, Oxford: Oxford University Press.

——(2001) *The Labyrinth of the Continuum: writings on the continuum problem, 1672–1686*, ed. and trans. R. T. W. Arthur, New Haven: Yale University Press.

Levey, S. (1998) "Leibniz on Mathematics and the Actually Infinite Division of Matter," *Philosophical Review* 107: 49–96.

——(1999) "Matter and Two Concepts of Continuity in Leibniz," *Philosophical Studies* 94: 81–118.

——(2002) "Leibniz and the Sorites," *Leibniz Review* 12: 25–49.

Lewis, C. I. (1960) *A Survey of Symbolic Logic*, New York: Dover.

Lewis, D. (1991) *Parts of Classes*, Oxford: Blackwell.

Lodge, P. (1998) *Leibniz's Anti-Cartesian Metaphysics of Body: a study of the correspondence between Leibniz and De Volder*, Dissertation, Rutgers University.

——(2001) "Leibniz's Notion of an Aggregate," *British Journal for the History of Philosophy* 9: 467–86.

——(ed.) (2004) *Leibniz and His Correspondents*, Cambridge: Cambridge University Press.

Loeb, L. E. (1981) *From Descartes to Hume*, Ithaca: Cornell University Press.

Look, B. (1999) *Leibniz and the 'Vinculum Substantiale'*, Studia Leibnitiana, Sonderheft 30. Stuttgart: Franz Steiner Verlag.

Loptson, P. (1999) "Was Leibniz an Idealist?" *Philosophy* 74: 361–85.

Machamer, P. K. and Turnbull, R. G. (eds) (1976) *Motion and Time Space and Matter*, Columbus: Ohio State University Press.

McGuire, J. E. (1976) "'Labyrinthus continui': Leibniz on substance, activity, and matter," in Machamer and Turnbull (eds) 1976, 290–326.

Mackie, J. L. (1973) *Truth, Probability and Paradox*, Oxford: Clarendon Press.

Martin, G. (1964) *Leibniz: Logic and Metaphysics*, trans. K. J. Northcott and P. G. Lucas, Manchester: Manchester University Press.

Mates, B. (1986) *The Philosophy of Leibniz*, New York: Oxford University Press.

Matson, W. I. (1968) *A History of Philosophy*, New York: American Book Co.

Melville, H. (1950) *Moby Dick or, The Whale*, New York: Modern Library.

Mercer, C. (2001) *Leibniz's Metaphysics: its origins and development*, Cambridge: Cambridge University Press.

Michalko, M. (1998) *Cracking Creativity: the secrets of creative genius*, Berkeley: Ten Speed Press.

Mugnai, M. (1992) *Leibniz' Theory of Relations*, Stuttgart: Steiner.

——(forthcoming) "Leibniz's Nominalism and the Reality of Corporeal Substances," *Studia Leibnitiana Supplementa*, Stuttgart: Franz Steiner Verlag.

Murray, M. J. (2000) "Critical Review of Cover and Hawthorne on Leibnizian Modality," *Leibniz Review*, 10: 73–86.

Nagel, T. (1986) *The View from Nowhere*, New York: Oxford University Press.

Nason, J. W. (1945) "Leibniz's Attack on the Cartesian Doctrine of Extension," *Journal of the History of Ideas* 6: 447–83.

Newton, I. (1952) *Opticks*, New York: Dover.

——(1934) *Sir Isaac Newton's Mathematical Principles of Natural Philosophy and His System of the World*, ed. and trans. F. Cajori, 2 vols, Berkeley: University of California Press.

Oates, W. J. (ed.) (1940) *The Stoic and Epicurean Philosophers: The Complete Extant Writings of Epicurus, Epictetus, Lucretius, Marcus Aurelius*, New York: Random House.

Okruhlik, K. and Brown, R. (eds) (1985) *The Natural Philosophy of Leibniz*, Dordrecht: Reidel.

Parkinson, G. H. R. (1965) *Logic and Reality in Leibniz's Metaphysics*, Oxford: Oxford University Press, reprinted New York: Garland, 1985.

Phemister, P. (2005) *Leibniz and the Natural World: Activity, Passivity and Corporeal Substances in Leibniz's Philosophy*, Dordrecht: Springer.

Plaisted, D. (2002) *Leibniz on Purely Extrinsic Denominations*, Rochester: University of Rochester Press.

Priest, G. (1987) *In Contradiction: A Study of the Transconsistent*, Dordrecht: Nijhoff.

Rescher, N. (1967) *The Philosophy of Leibniz*, Englewood Cliffs: Prentice-Hall.

——(ed.) (1989) *Leibnizian Inquiries: a group of essays*, Lanham: University Press of America.

——(1991) *G. W. Leibniz's "Monadology": an edition for students*, Pittsburgh: University of Pittsburgh Press.

Reston, J. Jr. (1995) *Galileo: A Life*, New York: HarperPerennial.

Riley, P. (1999) "Review of G. W. Leibniz, *Allgemeiner Politischer und Historischer Briefwechsel*," *Leibniz Review* 9: 65–85.

Robinet, A. (1986) *Architectonique disjonctive, automates systématiques, et idéalité dans l'oeuvre de G. W. Leibniz*, Paris: Vrin.

Robinson, H. (1982) *Matter and Sense: a critique of contemporary materialism*, Cambridge: Cambridge University Press.

Ross, G. M. (1984) "Leibniz's Phenomenalism and the Construction of Matter," *Studia Leibnitiana* Sonderheft 13: 26–36; pagination cited here follows the reprint in Woolhouse 1994, vol. 4, 173–86.

Russell, B. (1927) *The Analysis of Matter*, New York: Harcourt, Brace & Co.

——(1945) *A History of Western Philosophy*, New York: Simon and Schuster.

Russell, L. J. (1967) "Leibniz, Gottfried Wilhelm," in *The Encyclopedia of Philosophy*, Paul Edwards (ed.), New York: Macmillan.

Rutherford, D. (1990) "Leibniz's 'Analysis of Multitude and Phenomena into Unities and Reality," *Journal of the History of Philosophy* 28: 525–52.

——(1995) [Leibniz's] "Metaphysics: the late period," in Jolley (ed.) 1995b, 124–75.

Rutherford, D. and Cover, J. A. (eds) (2005) *Leibniz: nature and freedom*, New York: Oxford University Press.

Scarrow, D. S. (1973) "Reflections on the Idealist Interpretation of Leibniz's Philosophy," *Studia Leibnitiana Supplementa* 12: 85–93.

Schmidt, F. (1971) "Ganzes und Teil bei Leibniz," *Archiv Für Geschichte der Philosophie* 53: 267–78.

Schneider, M. (1988) "Funktion und Grundlegung der Mathesis Universalis im Leibnizschen Wissenschaftsystem," in Heinekamp 1988, 162–82.

Schopenhauer, A. (1896) *The World as Will and Idea*, trans. R. B. Haldane and J. Kemp. 3 vols, London: Kegan Paul, Trench, Trübner & Co.

Scott, W. L. (1970) *The Conflict between Atomism and Conservation Theory 1644–1860*, London: Macdonald; New York: Elsevier.

Shelley, M. (1969) *Frankenstein: or the modern Prometheus*, M. K. Joseph (ed.), Oxford: Oxford University Press.

Simons, P. (1987) *Parts: a study in ontology*, Oxford: Clarendon Press.

Sleigh, R. C., Jr. (1990) *Leibniz & Arnauld: a commentary on their correspondence*, New Haven: Yale University Press.

Smart, J. J. C. (1963) *Philosophy and Scientific Realism*, London: Routledge & Kegan Paul.

Smith, J. E. H. (1999) "On the Fate of Composite Substances After 1704," *Studia Leibnitiana* 31: 1–7.

——(2002) "Leibniz's Hylomorphic Monad," *History of Philosophy Quarterly* 19: 21–42.

Stace, W. T. (1955) *The Philosophy of Hegel: A Systematic Exposition*, New York: Dover.

Stewart, M. A. (ed.) (1997) *Studies in 17th Century European Philosophy*, Oxford: Clarendon Press.

Strawson, P. F. (1959) *Individuals: An Essay in Descriptive Metaphysics*, London: Methuen.

Unger, P. (1999) "The Mystery of the Physical and the Matter of Qualities: A Paper for Professor Shaffer," *Midwest Studies in Philosophy*, Vol. XXIII, *New Directions in Philosophy*, P. A. French and H. K. Wettstein (eds), *Journal of Social Philosophy*, Supplement.

Van Biéma, É. (1908) *L'Espace et le Temps chez Leibniz et chez Kant*, Paris: Félix Alcan.

Van Cleve, J. (1988) "Inner States and Outer Relations: Kant and the case for monadism," in *Doing Philosophy Historically*, P. H. Hare (ed.), Buffalo: Prometheus.

Van Inwagen, P. (1990) *Material Beings*, Ithaca: Cornell University Press.

Westfall, R. S. (1971) *Force in Newton's Physics: the science of dynamics in the Seventeenth Century*, London: Macdonald; New York: American Elsevier.

Wiggins, D. (1980) *Sameness and Substance*, Cambridge: Harvard University Press.

——(2001) *Sameness and Substance Renewed*, Cambridge: Cambridge University Press.

Williams, L. P. (1966) *The Origins of Field Theory*, New York: Random House.

Wilson, C. (1989) *Leibniz's Metaphysics*, Princeton: Princeton University Press.

——(1993) "Critical Notice: R.C. Sleigh, *Leibniz and Arnauld*," *Canadian Journal of Philosophy* 23: 661–74.

——(1994) "Reply to Cover's 1993 Review of *Leibniz's Metaphysics*," *Leibniz Society Review* 4: 5–8.

——(1997) "Leibniz and the Animalcula," in Stewart 1997, 153–75.

——(1999) "The Illusory Nature of Leibniz's System," in Gennaro and Huenemann (eds) 1999, 372–88.

Woolhouse, R. S. (ed.) (1994) *Gottfried Wilhelm Leibniz: critical assessments*, 4 vols, London: Routledge.

——(ed.) (1996) *Leibniz's 'New System'*, Firenze: Olschki.

Zimmerman, D. W. (1995) "Theories of Masses and Problems of Constitution," *Philosophical Review* 104: 53–110.

Index

Index of Leibniz Texts